Lived Theology
for the Whole of Life

Lived Theology
for the Whole of Life

LYDIA F. JOHNSON

WIPF & STOCK · Eugene, Oregon

LIVED THEOLOGY FOR THE WHOLE OF LIFE

Copyright © 2024 Lydia F. Johnson. All rights reserved. Except for brief quotations in critical publications or reviews, no part of this book may be reproduced in any manner without prior written permission from the publisher. Write: Permissions, Wipf and Stock Publishers, 199 W. 8th Ave., Suite 3, Eugene, OR 97401.

Wipf & Stock
An Imprint of Wipf and Stock Publishers
199 W. 8th Ave., Suite 3
Eugene, OR 97401

www.wipfandstock.com

PAPERBACK ISBN: 979-8-3852-2205-6
HARDCOVER ISBN: 979-8-3852-2206-3
EBOOK ISBN: 979-8-3852-2207-0

VERSION NUMBER 061224

Permission has been granted to cite the poem, "The Language of Trees and Clams," by Wardley Barry-Igivisa, from the book *From the Deep: Pasifiki Voices for a New Story*, by the publisher, Pacific Theological College.

To my grandchildren, light and hope for the future:
Owen, Luke, Percival, Aaralyn, Solomon, and Raphael

Contents

Acknowledgements | ix
Preface | xi

PART 1: Interrelational Theology
  1 Theological Underpinnings: Divine Indwelling | 3
  2 Gathered Life in the *Kindom* | 21

PART 2: Being Human
  3 Human or Post-human? | 41
  4 Living with the Pain of Being Human | 51
  5 Lifting the Mat of Forgiveness | 64

PART 3: A Widening Spiral of Relatedness
  6 All Lives Matter | 75
  7 "Blessed Are You Who Are Poor" | 100
  8 This Land Is Our Land | 112
  9 Lawn Transformations—Oddly Satisfying? | 124

PART 4: A *For-Life* Ethic Confronts a *For-Death* World
  10 The Evil That Is Empire | 141
  11 Pacifism, Just War, and Empire Proxy War | 165
  12 Father Abraham Was a Colonizer (and the Road Leads to Gaza) | 191
  13 What If? | 216

Bibliography | 227

Acknowledgements

THIS BOOK HAS BEEN like a slow-growing but resilient plant, and it has taken the planting, tending, pruning, watering, weeding, and appreciation of others besides myself to enable this plant to finally bear fruit. It is important to acknowledge, first, that this theological plant has been grafted from other plants, in particular those of theologians, colleagues, and friends in the non-Western cultures which have been my home for most of my adult life. I am particularly grateful to my Pacific Islander fellow gardeners for enabling me to graft my theological plant from theirs. I especially wish to thank Upolu Vaai and Aisake Casimira at Pacific Theological College in Fiji for their warm collegiality, as well as my Pacific Islander students who have become part of my extended family over the years. Their collective wisdom has, in many ways, provided the roots in which the theological plant that is this book has been able to grow and flourish. *Fa'afetai lava* and *vinaka vakalevu*.

This book has also benefitted from the support of my family throughout my theological (and cross-cultural) journeying. My theologically sharp siblings have always given me the space and encouragement to take a "path less travelled" in my theological gardening, offering loving "plant food" even when, at times, their unorthodox sister's path must have given them headaches. Thank you, Barbara and Jim McLean, and John and Debbie Johnson. My beloved daughters and sons-in-law, Kelly and Tom Gilson, and Erin and Ed Johnson-Williams, have been the most loving presence imaginable throughout my theological explorations, and they have always encouraged me to keep writing, even in trying times. I have dedicated this book to their children, my treasured grandchildren, who make me want to keep trying to bring theology to life.

I am also blessed to have a "cloud of witnesses" who offer support and encouragement as I tend my theological garden. I mention with gratitude a few of these cherished friends: Cissy and Steve Moore-Swartz, Mercy Ah Siu-Maliko, David and Anne Denham, and Joe Mitchell. Finally, I am genuinely grateful for the helpful and professional team at Wipf & Stock, especially Matthew Wimer, Jordon Horowitz and Emily Callihan, who have graciously steered me through the minefield of preparing this book for publication.

To my worldwide "family," thank you from my heart for the many ways you have helped me to bring this labor of love to fullness of life.

Preface

DURING MY LONG TEACHING career, I would sometimes say to my theology students as they were embarking on an important assignment, research project, or thesis, "you need to be guided in your work by two words—*'so what?'*" As a practitioner of practical theology, that was my way of reminding my students that their work should have relevance; it should matter in some consequential way. It should be more than simply a recitation of abstract concepts and ideas. It should stimulate associations with real-world concerns.

I have asked the "so what?" question of myself many times in relation to my own work and life. How is theology germane to what is happening within us and around us? Is it more than wordy debates about the intricacies of this or that doctrine, or the exegesis of this or that phrase in a passage of scripture? Does it matter beyond academic circles? As a person of faith, I believe theology does matter; it has to matter. But this is only true when it is *lived theology*. Lived theology is our reflection as people of faith on experience, and our response. I believe that is where theology should be situated.

My commitment to lived theology leads me to "do theology" in a way that differs from what I was taught in my theological studies. There I learned to engage intellectually with various forms of and movements in theology, with doctrines and beliefs, with the evolution of theological ideas, with historical theological debates (who can forget the arguments over *homoousias* versus *homoiousios*?). At the higher levels of study, theology was about articulating one's own theological position—constructing a "theology of this" or a "theology of that." The higher one went, the narrower one's path became. But what did any of this have to do with the life I was actually living, and the world in which I was actually living?

Reflecting and acting on lived theology necessitates a much broader and deeper way of doing theology than what I learned in academia. I am attempting in this work to put the dynamics of lived theology into practice in the way I think and write. That means that this book travels down a wide path rather than a narrow path, a path with many intersections. Lived theology comes to life at those intersections, where the varied aspects of experience meet and interact. This means that my task in this book is multifaceted and thus not confined to one methodological approach. What does that mean?

First, lived theology is *personal*. This is an unorthodox way to bring theology into public discourse. Academic theology usually speaks with an assumed dispassionate, detached voice, leaving the person of the author out of the picture. We can read tomes of theological works and have no sense of who the writer is. But that is not how theology is *lived*. It is "lived" theology because it emanates from the lived experiences of human beings. I did not start out in this work to include myself, but I found as I went along that, in order to be true to what lived theology is all about, it was not possible to divorce theological reflection from the person doing the reflection. The book is not about me (and including some of myself has made me at times uncomfortably vulnerable), but I include myself from time to time as a way to be honest about what lived theology is, and to invite readers to do the same. It is *we*, ourselves, living human beings, who "do" theology all the time, in every situation.

This is another way of saying that lived theology is *experiential*. Our lived experience, personal and collective, is the starting point of theology, not beliefs, creeds, scripture, or the theological traditions we have inherited. It is our experiences that stimulate our theological reflection and inform our faith responses to everything that happens. We are doing theology when we open ourselves to the presence, power, calling, and guidance of the divine Spirit in relation to experience.

Because lived theology is experiential, it is also *storied*. It takes shape and finds its voice through the stories of our lives, the stories that are shared with us, the stories we hear from others and witness all around us. The texts of theology are storied texts. Again, I did not start out to intentionally tell stories in this work, but the stories told themselves. As I explored a particular facet of lived theology, stories bubbled up to the surface of my consciousness, and these stories gave shape to the theological reflection I was undertaking. This is actually how we navigate our way through life; we are grounded in stories.

Lived theology is also *multidisciplinary*. This is perhaps the greatest challenge I faced in attempting to give voice to a lived theology engagement with life. I found that if I was going to theologize around a particular experiential concern, I had to understand that concern not just in a surface way, but in some depth. I had to do research. I had to "go down a rabbit hole," as the saying goes, in order to accurately understand what I was attempting to address. It was not enough simply to have an opinion or a hypothesis.

This means that this is an unusual theological text. The range of sources in the bibliography could cause the typical reader of theology to shake his or her head. I have had to become an investigative journalist, a scientific researcher, a historian, a social scientist, a geopolitical analyst, a psychologist, as well as a biblical explorer and conversation partner with other theologians. I do not claim to be an expert in these "non-theological" fields of study, but I have taken my interdisciplinary excavations very seriously. This way of doing theology requires a lot of digging.

The fact that lived theology is multidisciplinary means, of course, that it is *many-faceted*. Because it is about life itself, it addresses the "whole of life." Obviously, I have not been able to address the whole of life in this undertaking—that is impossible. The point is that there is no dimension of lived experience which is not a potential subject of theological concern. I have focused in this work on the aspects of experience that seem most pressing today, and so there are excursions into many subjects of concern, from post-humanism to immigration to abortion to poverty to forgiveness to fear to racism to disabilities to climate collapse to war to imperialism—and more. Because my understanding of lived theology is that it is interrelational, all of the facets of lived experience I cover are connected in some way; they are interwoven strands of the whole, and that interconnectedness guides my thinking throughout.

There are certain risks entailed in doing theology in the unorthodox way I have undertaken. My attempt to situate every concern within what I call a consistently *for-life* ethic that emerges from an interrelational God has led me to abandon some of my previously taken-for-granted ethical stances. This puts me at odds with some positions held by many of my closest relatives and friends, as well as the broader theological and ecclesial community in which I was formed.

Moreover, many of the issues I have addressed are typically politicized, such that those holding one view are in one political "camp," and those holding the opposing view are in another. I want to make it clear that this work is not intended to be political. I am not a member of any political party, nor do I place much stock in political parties or electoral politics. Although social policies tend to be associated with particular political ideologies, I have made every effort to let the interrelational theology that shapes my faith be the lodestar that guides my responses to the challenges that confront us in the "whole of life." It is lived theology that I want to inform my decisions and actions in the world, not politics.

At its heart, this work is an invitation to readers to imagine what lived theology means in your own life, your community, your faith experience, your orientation to being in the world. This is an invitation to dialogue, to gathering with your friends, loved ones, and faith community to explore together "what the Spirit is saying" to you in this challenging time in which we live. May theology *live* in all of us, in freshness and new discovery.

Part 1

Interrelational Theology

1

Theological Underpinnings
Divine Indwelling

THE ONGOING BEGINNING—GOD IS GOOD

AROUND 14 BILLION YEARS ago or thereabouts, something happened. Scientists sometimes call this the Big Bang. An unimaginable energy erupted, creating everything in the universe. Before there was matter, there was a "dark energy," but it expanded in an explosive creative act. Then there were atoms, molecules, and particles, and eventually air, water, planets, stars, plants, animals, and human beings. We call that creation. Throughout human history, in every place and culture, people have imagined some notion of a divine creator in an attempt to give voice to the miraculous beyond-ordinariness of this act that birthed everything into being.

In the first creation story in the book of Genesis (Gen 1), God is described as a moving wind hovering over and interpenetrating "the deep" that birthed creation. This dynamic energy is more a verb than a noun. God is the ongoing, ever-present creating that permeates the universe. The universe is still expanding, and at an accelerated pace, but this dynamic cosmos continues to consist of all those atoms and molecules released at the very beginning, at the birth of divine creating.

What happened then is the foundation of all that the universe has, or is, or ever will have or be. The atoms and molecules that came together to form you and me and every life form are all part of that initial burst of creating energy. We are part of the beginning, and when we die our essence will continue into infinity in other forms. The atoms and molecules of God are forever being reshaped into the never-ending material of creation. We are part of the eternal activity of *godding* whose purpose is to create and sustain life.

Because that divine creating energy is *for life*, it is good. In the first creation story in Genesis, at every stage of creation, metaphorically described as taking place in seven days, God speaks, and what God says is that "it" (each expression of created life) is "good." Because creation is *for life*, it exists to make and sustain life, not to destroy life. And therein lies the ethical framework of existence—and the reason for religions.

There are many dangers inherent in elevating human beings in this great household of creation, and our sense of self-importance has been our great downfall as a species. We have desacralized and misused the unique place we occupy in the created/creating world. Although Gen 1:27 tells us that we humans are made "in God's image," this does not mean that we should place ourselves above everything else in creation. It means that we are made to be *for life* because we partake of God's *for-life* creating. So does every *for-life* being and thing in creation; creation itself is "God's image."

In the Judeo-Christian religious tradition, we have all too often interpreted for our own ends the divine command in Gen 1:26 that humans take responsibility for creation, construing the words typically translated as human "dominion over" creation to mean "domination over" creation, rather than "stewardship on behalf of" creation. Stewardship of creation does not mean control but, rather, attentive care and respect. Yet even some well-meaning attempts by people of faith to speak, in light of the climate crisis, of "creation care" sometimes have a paternalistic ring to them. Creation care can be interpreted as a kind of parental oversight by we superior humans, who know best what to do because we see ourselves as the pinnacle of creation.

In contrast, the lived theology I embrace places us not at the pinnacle of creation, or at its center, but commingling with creation as relational equals with all that has been created and is being created. What ought to distinguish us as humans is not any inherent superiority that entitles us to "manage" creation so as to buttress our own interests but rather our *consciousness* of God, the *for-life* creating energy.

It is our intuitive awareness of this creating energy—the *godding* that created and creates everything, including us—that has led humans since they evolved into *homo sapiens* to be religious beings. This innate religiosity has been not only a response to our consciousness of the need to show gratitude for the divine gift of creation but an acknowledgement of the ethical implications of divine creating. Since this divine creativity is and has always been *for life*, the religious impulse is about honoring and practicing a *for-life* ethical orientation. This is why we say *God is good*, which is the same thing as saying *God is love*, a claim that was my first introduction to religious awareness as a very small child.

Religions fall far short of this originary impulse. Humans' awareness that there is an all-encompassing divine love for creation has all too easily been manipulated to suit our own needs and desires. The paradox that God is both transcendent (beyond us) and immanent (with us) has led to theological missteps. Because it is so difficult for humans to envision what a transcendent God looks like, we have anthropomorphized God. We have wanted to bring this mysterious, unfathomable creative energy closer to us, to make it more understandable and relatable. We have therefore imagined that God must be something like a super-hero, extraordinarily powerful in some magical way but also open to being appeased through our acts of sacrifice or pleading.

We see this tension between God as transcendent creator and God as intimate companion in the Judeo-Christian creation narratives. The first creation story in Gen 1 is a story of godding activity writ large. Out of the void of darkness, the divine energy "sweeps over" the face of the deep and creation takes shape. And at the end of each phase of creation, as noted earlier, the divine ethic is revealed: God sees the great *yin-yang* of what has come into being (light/darkness, day/night, water/earth, flora/fauna) and, because it is *for life*, it is *good*.

HUMANS MUDDY THE WATERS

But then this good creation encounters human beings, and in the second creation story in Gen 2 we find the mythical first humans struggling with their role in creation. Humans came into being as part and parcel of creation—literally created from dirt,[1] we are told—but God gave them something which the other creatures seemingly did not have—free will, the ability to choose between good and evil. That changed everything and has caused no end of problems.

The age-old theological conundrum of good versus evil is made starkly manifest in the second creation story of Adam and Eve. It raises profound questions: If creation is *for life*—an ethical and good design—why were

---

1. In Gen 2:7 we are told, "Then the LORD God formed man from the dust of the ground, and breathed into his nostrils the breath of life; and the man became a living being." For a provocative interpretation of this passage, and what it means to be "dirt people," see Vaai, "'We Are Earth,'" 40–54. *[Please note that all citations of Scripture in this work are from the New Revised Standard Version (NRSV), unless otherwise indicated.]*

humans created with the capacity to choose evil, to be not *for life and love* but *for death and evil*? The answer must be that it is the very fact of choice that makes ethical life possible.

On one level, this seems to fly in the face of the goodness inherent in divine creation. We humans could have been created *only* to be *for good*. But that would have been meaningless. Nothing comes into focus without contrast. It was only in the context of the dark void in the first creation story in Gen 1 that the creation of light had meaning. Creation can be recognized as good only by comparison with the alternative. And so God gave us our greatest yet most trying and frustrating gift—the capacity to recognize and choose either good or evil.

In the second creation story in Genesis, this divine gift of choice is symbolized by a tree—the "tree of the knowledge of good and evil," the only tree in the Garden of Eden whose fruits are forbidden. It is in their engagement with this tree that the human characters in the story, Adam and Eve, grapple with their humanness. When I first seriously reflected on this story as a teenager, it seemed ironic to me that Adam and Eve were punished because they desired knowledge (the woman more so than the man, which I found interesting). When I first contemplated this story, I intuitively admired Eve for wanting knowledge and found Adam less interesting precisely because of his passivity. Yet God punished Eve's desire for knowledge of good and evil *and* Adam's collusion in her rebellion. Why? Wasn't this desire a good thing?

I finally concluded that Adam's and Eve's punishment for eating the forbidden fruit of knowledge was a cautionary tale, a warning that our moral choices as humans are not a simple matter of eating whatever fruit hangs low from the tree because we want it. There would always be consequences for the choices we make. This *life-of-choice* we have been given as humans is difficult precisely because our human nature (not to be confused with our divine nature) predisposes us to choose what pleases us. We affirm our divine nature only in those holy moments when we are able to make the difficult ethical choice *for life*—not just for our own life, but for the life of all creatures and all creation.

The story of Adam and Eve is also a morality tale about the need for restraint. I will return to this in my exploration of a faithful *for-life* response to the climate crisis and to poverty. We are not entitled to consume everything in the garden. It does not belong to us. We do not own the garden nor its fruits. When Jesus offers us "abundant life," this does not mean over-stuffing ourselves; it means the fullness of our existence as interrelated beings. Yet the divine call for restraint bumps up against our human-natured desire to have it all, to have whatever we desire, to fill up our plates until we cannot cram anything else into our lives, whether as individuals, as persons in relationships, as communities, cultures, nations, or empires.

IS GOD HERE OR THERE?

It is in the throes of this struggle to be ethical beings that we humans have always sought to bring God down to earth, close to us, in an effort to feel God's presence, or to bend God to our will, or to appease God in the hopes of receiving a divine blessing. In the Garden of Eden story, God is in fact depicted not as distant, disembodied, and spiritualized but as an imposing being walking around in the garden, snooping on Adam and Eve, talking to them. Adam and Eve may have felt that they could convince this God to let them enjoy everything in the garden, but this could not be. Because of their greed, God banished them from the garden like a stern parent sending the children to "time out." This is the God we often encounter in the Old Testament. This God meets with and speaks to people, appears in nature, in a burning bush, in a sea that opens up, in a whirlwind, in food falling from heaven, in manifold dreams and visions. This God admonishes, instructs, comforts, nudges, berates, grieves, rejoices, rewards, and punishes.

Interestingly, the anthropocentric God we encounter in Hebrew Scripture is depicted not only as the imposing masculine Yahweh but, in a subversive undercurrent, in feminine guise. In Neh 9, God is described as taking care of the Israelites in the wilderness like a mother. In Ps 22:9, along with similar passages in Ps 71, Job 3, and various passages in Isaiah, God appears as a midwife: "It was you who took me from the womb; you kept me safe on my mother's breast." In Isa 42:14, God says, "I will cry out like a woman in labor; I will gasp and pant." In Isa 66:13, God says, "As a mother comforts her child, so I will comfort you." This undercurrent of feminine images of God may be the most striking sign of our human need to draw God close to us, to make God relatable.

The creation stories in Genesis, like creation stories found in many other cultures, and the broader depictions of God throughout Scripture, are not only efforts to make God relatable; they are attempts to come to terms with the divine expectation that we become ethical beings. Our paradoxical relationship with God—with the transcendent creative force beyond us and the relatable God we pull toward us—can be seen in all religious traditions. Behind them all is an awareness, however inchoate, that we are, indeed, created to be *for life that is good*, just as the universe came into being as the great divine impulse *for life that is good*.

"NATURE" GETS ITS WAY

This good creation should not be confused with "nature." Nature is not ethical; it can be fickle and capricious, although it has its own set of governing principles. It functions according to a system of natural laws that attempt to regulate and sustain it, but it can be destructive. Earthquakes, volcanic eruptions, hurricanes, floods, and wildfires wreak devastation on the earth and the humans and animals who dwell there. Some of these animals devour other animals; nature has both predators and prey. We humans are a part of this natural order. Left to our own devices, we tend to succumb to oppositional categories of conflict—predators versus prey, friends versus enemies, winners versus losers, haves versus have-nots, powerful versus powerless. Our inbuilt biological nature is *not* instinctually *for all life* but for self-preservation and self-promotion amidst relentless conflict.

It is abundantly clear, of course, that we humans cannot control nature's capriciousness. We cannot stop the earthquake, the volcano, the raging storm. Nature has its own quest for self-preservation and goes its own way. To the extent that nature has an ethical dimension, it is *us*. We have been given a divine mandate to be good stewards of nature, to promote its balance—the viability of its complex interconnected parts—and its sustainability. We cannot ultimately control nature, despite our human efforts to do just that, but we can promote its balance if we so choose. The climate crisis we now face is the end result of our failure as a human species to do that.

CONTEXTUAL COMPLEXITIES

This is a brief snapshot of the theological framework within which I ponder the ethical mandates of faith today. I approach this quest from within a specific sub-framework, that of the Christian tradition. Every religious tradition has emerged out of some context-specific connection to the larger framework of the inherent goodness of divine *for-life* creativity. Every religious tradition has its own distinctive storied wisdom—and its own shortcomings. Religious traditions, after all, emerge from human communities, and they are therefore all both precious and flawed. I acknowledge the capture and manipulation of religious imagination by human beings. We humans all left the Garden of Eden long ago, exiled by our own self-centeredness.

Still, I find sources of wisdom in the religious tradition most familiar to me, the Christian tradition. I value other traditions, but I am steeped in this one; it is my home, just as families are home, with all their strengths and flaws. And so I look to the teachings and witness of Jesus, and the religious tradition which shaped him, for guidance as I seek to answer questions about my calling as a religious person to respond to the ethical challenges that bedevil us in the present age—challenges within ourselves, in our relationships with others, and in our interrelatedness with the world.

But no religious calling takes place in a cultural or sociological contextual vacuum. I embrace my religious calling as an American by birth, albeit one who has largely rejected American culture and who has spent most of my adult life living in other cultures around the world. They have significantly informed and altered my worldview. Indeed, I would describe the theological perspective that now defines me as, in large part, a rejection of the Eurocentric[2] theology I inherited.

One of the insights I have gained in my faith journey in recent years is that what I have embraced as ethical principles that I attempted to fit neatly within a Christian ethic were in fact influenced, more than I realized, by my own contextual background. These principles were at times more culture than gospel. Thankfully, because of my exposure to other cultural worldviews and value systems, I came to see that the American worldview into which I was born and bred is in many ways antithetical to the Christocentric worldview I espouse, or to any religious worldview. It is a worldview that values individualism much more than it values the common good.

INDIVIDUALISM VS. THE COMMON GOOD

The notion of the common good was first articulated by Plato, Aristotle, and Cicero, but has been summarized by the ethicist John Rawls as *general conditions that are equally to everyone's advantage*.[3] This is affirmed when the "social systems, institutions, and environments on which we all depend work in a manner that benefits all people."[4] More specifically, the common good refers to "those facilities—whether material, cultural or institutional— that the members of a community provide to all members in order to fulfill a relational obligation they all have to care for the interests that they have in common."[5]

---

2. Eurocentrism has been defined as "an attitude, conceptual apparatus, or set of empirical beliefs that frame Europe as the primary engine and architect of world history, the bearer of universal values and reason, and the pinnacle and therefore model of progress and development." Sundberg, "Eurocentrism," 3:638. Eurocentric societies include not only those in Europe but other Caucasian-dominant societies such as the United States, Canada, Australia, and New Zealand.

3. Rawls, *Theory of Justice*, 217ff.
4. Hussain, "Common Good."
5. Hussain, "Common Good."

Unfortunately, efforts to promote the common good are hindered in American culture by its core value of individualism, with its appeal to individual rights and freedoms. In simplest terms, this can be captured in the American catchphrase "do your own thing." Here society consists of autonomous individuals who believe that they should be free to "do their own thing" with the fewest possible constraints. A popular American motto sums this up neatly: "Don't tread on me." Manuel Velasquez concludes that "In this individualistic culture it is difficult, perhaps impossible, to convince people that they should sacrifice some of their freedom, . . . some of their self-interest, for the sake of the 'common good.'"[6]

In her articulation of a Pacific Islands (Pasifika)[7] public theology, Mercy Ah Siu-Maliko argues that a Christian perspective on the common good is best summed up in Jesus' second great commandment—"In everything, do to others as you would have them do to you" (Matt 7:12) or "You shall love your neighbor as yourself" (Mark 12:31).[8] The public theologian Andrew Bradstock notes that Catholic social teaching "equates the common good with Christians' desire that God's 'will be done on earth,' for which Christians pray in the Lord's Prayer."[9]

Walter Brueggemann describes the erosion of the common good in postmodern Eurocentric societies such as the United States as the greatest crisis confronting these societies today: "The great crisis among us is the crisis of the 'common good,' the sense of community solidarity that binds us all in a common destiny—haves and have nots, the rich and the poor. We face a crisis about the common good because there are powerful forces at work among us to resist the common good, to violate community solidarity, and to deny a common destiny."[10]

The core value of individualism that has eroded the common good in Eurocentric societies is the antithesis of a *for-life* ethic in which humans co-exist as interrelated beings linked inextricably to others, to communities, to the world, to creation, treating all created beings and things with the

---

6. Hussain, "Common Good."

7. Although this region is typically referred to as the South Pacific, the Pacific Islands, Oceania, or simply "the Pacific," there is now a move to refer to this vast "watery continent" of islands in a more authentically indigenous way, as Pasifika. I will generally use that designation in this work. The designation "Pacific" is rejected because it was foisted upon the region and its ocean (*Moana*) by European colonizers, who not only wrongly characterized the *Moana* as a *pacific* (peaceful, placid) sea but applied that same label to its inhabitants (*Pacific* Islanders), as a way of suggesting that they too were docile and thus easy to control.

8. See Ah Siu-Maliko, *Embodying Aga Tausili*, 10ff.

9. Bradstock, "Recovering the Common Good."

10. Brueggemann, *Journey to the Common Good*, 1.

same love and respect. That is why my faith pulls and tugs at me to unmask the Eurocentric (and, in particular, the American) worldview and to look anew, through a Christocentric lens, at the serious ethical challenges we face today, as individuals, communities, and societies.

This is in part a search to *reclaim the consistency of God*. If God is indeed the divine creative thrust *for life* in all its goodness, then our ethical actions must likewise be consistently *for life*. My theological quest is to discern what that means in specific cases, across the whole of life—personal, interpersonal, ecological, societal. We cannot choose to be *for life* in one situation or setting but not in another. It is not possible, for example, to be for non-violence and yet to support war, to be anti-abortion and simultaneously pro-death penalty, to be pro-democracy and pro-empire. It is not possible to espouse the divine commandment "thou shalt not kill" and tolerate killing of any kind. I am compelled to explore what it might mean if we took the consistency of God more seriously.

LETTING GO OF EUROCENTRIC THEOLOGY

One of the greatest gifts of my many years of living in non-Western cultures has been the opportunity to see the worldly and the divine, the material and the spiritual, not as separate spheres, which was my Eurocentric heritage, but as the diverse ways in which God, creatures, and creation are inextricably woven together like the strands of a rope. Or, as in the Pasifika cultures which have most profoundly impacted my life, we might say that all of the divine expressions of life, in whatever sphere of being, are like the interwoven strands of the straw mats on which islanders traditionally ate, slept, made decisions, and socialized.

I have discovered over time that it is the surviving indigenous communities around the world which seem to come closest to holding on to a sense of the interrelatedness of creation, creatures, and creator. This way of viewing the world upends the Eurocentric worldview as it evolved historically. The separation of creator, creation, and creatures into separate spheres has had a long history, one which was already articulated clearly by the time of the ancient Greek philosophers. This orientation was not only about the separation of spheres but about hierarchies, some spheres being more valued than others. This philosophical tradition can be seen, to a degree, in the way of thinking of the apostle Paul in the New Testament, and it continued to influence the theological thinking of European Christianity through the centuries, persisting in certain respects to the present day.

This way of thinking accompanied the rise of modern European societies and was ultimately cemented in the Enlightenment and the Industrial Revolution. It was a worldview in which the sacred was severed irrevocably from the secular. This separation assumed the compartmentalization of existence—God versus the world, the material versus the spiritual, reason versus emotion, masculine versus feminine. Such compartmentalization relegated spirituality to private devotion or to confinement within the four walls of the church, leaving the "things of this world" to be managed by secular agents of power who were not constrained by any assumed connection to the sacred.

Prior to this decisive rupture that was the hallmark of modernity, a kind of co-dependency of secular and sacred had characterized the approximately ten centuries of Christendom, starting with the Emperor Constantine's conversion to Christianity in the fourth century, after which he decreed Christianity to be the religion of empire. This co-dependent relationship between religious and secular spheres continued through centuries of so-called "holy wars," papal armies, and churchly meddling in affairs of state (and vice versa) across Europe, until the onset of modernity. This was not genuine interrelatedness, because worldly powers had the upper hand and used Christianity to legitimize and bolster their power.

As feudalism gave way to burgeoning capitalism, "the world" became a materialist arena no longer tied to the sacred or answerable to religious authorities. The illusion of Christendom was abandoned, and "the world" was acknowledged to be a place to be controlled by wealthy elites whose power was no longer dependent upon the approval of the church. "The world" was there to be exploited by secular agents of power; it was in no way an intrinsic part of God's very being. This is a denial of the holism implied in alternative framings of God-and-world, such as Pasifika theologians' construal of the world as "the womb of God" (see Marc Pohue's "the living womb" in chapter 9) or the theologian Sallie McFague's depiction of the world as "God's body."[11]

Indigenous and non-Eurocentric societies do not subscribe to a compartmentalized worldview but to a holistic vision of God as infused in every expression of created life. I will return to this alternative worldview shortly, but first it will be helpful to recall briefly the underlying theological framework which emanated from the Eurocentric worldview—the so-called *classical theology* that dominated Christianity for centuries.

---

11. See McFague, *Body of God*.

Classical Theology and Patriarchy

John Markley defines classical theology as "most commonly used to describe the religious beliefs and doctrines that have been traditionally associated with mainstream Christianity in the Western world and that have been regarded by many Christian churches and theologians as authoritative."[12] This classical theology has been constructed and expressed through a male Eurocentric lens.

In the first instance, then, classical theology can be understood as a projection of patriarchy. One of the seminal first-wave[13] feminist theologians, Mary Daly, rejected classical theology's patriarchal assumption that God is "he," an assumption which has had profound implications for how Christianity has historically understood not only God but women, men, and religious leadership. God's assumed maleness has diminished women's importance, since men are seen as inherently more like God the Father and his son Jesus, and therefore the only gender suited for leadership.

The male God of classical theology has been described using patriarchal terms such as Lord, King, Judge, and Father, and the church's leaders throughout most of church history were expected to emulate this masculine, all-powerful God. This theological orientation legitimated the patriarchal underpinnings of Eurocentric theology and ecclesiology. As Elizabeth Johnson writes,

> Male self-definition has shaped the metaphysical concept of God which developed from the encounter of biblical and Greek philosophical traditions. The latter equated male reality with spirit, with mind and reason, and, most importantly, with action, reserving for female reality a contrasting intrinsic connection with matter, with body and instinct, and with fertility. This assumption and its attendant androcentric presuppositions permeate the classical Christian philosophical doctrine of God as well as the specifically Christian doctrine of the Trinity.[14]

I noted earlier that the patriarchal conception of God in Scripture which came to dominate in classical theology was counterbalanced, to a

---

12. Markley, "What is Classical Theology?"

13. "While First Wave feminism began with struggles for women's right to vote and workplace rights going back to the nineteenth century, First Wave feminist theology came into prominence in the late 1960s and 1970s, largely among white American feminists. Second Wave feminist theology (still largely Euro-American) is associated with the 1980s, and Third Wave (non-Western) feminist theology with the period from the 1990s onward." Ropeti-Apisaloma, *Nafanua Theology*, 31.

14. Johnson, "Incomprehensibility of God," 443. See also her "Naming God She."

degree, by the feminine divine imagery that existed as a kind of underground stream. However, simply switching from patriarchy to matriarchy in God-talk would not have solved the deeper issue: the patriarchal theology of God has been a huge problem in classical theology, but the larger problem is the anthropomorphizing of God in the first place, reducing the divine to a super-person, whether male or female.

Classical Theology and Monotheism

There is a related problem with classical theology, and that is its linkage with monotheism—the concept of *one* God, a discrete divine entity—who rules from an exalted position "above and beyond" humans and creation. The language of "one God" would not be problematic if it referred to the unity and inclusiveness of all things and beings that partake of divine creativity, but it has instead meant "one over against the many"—an overpowering monarchical god.

Although it is indigenous theologians who have been in the forefront of pointing out how monotheism has been used to support dominating "power-over" ways of relating, in which human leaders imitate the God who rules with absolute power, a few Western theologians have also acknowledged the problem of monotheism. Laurel Schneider, for example, argues that the concept of monotheism is "relationally bankrupt" because it is shaped by a *logic of the One* that makes God synonymous with absolute domination. She calls, instead, for a *logic of multiplicity*, and argues that "divine multiplicity" was in fact always present in the Judeo-Christian tradition, alongside the concept of the one God Yahweh which came to dominate.[15]

Monotheism was certainly not a settled concept in ancient Judaism. Yahweh is often described in the Old Testament as "the greatest" of the gods, or as a kind of CEO in "the council of the gods" (as in Ps 82:1: "God has taken his place in the divine council; in the midst of the gods he holds judgment"). It would be more accurate to describe this as *henotheism*, the worship of a favored god among others, with no one god having complete sovereignty.[16] Or at times what we see is *monolatry*, the exclusive worship of one god without denying the existence of others. It was perhaps in an effort to distinguish the evolving Jewish religion from other polytheistic religions in the Ancient Near East, with their array of gods, goddesses, and divinities housed in natural objects, that Hebrew Scripture came to voice the affirmation "Hear, O Israel, the Lord our God is one Lord" (Deut 6:4, NIV).

---

15. See Schneider, *Beyond Monotheism*.
16. Yusa, "Henotheism," 6:266.

Overall, Hebrew Scripture presents a hybrid of monotheism, henotheism, and monolatry. Old Testament passages abound with henotheistic or monolatrous affirmations about God, of which the following are only a few examples: In Deut 17:3, Yahweh chides the people of Israel for breaking their covenant by ". . . going to serve other gods and worshiping them—whether the sun or the moon or any of the host of heaven—which I have forbidden." Deuteronomy 29:26 again berates the Israelites because "They turned and served other gods, worshiping them, gods whom they had not known and whom he [Yahweh] had not allotted to them." In Exod 15:11, part of the Song of Moses celebrating the Israelites' escape from bondage in Egypt, we hear "Who is like you, O Lord, among the gods?" Deuteronomy 10:17 elevates Yahweh above the other gods with the title "God of gods."

Where the "one God" concept has the upper hand, God is depicted as the almighty Yahweh ruling from the heavenly realm, who can be a vengeful god of wrath as well as a god of mercy, at "his" whim—although, as we have seen, Yahweh is also portrayed at times as being in intimate relationship with people and the world. Notwithstanding this diversity of divine portrayals and roles, it is the shrinking of God to *one* that makes God only about power.

Schneider echoes the understanding of a growing body of indigenous theologians that "divine multiplicity" is in fact an experiential reality, located in our human experience of God as relationally present in all expressions and beings of the created world. It is therefore regrettable that Eurocentric Christianity, both as it developed in the West and was spread around the world through missionary activity, promulgated the *one God* of monotheism—an all-powerful divine king, seated on his throne of glory, ruling and judging, removed from his subjects. The challenge for indigenous Christians today, as the Samoan theologian Upolu Vaai points out, is this: "How do we continue to worship one God but at the same time continue to relate to a relational God who embraces everyone and everything?"[17]

The concept of the monotheistic God of Eurocentric theology, which was transplanted around the world along with imperial conquest, has indeed undermined the holistic experience of divinity as infused in all things and beings. This holistic God has thankfully not been completely eradicated, especially among indigenous communities. Nonetheless, as the World Council of Churches has recognized, it must also be acknowledged that the missionized churches which were recipients of foreign concepts of the one almighty God have all too often, like their Eurocentric colonizers,

---

17. Vaai, personal communication, cited in Ropeti-Apisaloma, *Nafanua Theology*, 125.

> ... perceived God in terms of power and perfection, as ruler, king, almighty, lord and father. Though God is merciful, loving, caring, compassionate, a comforter and liberator who shares in our suffering and, through Jesus Christ, taught us to care for one another, we have tended to over-emphasize the victorious images of God. These images of God have made Christianity a religion of rulers, of elites... [Christians must] reject any notion of a God who is an external monarch ruling from above, imposing his divine laws on the world.[18]

Monotheism, in short, has been a convenient model for "power-over" ways of relating, rather than "power-with" or "power-for" ways of relating. This has had dire repercussions for the recipients of the colonizing and neocolonizing projects of empires, as Upolu Vaai reminds us:

> Monotheism has been the epistemological foundation that underpinned the colonial project. This can be ascertained if we dig deeper into the Doctrine of Discovery and *terra nullius* that impacted many indigenous communities around the world, as a justification to take their lands, resources, and knowledge to build the royal empire. This monotheistic philosophy still continues today in the neoliberal economic philosophy of growth, and many development policies in the Pacific that promote the idea of extracting from one culture or peoples to benefit another.[19]

RECOVERING AN INTERRELATIONAL GOD

In rejecting Eurocentric classical theology, I have gravitated toward what many Pasifika theologians call *relational theology*. Other indigenous theologians articulate a similar theological framework.[20] I find the term *relational theology* helpful but perhaps not the ideal designation. While I share its intention and substance, it could be misconstrued at first glance as referring to a theological orientation that focuses on building healthy relationships between individuals—or between people and God or creation.

Those are essential aspects of relationality, but the term *relational theology* does not explicitly address the core grounding of theology in the

18. World Council of Churches, "Indigenous Theologians' Reflections."
19. Vaai, "Theo-ethical Reflections from Oceania."
20. See, for example, Yunkaporta, *Sand Talk*; Clark, *Reclaiming Stolen Earth*; Chibuye and Buitendag, "Indigenisation of Eco-theology"; and Kerber, "Climate Change and Southern Theologies."

*inter*relatedness of everything in the cosmos, although this is its intention. We may relate "to" God while still envisioning God as being "out there"—a "wholly other" being, radically separate from us. We may relate "to" creation, but I noted previously the potential theological shortcomings of "creation care" if we conceive of ourselves as benevolent parents relating "to" the damaged earth from a position of assumed superiority.

Interrelational theology is thus a more fitting way of speaking of my theological orientation. As alluded to already, this is an orientation which draws on the wisdom of indigenous cultures that have not artificially separated humans from creator and creation in the way that Eurocentric theology has done. There are of course distinctions between creator, creation, and creatures. However, returning to my description of the originary creating act, *all* of creation, human and non-human, partakes of the same atoms, molecules, and particles that burst forth in the birthing of *life*. That "stuff of life" is God, and all of creation partakes of that divine substance.

A core claim of interrelational theology (and relational theology), therefore, is that humans are not privileged or entitled as participants in this divine creation. We are given the gift of being human, but our response to that gift should be humble gratitude, not any innate prerogative to exploit our relationships with creation or others for our own selfish ends. An apt analogy for our human place in creation is what happens when Pacific Islanders weave the straw mats which are central to their communal life. Through a lengthy process, some of the strands, typically made from dried palm or pandanus fronds, take on distinctive hues. Traditionally, at least in the Tongan tradition of which I am aware,[21] darker colors emerged by leaving some strands for a time in the mud flats of the mangrove swamps, or soaking them in vats colored by various tropical fruits.

The end result when all of these strands are woven together is a mat with intricate designs highlighted by distinctive hues. These varied strands are each unique, but all are of equal value. Each strand is valued because of its unique beauty but, most importantly, because of what it contributes to the overall design. Every strand is necessary to create the flawless design which is revealed when one views the mat in its totality. In an interrelational theology, humans, earth, sea, sky, stars, sun, moon, trees, plants, animals, and every aspect of creation are all essential strands that are needed to weave the mat of life. God is the mat in its totality.

I wish to give full credit to my Pasifika brothers and sisters whose relational theologies have inspired me as I have developed my own theological perspective. I am closest to them theologically, having lived and worked in

---

21. See Palu, "Tapa Making in Tonga," 64–67.

Pasifika for the most significant years of my adult life.[22] Their insights have contributed profoundly to the shaping and reshaping of my own theological journey.

"We Are"—not "We Have"

Among contemporary Pasifika theologians who espouse relational theology, the best-known is the Samoan theologian Upolu Vaai.[23] According to Vaai, spirituality for Pacific Islanders is not about the spiritual world as distinct from the physical world. Instead, spirituality is the holistic manifestation of the divine in the created world and in all relationships, human and non-human. It defies the dualistic splitting of reality into opposites. As Vaai puts it, "The spiritual is 'embodied' in the physical and the physical is 'enhanced' in the spiritual."[24]

This theological understanding has far-reaching implications for the climate crisis, political systems, economics, the evils of empire and colonialism, the struggle for decolonization, and relationships between men and women. This is because, as Vaai writes, relational spiritual consciousness ". . . promotes the 'we are' over the 'we have.'"[25] Embracing a "we are" rather than a "we have" way of being in the world means that we do not measure our success as persons, communities, or nations by what we "own." Vaai's critique of the "we have" paradigm is that it

> . . . promotes competition over the limited resources of the earth. The 'we are' paradigm means that the earth 'owns' us and not the other way around. It is a principle that decentralises power . . . [it] promotes the idea of 'enoughness' that encourages sharing

---

22. I taught at Pacific Theological College in Suva, Fiji for some years. PTC is a regional theological institution whose students hail from across Pasifika (in its sub-regions of Polynesia, Melanesia, and Micronesia). In addition to its ethnic and cultural diversity, PTC is unique in terms of its ecumenical breadth, representing the Protestant churches in the region and having a cross-fertilizing relationship with the nearby Roman Catholic Pacific Regional Seminary. PTC has produced a number of significant theologians in recent decades. As of 2025, it will become Pasifika Communities University.

23. Upolu Vaai is the principal of Pacific Theological College, where he is also professor of theology and ethics. Among his many publications, see, for example, "Tino Theology"; "E Itiiti a Lega Mea—Less Yet More"; "Relational Hermeneutics"; "We Are, Therefore We Live"; and "'We Are Earth."

24. Vaai, "We Are, Therefore We Live."

25. Vaai, "We Are, Therefore We Live."

and distribution of wealth equitably, and challenges the greed and individualism found in the 'more is better' paradigm.[26]

This "we are" ethic directly challenges the Eurocentric worldview that was transported to and transplanted in so many indigenous communities around the world through missionization, colonization, and empire-building. This is a worldview in which, as noted earlier, spiritual experience following missionization came to be confined to the church or to explicitly religious personal activities. This could not be more different than the Pasifika worldview, and that of many other indigenous cultures, in which spirituality is everywhere: all of life is sacred and "woven together in the mat of life."[27] "We are" part of God.

Relationality, in other words, refers to the mutual interdependence of the multiple networks of creation. In the Maohi[28] theologian Marc Pohue's interpretation of Vaai's relational theology, he concludes that this interconnectedness "creates the link between wholeness and relationality."[29] The denial of the interrelatedness implicit in creation "promotes negative and destructive behaviours toward the living womb [creation], leading to discrimination and oppression, and ultimately to imperialism and neglect of the marginalized."[30] As humans, we are born into multifaceted interwoven relationships, not only with families, communities, and non-human creation, but with the whole cosmos.[31] I will return to Pohue in my discussion of the climate crisis in chapter 9.

Movement Toward a *For-Life* Ethic

I find inspiring insights in the indigenous voices from the non-Eurocentric world who have rejected any understanding of God as an all-powerful, domineering figure who rules the world by controlling and pontificating from a

26. Vaai, "We Are, Therefore We Live."
27. Vaai, "We Are, Therefore We Live."
28. In the context of the struggle for decolonization in Pasifika, the indigenous people of the colonized (French) territory known as French Polynesia insist that their land is Maohi Nui and that they are the Maohi people, whose mother tongue is the Maohi language. They also resist the common designation of themselves as Tahitians (the only island in Maohi Nui that is widely known, thanks to the tourist industry, Gauguin's paintings, and the filming of *The Mutiny on the Bounty*). Tahiti is only one of the 121 islands that make up the Maohi Nui archipelago.
29. Pohue, "Navigating with the Womb of Life," 80. Marc Pohue completed his PhD in theology at Pacific Theological College in 2022.
30. Pohue, "Navigating with the Womb of Life," 80.
31. Vaai, "Faith and Culture."

heavenly throne, above and beyond creation and creatures. This separation of creator from creation and creatures has had destructive consequences for ethics. It has countenanced an authoritarian, top-down framework in which males have emulated the presumed masculine, dictatorial God in their practice of a "power-over" orientation to the world—power over creation, power over the weak, power over the poor, power over women, power over perceived inferior races, power over competitors. This is a denial of the original divine intention for creation, which did not privilege one entity over others but celebrated the divinely infused life of all creation and all creatures.

This divinely interrelated understanding of life has led me to examine and re-examine what a *for-life* ethic means when applied to our inner life as persons, our relational life with creation, and our life-lived-together—our social existence in the world. If we are called as God's creatures to be *for life* in our interconnected life with all beings and things of creation, how should this motivate us to act?

In this work, I attempt to apply the ethical implications of a *for-life* theology to a number of realities that impact us and at times confound us. This is not an exhaustive exercise in discernment and application. It is a patchwork quilt stitched together through the lens of my experience and the wisdom of others, and an invitation to readers to envision their own quilted tapestry of responses to the divine invitation to live an interwoven life of gratitude in the light of God's *for-life* ethical imperative.

This book, then, is a praxiological theological exploration, in which I have allowed the existential realities that most press in on my consciousness to inform the ways I have explored them. This has meant that each chapter assumes its own distinctive style and approach, tied together by my underlying quest to apply a *for-life* ethic to these lived realities. Because I ground my exploration in a Christian worldview, it is also essential to situate the experiential threads of this ethic in the communitarian core of the Christian faith—the ecclesial community known as the church—and it is to that phenomenon that I turn next.

2

Gathered Life in the *Kindom*

ALL RELIGIONS HAVE A communal aspect, habitual patterns and rituals of being-together for shared prayer, moral instruction, spiritual guidance, and fellowship, whether in a temple, mosque, synagogue, church, or at a shrine or other holy place. This communitarian thrust is very pronounced in the Christian religion, which prioritizes the regular gathering of Christ-followers in what came to be known as the church.

The church is, in simplest terms, any gathered community of Christians, and it has been assumed since the church's beginning that it is essential for Christians to set aside time, energy, talents, and resources to support and nurture one another in the life of faith through such communities. The church had its birth in Jerusalem at Pentecost (Acts 2:1–13) among a remarkably diverse gathering of people. Although those who had initially gathered in a house to await the inbreaking of the Holy Spirit are identified in the text as "Galileans" (presumably mostly Jews), those in the growing crowd were astonished to hear that these "insiders" were speaking their "outsider" languages. As a child, I used to delight in trying to pronounce the names of these different ethnic groups that were present: "Parthians, Medes, Elamites, residents of Mesopotamia, Judea, Cappadocia, Pontus, Asia, Phrygia, Pamphylia, Egypt, the parts of Libya belonging to Cyrene, Romans, Cretans and Arabs" (Acts 2:9–11).

While we sometimes focus on the more overtly miraculous manifestations of the Holy Spirit amongst those gathered at Pentecost—such as the flames of fire appearing over their heads—what strikes me as the most significant occurrence on that occasion was the fact that all present could communicate with each other, "insiders" and "outsiders." The church was, from its birth, a sign to the world that the faithful were to be a heterogeneous community where very different people could understand one another.

Although there were arguments in the very beginning about whether the church should be Jewish or open to non-Jews, generically known as Gentiles, the latter perspective won the argument, as the Apostle Paul, formerly a strict, even repressive Jew, came to affirm. As he proclaimed in Gal 3:28, "There is no longer Jew or Greek; there is no longer slave or free; there is no longer male and female, for all of you are one in Christ Jesus." Christians did not lose their diverse cultural and ethnic identities, but what was most important was the way in which everyone was interrelated with everyone else, as a family of equals.

CHURCH AS BODY

The earliest church is perhaps best depicted in the New Testament in the Book of Acts, which describes a communistic community, gathering daily in people's homes to share not only prayer, worship, teaching, and reflection but food and worldly goods. As Acts 2:42, 44–45 tells us, "They devoted themselves to the apostles' teaching and fellowship, to the breaking of bread and prayers . . . All who believed were together and had all things in common; they would sell their possessions and goods and distribute the proceeds to all, as any had need." This early ecclesial community existed in large part to share, and this included sharing not just amongst themselves but with the wider circle of those in need—the poor, the "widows and orphans."

This community was symbolized in New Testament theology through the metaphor *body of Christ*. We come to understand the reason for the use of the image of "body" to describe the church in the well-known passage in 1 Cor 12:12–27:

> For just as the body is one and has many members, and all the members of the body, though many, are one body, so it is with Christ. . . . If the foot would say, 'Because I am not a hand, I do not belong to the body,' that would not make it any less a part of the body. And if the ear would say, 'Because I am not an eye, I do not belong to the body,' that would not make it any less a part of the body.' . . . The eye cannot say to the hand, 'I have no need of you,' nor again the head to the feet, 'I have no need of you.' On the contrary, the members of the body that seem to be weaker are indispensable, and those members of the body that we think less honorable we clothe with greater honor, and our less respectable members are treated with greater respect . . . If

one member suffers, all suffer together with it; if one member is honored, all rejoice together with it. Now you are the body of Christ and individually members of it.

The Samoan theologian Marie Ropeti-Apisaloma writes that "The church as 'body' is the organism through which Christ manifests his life in the world today. Members of the body of Christ share a common bond through their *tausi le vatapuia* (nurturing of right relationships) with all other members, who are connected to one another and to the whole body as equally valued beings, regardless of gender, race, or background."[1] The body of Christ metaphor is an interrelational way of envisioning and describing the church as a community in which all members have equal value.

KINGDOM OR KINDOM?

Regrettably, the body of Christ has at times been conflated with the kingdom of God. The phrase "kingdom of God" occurs often in the New Testament, usually spoken by Jesus, and it has generally been understood as referring to the spiritual realm over which God reigns as king. This is a paradoxical "already/not yet" reality: Christians can experience a sense of belonging in the kingdom of God since Jesus has ushered it into being with his incarnation, but it also refers to the future ultimate fulfillment of God's will on earth in an eschatological sense.[2]

Although the phrase "kingdom of God" is not explicitly used in the Old Testament, the imagery of God as "king" was certainly common in ancient Judaism. We do see occasional references to the "kingdom of the Lord" (as in 2 Chron 13:8), and to "God's kingdom" (as in Dan 6:26). The concept of divine kingship is thus well established in the Old Testament, and this may have influenced Jesus' adoption of kingdom imagery. But the Aramaic word for "kingdom" (*malkut*), which Jesus would have used, "does not refer to a realm nor to the people inhabiting the realm but, rather, to the activity of the king himself, his exercise of sovereign power."[3]

This is a problematic concept for interrelational Christians in relation to the church, because it undercuts the essence of the body of Christ as an organic community in which all are equally responsible for their shared life of faith. Although in Luke 17:21 Jesus said, "the kingdom of God is within

---

1. Ropeti-Apisaloma, *Nafanua Theology*, 11.
2. "Kingdom of God."
3. "Kingdom of God."

you," the word "kingdom" still connotes authority and sovereign rule by a king, not the oneness of all in the body of Christ.

Thankfully, some feminist and anti-empire theologians have pointed out the dangers of associating the church with a kingdom, which assumes a king who, by definition, is male and all-powerful. This anachronism was brought into contemporary theology of church discourse by the Cuban theologian, Ada Maria Isasi-Diaz.[4] She first heard the phrase *kindom of God* from a friend of hers who was a Catholic nun, who found the language of 'kingdom' to be "fraught with colonial oppression and imperial violence."[5] Although Jesus' intention was to ". . . use 'kingdom of God' to evoke . . . an alternative 'order of things' over and against the political context of the Roman Empire and its Caesar, the actual kingdom and king at the time,"[6] it makes no theological sense to use the word "kingdom" to describe the egalitarian community of the body of Christ.

Rather than Christians being submissive subjects living in a male-dominated kingdom, Isasi-Diaz adopted *kindom of God* as a way of describing an ecclesial community in which the faithful gather as one family. Although it could be argued that not all members of families are necessarily equal, especially in patriarchal families where the father is the "head," kinship here is about *collective intimacy*, a far cry from the experience of the passive subjects who live under a king.

Isasi-Diaz frames the kindom of God as an intimate place of *libertad*, the "liberation of God at work among people, [which is] good news for those who suffer at the hands of kings."[7] Kindom liberation "emerges from opening space where love invites us into kinship, invites us to join others at a table that grows. Liberation is found not in hope deferred to another world, to life after death, but in what can be created now."[8] Isasi-Diaz describes the kindom as a *community of solidarity* with all who are oppressed, who suffer from injustices of any kind: "From a Christian perspective, the goal of solidarity is to participate in the ongoing process of liberation through

---

4. Ada Maria Isasi-Diaz was born in 1943 in Cuba and migrated to the United States in 1960. She earned her PhD in Christian Social Ethics from Union Theological Seminary and became Professor of Ethics and Theology at Drew University in 1991, where she founded and was co-director of the Hispanic Institute of Theology. Isasi-Díaz is best known for her *mujerista* theology, a feminist liberation theology from a Latina (Hispanic women's) perspective. Some of her best-known works include *En La Lucha/In the Struggle*; *La Lucha Continues*; and *Mujerista Theology*.

5. Butler-Bass, "Kin-dom of God." Bass's comments here on the origins and essence of Isasi-Diaz' kindom theology are excerpted from her book, *Freeing Jesus*.

6. Butler-Bass, "Kin-dom of God."

7. Florer-Bixler, "Kin-dom of Christ," 2.

8. Florer-Bixler, "Kin-dom of Christ," 2.

which we Christians become a significantly positive force in the unfolding of the Kindom of God."[9]

Diana Butler-Bass traces the origins of kindom imagery far back in Christian history, revealing how the medieval theology of Julian of Norwich[10] used kinship language to speak of Jesus. She unpacks the way in which Julian of Norwich wrote of

> ... 'our kinde Lord,' ... summoning images of a gentle Jesus. But it was not that. Rather, it was a radical one, for the word 'kinde' in medieval English did not mean 'nice' or 'pleasant.' Instead, in the words of theologian Janet Soskice, 'In Middle English the words 'kind' and 'kin' were the same—to say that Christ is 'our kinde Lord' is not to say that Christ is tender and gentle, although that may be implied, but to say that he is *kin—our kind*. . . To say 'our kinde Lord' was to say 'our kin Lord.' Jesus is our kin. The kinde Lord is kin to me, you, all of us—making us one. This is a subversive deconstruction of the image of kingdom and kings, replacing forever the authoritarianism of earthly kingdoms with Jesus' calling forth a Kin-dom.[11]

A core feature of our life as Christians who are interrelational beings can therefore be said to be our shared life of kinship with others, with God, with Jesus, with creation, in the gathered community which is the kindom of God. This intimate life of connection and activism for the cause of justice is key to our collective life as Christians. It not only provides solace and solidarity; it calls us to action. It asks something of us. It is where we grow in discernment and insight, where we hold one another up in our weakness and times of doubt or sorrow and where we hold hands to find strength for loving and liberating action in the world.

A kindom image which comes to mind is that of worshipers who form a circle around the sanctuary at the conclusion of Christmas Eve services, leaving their pews—where they only see the backs of people's heads and gaze upward toward a raised pulpit which is the domain of clergy—to create an unbroken space of connection. In the darkened sanctuary, one person lights the first candle from the Christ candle and then lights the candle of the person standing beside him or her. This person lights the candle of

---

9. Isasi-Diaz, *Mujerista Theology*, 55.

10. The medieval English theologian Julian of Norwich (1342–1416 CE) is best known for her book, *The Revelations of Divine Love*, still considered one of the finest expositions of the spiritual life. Although she is thought of as a mystic, her theology could also be said to be interrelational, as she spoke of the inner life of God as intrinsically connected to God's relationship with creation.

11. Butler-Bass, "Kin-dom of God," 2.

the next person, and on it goes around the circle, until the dark sanctuary becomes first a faint light, a tiny glow, that then grows and grows until the whole sanctuary is suffused with light. This is kindom light. This is the kind of community in which we are meant to situate ourselves in our shared striving to be interrelated beings living out a *for-life* ethic.

KINDOM LIFE IS JUBILEE LIFE

Kindom life has "real world" economic and societal implications. The church is called to practice the theological imperatives suggested by the biblical Jubilee. The biblical concept and practice of the Jubilee is a reminder that God has expectations for how human communities are to live their earthly life. Jubilee life is a visible sign that no one owns the land or those who dwell in the land, but all are responsible to show gratitude for its gifts by keeping earthly life in balance, so that both the land and its inhabitants can live with justice and mercy.

The Jubilee Year, which in Scripture occurred every seven years, or in certain situations every fifty years, has four components, which are spelled out in Lev 25. In the Jubilee year, (1) the soil will be left fallow—no planting allowed; (2) debts will be forgiven; (3) slaves will be freed; and (4) all confiscated land will be returned to its original owners. I will explore each of these in turn, gleaning insights from John Howard Yoder's study of the Jubilee.[12]

First, we consider *the fallow year*. I can imagine that not planting crops every seventh year may have created anxiety for families as they approached this fallow year. Leviticus 25:20–21 gives voice to this concern: God speaks, saying, "Should you ask, 'What shall we eat in the seventh year, if we may not sow or gather in our crop?,' there will be a blessing for you in the sixth year, so that it will yield a crop for three years." This is an invocation of the divine intention to keep things in balance in creation, as the result of which wellbeing in fallow times will be assured. It has great relevance for our climate crisis today, when our land and waters certainly need a time of rest from over-use and over-extraction of resources.

Although Jesus does not speak overtly about the *fallow year* component of the Jubilee, Yoder suggests that he does seem to echo the promise of Lev 25:20–21 when he says in Luke 12:29–30, "Do not keep striving for what you are to eat and what you are to drink, and do not keep worrying. For it is the nations of the world that strive after all these things, and your Father [sic] knows that you need them." Jesus' reassurance here could indicate that his listeners were following the Jubilee prescriptions. Their concerns may

12. Yoder, *Politics of Jesus*.

have been particularly relevant during Jesus' ministry because the year 32 CE was a Jubilee year.[13] Jesus is implying that if people have planted carefully and stored food in advance, they will not have to worry during the Jubilee year, and the long-term blessing will be that the land will have time to be restored and replenished.

The second aspect of the Jubilee year is the *forgiveness of debts*, and this expectation was well known in Jesus' teaching. This principle is seen in several of his parables and in the Lord's Prayer (Matt 6:9–13; Luke 11:1–4), which says "remit us our debts as we ourselves have also remitted them to our debtors." This is Yoder's translation, and he points out the fallacies of modern translations which say "forgive us our trespasses" or "forgive us our sins." Yoder explains that the Greek noun used here, *opheilema*, "signifies precisely a monetary debt, in the most material sense of the term . . . Jesus is not simply recommending vaguely that we might pardon those who have bothered us or made us trouble, but tells us purely and simply to erase the debts of those who owe us money—that is to say, practice the Jubilee."[14]

It is interesting that Jesus, who objected to the strict laws of the Pharisees (as in Mark 2:27, where he upbraids the Pharisees for chiding the man who rescued his ox from a ditch on the Sabbath, saying, "The Sabbath was made for humankind and not humankind for the Sabbath"), was adamant about upholding the Jubilee command to forgive people's debts. As Yoder comments, when the law was compassionate and merciful, as in the Jubilee, "Jesus became more radical than the Pharisees."[15]

The Jubilee prescription to forgive all debts in the seventh year has been taken up by some economists today. The socialist economist and scholar Richard Wolff has explicitly called for a "debt Jubilee" to ease the suffering of millions of Americans trapped in debt. He has specifically advocated for the biblical Jubilee commandment regarding the forgiveness of debts to be adopted as a way to save millions of vulnerable Americans from bankruptcy, home foreclosures, credit card debt, student loan defaults, and more.[16]

I will consider together the third and fourth prescriptions of the Jubilee, namely the *freeing of slaves* and the *return of foreclosed land to its original owners*. I place these together because they are linked in Leviticus, and both have to do with liberation from poverty. Loss of freedom was the

---

13. Yoder, "Implications of the Jubilee," 62.
14. Yoder, "Implications of the Jubilee," 62.
15. Yoder, "Implications of the Jubilee," 65.
16. Wolff, "Interview." Among Wolff's many scholarly works, see *Occupy the Economy*.

consequence of farmers falling into poverty and subsequently losing their land. If a farmer could not repay debts to a creditor, who then seized his land as collateral, in the Jubilee Year his land would be returned to him (Lev 25:39–43). If a farmer became so indebted that he could no longer support his family, he was bound over to the creditor, becoming in effect a slave. As a bound laborer, he could work for wages, but his earnings could only be used to repay his debt. However, in the Jubilee year, he would regain both his land and his freedom, and his debt would be cancelled (Lev 25:41).

Some of these same economic stresses remained in first-century Palestine in Jesus' day. He often addressed the problem of poverty, and his followers were told to sell all they had and give the proceeds to the poor (Luke 12:30–33). Some have found this instruction to be preposterous, for if everyone gave away everything they had, everyone would be poor. Jesus' point was that our generosity as a kindom community must be extravagant, not restrictive. Devout Jews in Jesus' day, especially the Pharisees, still practiced tithing (giving ten percent of their income to help the poor), but Jesus pointed out flaws in the prevailing practice of tithing. In Luke 11:42, he said, "But woe to you Pharisees! For you tithe mint and rue and herbs of all kinds, yet neglect justice and the love of God; it is these you ought to have practiced, without neglecting the others. Woe to you Pharisees!"

The Jubilee provisions for the freedom of slaves from their bondage to wealthy creditors, and the return of land which had been taken from them, were practical means of periodically taking extraordinary steps to correct the imbalances which plague economic life. These were opportunities to make a fresh start, to restore hope for those who had become mired in hopelessness. What was most important for Jesus was generosity of spirit, not fulfilling the requirements of charitable obligations.

As Yoder concludes, "When comparing the generosity of the wealthy, who ostentatiously were throwing large offerings into the temple treasury, with that of the poor widow, Jesus exclaimed, 'This poor widow [who had given her only two coins] has put in more than all of them. They put in from their overflow but she from her poverty has given all that she had' (Luke 21:1–4)."[17] The Jubilee redistribution of capital and land, and freedom from indebtedness, is about this kind of generosity.

What are the implications of the Jubilee for kindom communities who seek to live a *for-life* ethic today? The Old Testament scholar Christopher Wright has addressed this question and has responded through three lenses: theological, social, and economic.[18] *Theologically*, the Jubilee affirms that

---

17. Yoder, "Implications of the Jubilee," 65.
18. Wright, *Old Testament Ethics*, chapter 9.

God's love encompasses all times, places, people, and spheres of creation. Living out the Jubilee is thus an affirmation of our commitment to emulate God's care and mercy for those whose protection, safety, and wellbeing are precarious. My way of rephrasing this would be to say that a Jubilee life is a way of reminding ourselves—whether every seven years, every year, every month, or every week—that as *for-life* beings our generosity and care for others and for the land must be wholehearted and all-encompassing. This must be evident in our kindom life.

The *social* lens of the Jubilee reminds us that a crucial aspect of our relationality is our ethical connectedness to the societies in which we live. The Jubilee, both in ancient Israel and today, provides "a socio-economic solution to keep families whole even in the face of economic calamity. Family debt was a reality in ancient times as it is today, and its effects include a frightening list of social ills. The Jubilee seeks to check these negative social consequences by limiting their duration, so that future generations will not have to bear the burden of their ancestors."[19]

This appeal to the common good is the antithesis of the fragmentation of social life in individualist societies like the United States, which has led to a "dog eat dog," "each one for himself" mindset. The wealthy find ways to avoid paying taxes almost completely and blame the poor for their poverty, telling them to "pull yourself up by your bootstraps." As kindom dwellers, we need to counteract this mindset with Jubilee lifestyles that reconnect us with our neighbors and communities across the divides of class and socio-economic status.

The *economic* lens of the Jubilee is a reminder that God desires the just distribution of the earth's resources. The Jubilee is about both redistribution and restoration. In practical terms, for example, as Wright points out, "The Jubilee stands as a critique . . . of massive private accumulation of land and related wealth. . ."[20] In the American context, this suggests the need for the dismantling of "Big Ag," the huge corporations that control more and more of America's commercial agriculture. Big Ag is about the profits of corporation owners and stockholders, not the welfare of the agricultural workers who barely earn enough in wages to feed their families. The antithesis of these corporate behemoths is the solution proposed by Richard Wolff and other socialist economists—a shift toward small-scale, worker-owned agricultural cooperatives. Kindom communities should support such efforts.

I have included the Jubilee in this chapter because of the need for us as interrelated beings to ground ourselves in kindom communities that lift

---

19. "Sabbath Year and the Year of Jubilee."
20. Wright, *Mission of God*, 296.

up those who have fallen, encourage the downhearted, bind the wounds of those who suffer, and create joyful communities that practice generosity, compassion, justice, and love. It may not be feasible to reproduce today the precise injunctions of the Jubilee laid out in Leviticus. But what if we were to take to heart the Jubilee theology of restoring what has been lost or wounded? How might we live in our communities and our societies? The biblical Jubilee gives us clues.

COMMUNITARIAN EXPRESSIONS OF CHURCH

An indispensable aspect of my quest to enflesh an interrelational theology in and through the church is the need to ask the "What if?" question in relation to the insights that emerge from such reflection. In relation to what the church should be, I must ask: are there living examples of kindom churches today? If so, what might this mean for Christians striving to be God's living kindom/body of Christ in their own contexts?

For much of my adult life, I have been drawn to alternative communitarian forms of church. This has been a tough juggling act at times, because I have never completely left the institutional church, and I remain an ordained minister in an established church. I have been a pastor in churches from Jamaica to Tennessee to North Carolina, but I have lived uneasily in those institutional spaces. At times I have situated myself in alternative expressions of church, but I have done so while still respecting my loved ones who are deeply committed to their mainstream churches, several of them as ministers.

I was thoroughly entrenched in traditional church life from my earliest beginnings, and as a child I found meaning there, largely due to the fact that my father was my minister and inspired me every Sunday with his thought-provoking sermons and heartfelt prayers. But by the time I left home for college at age 18, something had changed. I found church stultifying, even suffocating at times. I felt that the traditional routinized liturgy boxed out the movement of the Spirit, and left little space for spontaneity or substantive contributions to worship by worshipers. It began to bother me that the minister was "above" the congregation, visibly elevated. And why did he (when I came of age in the 1960s, ministers were almost all "he") wear a robe or a tight-fitting collar? What was the theological significance of that? Why was he "set apart" from the rest of us?

I came to believe that the institutional church did not seem to be taking too seriously the congregational refrain following the reading of the gospel, "hear what the Spirit is saying to the church." Where was this Spirit in our ecclesial life? Was the Spirit trying to speak but our formalities and structures were preventing us from hearing clearly? In seeking the Spirit's presence, I was not longing for a Charismatic or Pentecostal church, where the emphasis seemed to be more on emotional catharsis than on the provocative urgings of the Spirit to transform us for faithful life in the world. I was simply longing to be spiritually challenged in church, not only in my intellect but in the entirety of my being.

By this time, during my student years, I was very involved as an activist—motivated by my Christian faith—in the civil rights movement led by Martin Luther King, Jr. and the anti-war movement. But that impulse was not nurtured by the church but by my "listening" to a small group of inspirational role models. I was inspired by Christian exemplars from my father to Martin Luther King, to William Sloan Coffin (the minister of Riverside Church in New York City and prominent anti-war activist), to the Catholic priests Daniel and Philip Berrigan, who were arrested numerous times for protesting the Vietnam War.

During my student years, I did not lose my faith, but I did almost lose the church. After a few visits to local churches near my college campus, which left me staggering out into the sunlight after the service feeling as though I had been given a sedative, I had no desire to continue with what for me had become a sterile glut of words. Words, words, words—worship was inundated with words, with almost no time or space for pregnant silence, in which we might attune ourselves to the stirring, challenging, empowering, and comforting presence of the divine Spirit.

Despite my alienation from the institutional church, I continued to long for a faith community that could be central to my life. My faith was still the center of my existence, and I felt a strong calling to find a path toward ministry. After earning my bachelor's degree in music, and a further year of teaching piano at my college, I was accepted to study theology at Harvard Divinity School. This was a place that was theologically stimulating but not a place where one could easily find an alternative communitarian experience of church! However, I arrived at HDS in 1972 just as something important was beginning to emerge out of the barrios of South America, something which gave me new hope in my yearning to find a form of church that was a community rather than an institution—a kindom community.

In 1973, the groundbreaking book *A Theology of Liberation*,[21] by the Peruvian theologian Gustavo Gutiérrez,[22] was first translated from Spanish

---

21. Gutiérrez, *Theology of Liberation*. Among his many other books, see, for example, *God of Life* and *We Drink from Our Own Wells*.

22. Gutiérrez is *mestizo* (mixed race), part Peruvian of Spanish ancestry and part indigenous Quechuan. After completing degrees in medicine, philosophy, and

into English. It is considered the foundational text of liberation theology. Gutiérrez gave voice to a new spirituality rooted in solidarity with the poor and called on the church to embody this solidarity, using grassroots activism to nudge social, economic, and political institutions toward social justice. Here the poor become agents of their own liberation, and the church becomes a community that *practices* theology and interprets salvation through the lens of liberation from oppression. As Gutiérrez wrote, a theology of liberation "does not stop with reflecting on the world but rather tries to be a part of the process through which the world is transformed."[23]

My advisor at Harvard Divinity School was Harvey Cox, best known in theological circles as the author of *The Secular City* and other works that stimulate cross-fertilization between theology and society.[24] As soon as Gutiérrez's *A Theology of Liberation* was published, Cox straightaway offered the first course in liberation theology at HDS and had us read Gutiérrez's book, along with other emerging liberation theology texts. Liberation theology was eye-opening for me, and what left me most transfixed was its praxiological grounding. Here theology was not something abstract to be confined to classrooms in universities and seminaries but something to be lived in grassroots communities. The church could in no way be separated from struggles for social justice.

Alongside the rich repository of works in liberation theology emanating from Latin America that followed Gutierrez's *Theology of Liberation*, by theologians such as Leonardo Boff, José Míguez Bonino, Juan Luis Segundo, and Jon Sobrino, a revolutionary new way of being church emerged. This was the Base Ecclesial Communities (BECs), sometimes translated into English as Christian Base Communities. BECs were small groups of Christians whose gathered life was centered in a synthesis of spirituality and action. They were the poor, led mostly by lay people, meeting in homes, village squares, under trees in city parks—wherever people could gather. They emphasized community engagement and organizing, even political agitation. Their gatherings for prayer, reflection on Scripture, singing, and the sharing of food were intimately connected with their activism—one flowed into the other.

---

psychology, he earned his doctorate in theology at the University of Lyon in France. He had been ordained as a Catholic priest in Peru in 1959. Following his studies, Gutiérrez returned to Peru and served as a parish priest in a poor community in the city of Rimac, while also teaching in several universities. In 1974 he founded and directed the Bartolomé de Las Casas Institute in Lima, which situates theology in the praxis of the poor.

23. Gutiérrez, *Theology of Liberation*, 12.

24. See, for example, Cox, *Secular City*; *Future of Faith*; and *When Jesus Came to Harvard*.

These communities were guided by *conscientization*, a term first coined by the Brazilian liberationist educator and philosopher Paulo Freire.[25] Freire defined *conscientization* as "the process in which men [and women], not as recipients, but as knowing subjects, achieve a deeper awareness both of the socio-cultural reality that shapes their lives, and of their capacity to transform that reality through action upon it."[26]

This *critical consciousness* entails asking many "why" questions, and linking them together. For example, rather than imploring God in prayer, "please heal our sick children," a BEC community might ask, "Why are our children getting sick?" This would lead to a widening spiral of questions, which might reveal that the children are getting sick because the river from which they drink and in which they bathe is polluted. Why is the river polluted? Because the American corporation is dumping waste from its (fill in the blanks:) oil company/chemical company/mining company into the river. This awareness, and critical reflection on what it means in the light of their faith conviction that God is a God of justice, would then lead to the BEC joining together with others to demand that their government rein in the oppressive actions of the American Empire and its lackey corporations.

The BECs also taught basic skills such as reading and writing, as many peasants in South America were still illiterate in the 1970s. This was part of the BECs' efforts to empower the poor to bring about their own liberation. As they spread across Latin America, and later to other countries, "the base communities not only acted as a means to disseminate liberation theology, but also as a means of inspiration for the liberation theology movement. They allowed the poor to direct the movement and to keep the struggle of the oppressed in the forefront (of the church's mission)."[27]

BECs were the answer to my longing for a church-as-community that would link theology and praxis. In addition to their praxiological focus, I was attracted to their informality and egalitarianism. Leaders emerged, but these were not always (or even often) priests. They emerged from within these communities of lay Christians who believed that the church was a living link between spirituality and activism. The Vatican was not pleased with this development, but as time passed the BECs became more ecumenical in any event. Although they originated in the heavily Roman Catholic countries of Latin America, they were open to Protestants, or to any Christians seeking to link faith and life.

---

25. Among Freire's many works, see *Pedagogy of the Oppressed*; *Education for Critical Consciousness*; *Cultural Action for Freedom*; and *Pedagogy of the Heart*.

26. Freire, *Cultural Action for Freedom*, 27.

27. Tombs, *Latin American Liberation Theology*, 199.

During my years at Harvard Divinity School, I often travelled on weekends to visit close friends who were students at Union Theological Seminary in New York City. They were part of a group of eight or so UTS students who lived communally in a large apartment close to the seminary. Their spiritual mentor was Daniel Berrigan, the Catholic priest who, along with his brother Philip, was a guiding light in the anti-war movement.

This UTC commune was, in a way, a sort of American BEC. Although their activism was centered around the anti-war movement, they also sought to connect the gospel with the larger fabric of social injustices, such as the poverty that surrounded them at the edge of Harlem where they lived. They shared prayer, theological reflection, and meals together, and also placed a portion of their incomes (meagre though they were as students) into a "common purse." They adopted me into their community whenever I was able to join them.

The upshot of this personal history is that I have been seeking some version of the Base Ecclesial Communities ever since I first heard of them. During the three years I lived in Asheville, North Carolina, before leaving for Jamaica—and an adult lifetime of living in other cultures—I was a founding member, along with my husband, of an intentional Christian community there. Only a handful of us lived in a communal house, but our group of ten to twelve gathered weekly for worship, study, and fellowship, and we were involved in community projects in the mixed but predominantly African American neighborhood where we lived.

The struggles entailed in attempting to be an intentional community in Asheville, which fell short of the BEC theology of church, prompted me to write my doctoral thesis a few years later on why intentional Christian community is so difficult in the American context.[28] This was a sociological-theological analysis of the reasons for the failure of so many attempts at intentional Christian community in the United States, where the average lifespan of such communities is three years. Although there are some such communities which have lasted for more than a generation, such as the Bruderhof[29] and Koinonia Farm,[30] the vast majority of these communities

---

28. Johnson, "Clusters on the Vine."

29. The Bruderhof (see https://www.bruderhof.com/) is an international collective of Christian pacifist intentional communities in the Anabaptist tradition, founded in Germany in 1920. It has branches in the United States, England, Germany, Austria, Paraguay, and Australia. Bruderhof communities refuse military service, share a common purse, and are largely self-sustaining, involved in farming and making highly sought-after handmade crafts.

30. According to its website (https://www.koinoniafarm.org/), Koinonia Farm was founded in 1942 near Americus, Georgia, by Clarence and Florence Jordan and Martin and Mabel England, as an intentional community of Christians who "seek to follow

fall apart fairly quickly. That is indeed what happened to our community in Asheville after three years.

In a nutshell, what I discovered in my research was that the core problem for American intentional Christian communities is the same one I identified earlier in this work—the problem of individualism as the core value in American culture. Communalism and individualism are not a natural fit. Conflicts thus easily arise in American intentional communities over issues such as leadership and decision-making, sharing incomes in a "common purse," and sharing personal possessions. This was the heart of the problem in our Asheville community. A range of incomes existed among members, and those who were more affluent resented the fact that those who had little could not contribute much to the financial coffers.

There were also theological differences. For some, the community was an "add-on" to their membership in an established church. For others, like myself, our community *was* my church. We worshiped together weekly, took part in several activities to support our neighborhood and city, hosted classes for the public, and shared meals and quarterly retreats together. I would have liked to have been more directly engaged in social activism, but at least we engaged in genuine struggle and sharing with one another. However, in the end there was not a strong enough shared theological bond to hold us together.

I went from Asheville to Jamaica and thus began my many years of intense engagement with communities in non-Western cultures around the world. In these places, "intentional community" was not something one had to manufacture. It happened naturally because these were all collectivist rather than individualist cultures. There were many things I deeply appreciated about every place I lived outside the United States for most of my adult working life. However, what I never found was anything like the BECs, where "church" meant organic intimate communities who cultivated spiritual life in a way that did not separate faith from action for justice.

Although the BECs in Latin America may not have explicitly practiced the Jubilee, they were working to liberate the economically enslaved, restore lands to the dislocated and dispossessed, and undo the damage caused to their lands and water by unjust extraction of their resources. They lived a

---

the example of the earliest Christian communities." Their livelihood continues to come from their extensive farm, where they work sustainably in partnership with the land—in Clarence Jordan's words, "to conserve the soil, God's holy earth." Koinonia's local housing ministry evolved into Habitat for Humanity, which now builds housing for the poor around the world. For many years, Koinonia Farm's close neighbors, former President Jimmy Carter and Rosalyn Carter, participated annually in Habitat for Humanity housing builds, becoming staunch supporters of the community. Koinonia also founded Jubilee Partners, a community that welcomes refugees from war-torn countries.

form of Jubilee life. And they clearly lived as kindom communities, organically fleshing out together the connections between faith and life.

It is important to affirm here that I am respectful of all manifestations of church. God is present in every gathering of Christians, whether in a cathedral, a small rural or village church, an urban "First Church," a Catholic mass, or in small, informal gatherings of faith-seeking people in their own contextual versions of BECs. I come from a family of deeply committed Presbyterians. My father was a Presbyterian minister, my brother is a Presbyterian minister, my daughter is a Presbyterian minister, my sister has held numerous leadership roles at all levels of the Presbyterian Church in the United States, and I am also a minister.[31] I do not begrudge my family members their long-held commitment to the institutional church. They find meaning there. I also do not want to diminish the importance of the many initiatives which some mainstream churches take that demonstrate their care for the poor, for refugees, for victims of abuse or racism, and for creation.

My "what if?" question about church pulls me back to the ethical imperatives of living in a kindom community as followers of an interrelational God who is radically *for life*. I am searching for a sense of connectedness with others who are grounded in the kind of kindom life that challenges us to live out our theology in the everyday and the ordinary—in the trials we face relating to ourselves and others, in the ways we demonstrate our love for creation, and in the ways we seek to push our societies to practice justice for those who are left behind, dismissed, forgotten, or outright oppressed. I still hold on to the model of church I discovered in the Base Ecclesial Communities, and I end this reflection with a question: What might a contextually-rich BEC community look like for each of you, in the places and circumstances in which you find yourselves today?

---

31. I partially rebelled and was ordained in the Christian Church (Disciples of Christ), which emerged in the mid-1800s on the American frontier, largely from Presbyterian roots. This church is a unique blend of several traditions: Reformed, Free Church (practicing "believers' baptism" by immersion as in the early church), and even Catholic (in that the eucharist is central to its gathered life and celebrated whenever the church worships). It is strongly ecumenical, and has contributed significantly to ecumenism worldwide.

PART 2

Being Human

3

Human or Post-human?

TWO FAMILIES IN AN AIRPORT

I HAD A RATHER jarring experience in the Los Angeles International Airport in 2022, during a long layover between my arriving flight from New Zealand and my onward flight to North Carolina. This began while I was walking from the international terminal to the domestic terminal. As I made my way, it seemed that almost everyone was looking at their cell phones as they walked along. At times people who were staring at their phones, or talking into them, would jostle other travelers. There seemed to be a sea of people all attached to their cell phones as if they were extensions of their arms.

My musing about what this all meant went into overdrive during the next eight hours or so while I waited for my next flight. When I found my departure gate, it had an alcove off to the side of the main gate area, a small space with seats for perhaps twenty people. It was initially empty, but soon after I settled into my seat two families appeared, and they became a study in contrasts over the ensuing hours. I came to think of this scene as a contrast between humans and post-humans.

The first family was, I believe, Ethiopian, based on their traditional attire and features. It consisted of a mother, father, a boy who seemed to be ten or eleven, and his little sister, who looked to be around four years old. This family settled in one corner and began arranging things from their carry-on luggage to make themselves more comfortable. A small blanket and soft toy appeared out of one bag for the little girl. The boy drew pictures and read a book. The father occasionally looked at some papers or documents, but mostly he chatted with his family. The mother busied herself with caregiving activities, such as making a kind of bed on the floor for her little daughter, with the blanket and a makeshift pillow created by rolling up several jackets. For periods of time, she seemed to be knitting or crocheting.

The family chatted to one another softly, with the parents listening and responding to their children. At one point, the mother took food out of one of her bags, and the family had a kind of picnic. This seemed to be mostly bread and fruit, and I wondered if she had brought this food with her on her overseas flight and managed to get it through Customs, or if she had purchased it in the airport. It did not look like the typical fare in the overpriced eating establishments that lined the concourses. When the little girl needed a nap, her brother helped to settle her in her improvised bed. Over our long hours sharing the same space, the father occasionally glanced at a cell phone but only briefly, perhaps to check flight information about their upcoming flights.

This was what I called the "human family." The other family was sitting directly across from me, and occupied this space for almost the entire time I was there. This was a white American family consisting of a father and mother, a daughter of around sixteen years old, a slightly younger brother of perhaps fourteen, and a younger brother of nine or ten. In the many hours I was sitting across from this family, they never put their phones down. The family members did not talk to each other. They all looked at their phones constantly. At one point the father said, "I'm going to get food; what do you want?" The other family members looked up briefly from their phones and placed their orders but then immediately returned to whatever they were doing on their phones.

I was astonished that a family could sit side by side for that many hours and not talk to each other, and that they could remain attached to their phones over all that time. At one point, the younger brother did playfully begin to kick his older brother (while still playing his video game), but the older brother simply pushed him away without speaking to him or looking up from his phone. In my mind, this family became the "post-human family."

I should not stereotype these two families, of course. I did not know them at all. The Ethiopian family may have had serious character flaws, but that is not the point. And the American family could well have had many redeeming qualities, but that is also not the point. My characterizations of the two families were not about how nice or un-nice they may have been. I was interested in something much deeper—the question of what constituted their very humanness.

A RELATIONAL WAY OF BEING

My lifetime has witnessed the most dramatic and rapid developments in the relationship between humans and technology in human history. When I was a child, all the children on my street in the small North Carolina town where I lived played together, mostly outside, year-round. We played baseball until it was too dark to see the ball. We climbed trees, made "play houses" under bushes, and played every childhood game imaginable. We only went inside when our mothers insisted we come in for dinner or chores. In the summertime, I often went back outside in the dark after dinner to catch lightning bugs in a glass jar with my best friend and walk around watching them glow in the dark (I have heard that lightning bugs are now extinct). We all went to Sunday School and church and to Vacation Bible School. We walked to and from school.

My life growing up was completely absorbed in relationships. My immediate family was paramount. Because my father was a minister and my mother a church educator, our family life centered around the church. Church folks and neighbors were in and out of our house, and likewise I was able to wander in and out of our neighbors' houses. Our home life was filled with music (piano lessons starting at age six) and books. After church on Sundays, we discussed my father's sermons over lunch. My best friend from the age of three (still my best friend after all these years) lived two houses away, and we were constant companions, often getting in trouble for our more adventurous escapades.

This depiction of life growing up in the 1950s may sound over-romanticized, but it is not meant to be. We and our neighbors had all the challenges that families everywhere face, as persons in families all have distinct personalities, idiosyncrasies, and foibles. The point is that we were intimately enmeshed in a web of relations—with our families, our friends and neighbors, our church family, our school family, and our physical surroundings (I can still picture every tree in our yard, hear the cicadas and songbirds, smell the damp earth, feel the shiny pieces of quartz under the bushes, see the view from my 'nest' in the top branches of our crepe myrtle tree, and taste the figs from our fig tree). We were enmeshed in relationships.

This inherited relational orientation continued as I came of age. I was deeply impacted by the civil rights and anti-war movements during my adolescence and college years, and developed very close relationships with likeminded friends who explored with me what those commitments meant. As a music major in college, I had a whole different set of relationships with musicians, who tended to be less political and more poetic. My relationships expanded when I began exploring other cultures, beginning at age nineteen when I spent a summer living in an indigenous Mesquite village on the east coast of Nicaragua.

Although many of our neighbors had televisions when I was growing up, we never had one in our house until I was in high school. I never missed TV as a child; I was too busy being with my friends, playing the piano, immersed in school work, running around outside, and doing all things church-related. But on the Sunday after President John F. Kennedy was assassinated on Friday, November 22, 1963, when I was fifteen, one of our church members brought his old black and white TV to church and gave it to us after the service, along with a table-top antenna which everyone called "rabbit ears," which was fine-tuned by wrapping pieces of tin foil over the ends when the signal faded. We brought this used television home, plugged it in, adjusted the rabbit ears, and turned it on just in time to see Lee Harvey Oswald, Kennedy's alleged assassin, being assassinated himself in real time.

That was my introduction to the world of TV, and in the days that followed we watched the events surrounding Kennedy's state funeral and burial in stunned silence. After that, very firm restrictions were put in place by our parents about what we could and could not watch on TV. We could watch for one hour a night, but the program had to have parental approval, and we could only watch it after completing all of our chores, homework, and music practice. We were not allowed to watch violence on TV, and we could not watch commercials. This was before the invention of remote controls, but my father rigged up a long extension cord with a switch on one end, and we had to turn the switch off during commercials. My father told us that companies trying to sell us things on TV were attempting to brainwash us, and he did not want our minds to be infected with such advertising gimmicks.

I never personally owned a television until many years later, when I was in my thirties. By then there were remote controls, and I still put commercials on "mute" to honor my father's wisdom. Later still, I had to learn how to use a computer and then finally to venture forth into cyberspace and the internet. But I only wanted to learn what I absolutely had to know in order to do my work. I had to send e-mails because that was how everyone was communicating, but I was very sad when no one sent personal letters anymore. I had always loved going to the mailbox and eagerly looking for personal mail. I loved reading and writing letters, knowing that we both (sender and receiver) had touched the same paper, and that our handwriting revealed something unique about us. At times we pressed dried flowers between the pages of our letters. Some people close to me gently tease me today for writing e-mails as though they were letters (read: lengthy).

It was not until the mid-2000s that I had my first cell phone, and I was always content to use the old simple flip phones. Even though certain solicitous loved ones gave me a smart phone a few years ago, I still only use it for calling or texting. I have no interest in using the internet on a tiny screen, and I do not know to this day exactly what an app is. Some family members have occasionally playfully called me a Luddite.[1] But it is not that I am opposed to technology *per se*, only that I hail from a different time, in which being human meant personal encounters and connections with people. I come from a time when what mattered most was one's web of relatedness. Being a product of that earlier worldview, technology has always been nothing more than a tool—one that is peripheral and secondary to embodied ways of relating.

A WIRED WAY OF BEING

I have been wondering for the past few decades what is happening to the human species, now that our connections to others seem to be more and more removed from face-to-face ways of relating. Most young people today spend more of their waking hours communicating or absorbing information through a screen than in person. This has led to a host of problems, physically, mentally, emotionally, and spiritually.

On a physical level, today's technologically preoccupied youth are being diagnosed at alarming rates with medical conditions such as sleep deprivation and eye damage from spending so much time looking at screens. Changes in brain activity are occurring, a decrease in reaction times, and a reduced ability to concentrate. The radiofrequency energy emanating from cell phones is now known to cause genetic, neurological, and other forms of bodily damage. It is a form of electromagnetic radiation that is absorbed into human tissues.

In 2011, the International Agency for Research on Cancer classified mobile phone radiation as likely carcinogenic, and there has been an increase in brain cancer among heavy cell phone users, and testicular cancer among male users who leave their phones turned on in their pockets. Brain cancer among children using cell phones is significantly higher than in other age groups, or among children who do not use cell phones. Youth

---

1. "Luddite" is a term that is used today to refer to people who dislike new technologies—Luddites may refuse to own a computer, for example—but its origins date back to an early nineteenth-century labor movement in England that resisted the ways in which mechanized manufacturing was undermining the livelihoods of skilled craftsmen.

who drive are four times more likely to be involved in a car accident due to being distracted from cell phone use, even if they use hands-free devices.[2]

There is also troubling evidence of a significant increase in psychological problems among youth who are heavy users of cell phones and online technologies, especially those who are active on social media platforms. One of these problems is social isolation. Although social media platforms (e.g., Tik Tok, Instagram, Facebook, Snapchat, YouTube) ostensibly increase interaction with others online, the result is actually an increase in isolation, for these are not in-person ways of interacting. One recent study has shown that frequent users of these online platforms are three times more likely than others to experience severe social isolation.[3]

There is also increasing evidence of a rise in depression and anxiety among frequent users of social media platforms, especially in light of the explosion of cyberbullying in recent years. Cyberbullying is bullying by means of digital technologies. It can take place on social media, messaging platforms, and mobile phones. Cyberbullying is defined as

> . . . repeated behaviour aimed at scaring, angering or shaming those who are targeted. Examples include: spreading lies about or posting embarrassing photos or videos of someone on social media; sending hurtful, abusive or threatening messages, images or videos via messaging platforms; and impersonating someone and sending mean messages to others on their behalf or through fake accounts.[4]

In addition to increases in depression and anxiety due to online exposure to cyberbullying, it has led to an upsurge in suicide. A 2020 study revealed that "Students who are involved in . . . cyberbullying (both offenders and victims) have a significantly elevated likelihood of experiencing suicidal thoughts, suicide attempts, or completed suicide."[5] It is easy to be a cyberbully because one does not have to face one's victims and can thus bully with impunity, without any accountability, but the bully pays a heavy cost psychologically, along with the victim.

A further psychological consequence of the over-use of these technologies and online platforms is the alarming impact of sexting and other forms of online sexual activity among youth, now affecting children as young as twelve. Sexting is sharing explicit sexual messaging, photos, or videos through a cell phone, social media site, or e-mail. Although the sender may

2. Naeem, "Health Risks Associated with Mobile Phone Use," 5.
3. Primrack, et al., "Social Media Use and Perceived Social Isolation."
4. "Cyberbullying."
5. Baiden and Tadeo, "Investigating the Association," 104.

believe that such sexting is private, it can end up being spread far and wide. This can lead to name-calling, social exclusion, and shaming, and this is a leading contributor to teen depression and suicide. A growing problem is *sextortion*, in which a male convinces a young girl to send him a nude or sexually explicit photo or video and then threatens to release it publicly unless she does as he asks.[6]

A serious ramification of the spread of sexting concerns how it is changing the ways in which youth relate to others sexually in "real life." Since the beginning of human history, sexuality has been an intimate, *embodied* way of relating to another. In contrast, "virtual" sexual activity takes away the embodied encounter. It is impersonal and detached from genuine feeling. It is performative rather than intimate. This is redefining, in a dangerous way, what it means to be human, and what it means to be a sexual being.

There is now growing evidence that participation in online sexual activity negatively impacts the ability to engage in actual sexual relationships. It turns out that "virtual sex" seems to deaden the capacity for real sexuality. Recent research shows that participants in virtual sexual activity exhibit "decreased feelings of sexual desirability and sexual desire, decreased sexual satisfaction, and less frequent sexual intimacy."[7] So while young people are taking part in high levels of sexual activity online, the irony is that they seem to be less and less able to enter into or sustain "real-life" sexual relationships. There is even a hypothesis among some researchers that one reason for the decline in teen pregnancies in some Western countries in recent years is because fewer teens are having actual sex.

This situation raises profoundly disturbing questions about what it now means to be human in the face of the "virtual" life that has been created by technology, including what it means to be a sexual human. If we relate to others through a screen on a phone or other device, rather than in person, what does this do to our innate divine predisposition to be relational people, relating to others through personal proximity, listening intently to one another, looking into the other's eyes, and, when appropriate, touching the skin of the other? If we lose the ability to relate person-to-person, even skin-to-skin, are we still human? Or are we becoming post-humans?

---

6. "Dangers of Sexting."
7. Grov et al., "Perceived Consequences," 431.

HUMANS CANNOT BE POST-HUMANS

Until I began to be increasingly concerned about how our reliance on technology may be diminishing our capacity to be relational beings, I had not spent much time thinking about post-humanism. When I heard the term "post-humanism," it conjured up images in my mind of artificial intelligence, robots, cyborgs,[8] and other fantastical constructions of futuristic humans which I associated with science fiction. It all seemed a bit far-fetched. But in light of my growing worry about 'what the human race is coming to,' especially for our youth who are moving into adulthood, I began to give post-humanism a second look.

Post-humanism is a postmodern reaction to humanism. Humanism describes "a broad range of philosophical and ethical movements that are unified by their unshakable belief in the unique value, agency, and moral supremacy of human beings."[9] Humanism began to emerge in Europe as far back as the Renaissance, as a reaction against the "religious authoritarianism" associated with the medieval worldview. It "wrested control of human destiny from the whims of a transcendent divinity and placed it in the hands of rational individuals (which, at that time, meant white men). In so doing, the humanist worldview, which still holds sway over many of our most important political and social institutions, positions humans at the centre of the moral world."[10]

Post-humanism, which emerged as a philosophical discipline in the 1990s, challenges the notion that humans are the only agents of the moral world. Post-humanists argue that "in our technologically mediated future, understanding the world as a moral hierarchy and placing humans at the top of it will no longer make sense."[11] This way of understanding the human has gone in two different directions.

The first branch of post-humanism, sometimes called transhumanism, is closer to my stereotypes mentioned above. It posits that, before the end of the twenty-first century, humans will be so radically altered by the intrusions of artificial intelligence, bio-implants, cognitive enhancements, and other biomedical technologies that we will have evolved into a species that

---

8. The term "cyborg" was coined in 1960 by Manfred Clynes and Nathan S. Kline, to refer to a human-machine hybrid consisting of both organic and biomechanical body parts.

9. "Post-Humanism."

10. "Post-Humanism."

11. "Post-Humanism." Important scholars of post-humanism include Ihab Hassan, Michel Foucault, Jacques Derrida, Judith Butler, Gregory Bateson, Donna Haraway, Elaine Graham, Benjamin Bratton, Timothy Morton, and Douglas Kellner.

will be unrecognizable in relation to our previously taken-for-granted assumptions about what a human is. We will be, in effect, cyborgs, but it is not clear how these creatures will engage in the relationality that has characterized humans since the beginning of human history.

However, there is another branch of post-humanism which I find slightly less frightening and more engaging from an interrelational perspective. The philosopher Donna Haraway is among those who argue that the fusing of humans and technology, while it will not physically improve human beings, will help us "to see ourselves as being interconnected rather than separate from non-human beings . . . [It] will help us understand that the oppositions we set up between the human and non-human, natural and artificial, self and other, organic and inorganic, are merely ideas that can be broken down and renegotiated."[12]

Haraway and those in her camp differ from the first stream of post-humanism in that, while the former embraces a technological future which changes (and hypothetically enhances) human capacities, the latter vision ventures into ethics. For Haraway, "post-humanism is an ethical position that extends moral concern to things that are different from us and, in particular, to other species and objects with which we cohabit the world."[13]

Haraway's vision of a post-human future is of a time "when species meet" (the title of her best-known book) and "when humans finally make room for non-human things within the scope of our moral concern. Post-human ethics, therefore, encourages us to think outside of the interests of our own species, be less narcissistic in our conception of the world, and take the interests and rights of things that are different to us seriously."[14]

This ethical vision has affinities in certain respects with the ethics of relational and interrelational theology. Where I depart from Haraway is that I do not privilege technology in the divinely interrelated way of being. I completely agree with her that humans should be less narcissistic; they should recognize that they are not superior to the rest of creation. But I do not see evidence that technology is the catalyst which will ensure that we arrive at this ethical awareness. I return to my assertion that technologies are only tools—tools which can be useful or dangerous, helpful or destructive. It is not technologies that make ethical decisions but the humans who use them.

All of this leads me back to the core question which has guided the discussion in this chapter: what does it mean to be human? In a way, the

12. Haraway, *When Species Meet*, 21.
13. "Post-Humanism."
14. "Post-Humanism."

term "post-human" is a contradiction. 'Post' refers to something that is in the past, that is no longer. But humans cannot be human and no-longer-human at the same time. Cyborgs who are controlled by technology are something other than human. I should therefore not have referred to the cell phone-obsessed family in the airport as post-humans. They were of course humans, it was just that their obsession with their phones made them "relationally challenged humans."

Instead of embracing post-humanism, I would call for us to become more and more what we were divinely created to be, from the beginning of human creation until now, and into the future. Instead of moving *past* our humanness, we should be becoming more and more the interrelated humans we were created to be. *Embodied relationality* is the key to being human. This is a spiritual quest, a religious commitment, a theological calling, and an ethical imperative. It is not technology that will get us there but spiritual awareness and ethical engagement with ourselves, others, and the world.

4

Living with the Pain of Being Human

This chapter is a compilation of three meditations on some of the challenges we face as humans who have to live with ourselves. Living with ourselves is at the very heart of theology, yet what this entails is rarely addressed in published theological works. At the deepest personal level, all humans desire to live an integrated life, a life which balances all of the complex facets of being relational human beings. We strive for this balance, but finding it is not always easy. We cannot find this balance without faith. This chapter looks honestly at several ways in which we confront the challenges of being human, through the lens of faith.

THE CURE FOR THE STING IS IN THE THORN

I once saw an interview with the psychotherapist Phil Stutz, who coined the term "X Parts."[1] It is not the most descriptive of terms, but I was curious and so I listened. In his understanding, we all have numerous X Parts—our ingrained defensive responses to the challenges we face. These are our at times less-than-helpful ways of coping with the things that go wrong, that hurt or disappoint us. These coping mechanisms may take the form of anger, judgment, retreat, self-pity, escape, other-blaming, aggression, or saying things that will hurt the person or group or institution that has harmed us.

We tend to have two ways of dealing with our X Parts. The most common is to ignore their existence, even though we are making use of them all

---

1. He is featured in the documentary *Stutz*, produced by Jonah Hill and available on Netflix.

the time. We simply respond to disappointment or pain as we always have, without stopping to analyze why we respond as we do, or whether these are the most helpful responses. The other way of dealing with our X Parts is to view them as personal demons and attempt to vanquish them. For some of us, this may partially stem from a "depraved humanity" Protestant worldview, where we blame ourselves for what goes wrong.

There is a third path, and this is what the psychotherapist was advocating. Rather than ignoring our X Parts, or trying to atone for them, we should begin by first accepting that they are deeply ingrained in our identities; they are hardwired into our psyches from a lifetime of coping with everything that has gone wrong. What if we neither ignored them nor hated them? What if, instead, we might see in the inner depths of our X Parts the seeds of a more positive way of being in the world? What if we allowed our X Parts to teach us?

In his PhD thesis on a Samoan contextual theology of grace, Piula Samuelu[2] uses as a metaphor a Samoan saying about the *alamea*, the crown-of-thorns starfish. The adage says that the cure for the sting of the *alamea* is found in the *alamea* itself (*"E fofo e le alamea le alamea"*).[3] When one is stung (which can be fatal), one quickly places the underside of the *alamea* on the sting, and it sucks out the toxins. This traditional remedy for the sting of the crown-of-thorns starfish is found not only in Samoa but throughout Pasifika.

This seems like a wonderful metaphor for how we might be able to relate in a more positive way to our X Parts. Perhaps our healing resides in the underside, the hidden recesses, of our pain and our inbuilt reactive ways of responding to it. The Catholic mystics allude to this when they say that the pathway to healing from despair resides in our darkest moments of despair—what they call the "dark night of the soul." But how can this happen? What is the catalyst for this opening? What can possibly dissuade us from our habitual ways of responding to pain?

First, we need to get to the bottom of what has caused our X Parts to develop as they have. They have been in the making since our early childhoods, and many factors have predisposed us to fine-tune them as we have—parents, families, communities, social environments, impinging circumstances, health challenges, our own idiosyncrasies and personalities. We cannot begin to turn them over to their undersides, wherein lies the pathway toward healing, unless we first honestly acknowledge what they mean to us.

2. Samuelu, "Decolonising Grace."
3. Samuelu, "Decolonising Grace," 2.

Our X Parts are in fact our friends, flawed though they are; we rely on them without thinking. They have become over time as taken-for-granted as the air we breathe. They have been our friends because we have always been able to count on them to provide momentary relief in times of stress or crisis. When someone or something "pushes our buttons," as the saying goes, we instinctively react as we always have, and this makes us feel momentarily secure in the midst of insecurity. If we lash out in anger? The other person deserves it! If we retreat while playing the "silent treatment" card? That'll make the other person feel bad! Such automatic reactions are a bit like the behavior of the drug addict, who may know at some level that the drug is not life-giving but still turns inexorably to it because it temporarily numbs his or her pain.

What recovering addicts come to know, of course, is that there are alternative ways to lessen pain. The key to discovering this alternative path is *consciousness*, which is not always a pleasant thing. The old axiom "ignorance is bliss" describes our preference for maintaining the status quo, the known, rather than venturing into the unknown. Yet it is only in the act of opening ourselves to a new consciousness which shatters the status quo that we can come to trust that God resides in the healing balm of the underside of the *alamea* that has stung us. It is in the nature of such creatures to sting, and life is full of people and forces whose purpose seems to be to inflict pain upon others. We can never change them, as their own healing also has to come from within themselves. But we can deal with our own stings.

With consciousness comes liberation and empowerment. This enables us to remind ourselves, when we react in default mode, "yes, you just responded like you always do; you know why, but there's no need to dwell on that, just know that you have the power to take a different path." I always remember the Pentecost weekend retreat I attended years ago in Dunedin, New Zealand, led by the wonderful Presbyterian minister Neal Churcher. He put it so simply: he was standing at one end of the room, and he said, "I've always been walking this way, but I can turn and walk this other way." And he did—he turned and walked "another way" across the room to demonstrate the power of choice, of agency, of turning around (*metanoia*),[4] of becoming "new creatures altogether" (2 Cor 5:17).

---

4. *Metanoia* is the New Testament Greek work often translated as "repent" but understood more broadly, in relation to its literal meaning of "turn around," as referring to turning radically away from the old to embrace transformation. Perhaps the most common New Testament passage which uses the word *metanoia* is Acts 3:19, where Peter tells the people, "Repent (*metanoia*), then, and turn to God, so that your sins may be wiped out."

We may have been trapped in our X Parts for years, but it is never too late to overturn the *alamea* and place the underside on our wounds. We can only do this through an intense attunement to prayer. That is the element which the psychotherapist left out. In overturning the *alamea* to illuminate the sources of healing imbedded within the sting, we can discover through prayer the miracle of transformation, without which we would still continue to replay our old X Parts *ad nauseum*.

This discovery, of course, entails being honest and discerning about the miraculous possibilities of prayer. Prayer is not begging God to give us what we want. The older I get, the more I find this tendency in the prayers I hear jarring, with their statements such as "God, bless this gathering" or "God, please give us a safe trip." As sincere as those kinds of prayers are (and I have uttered that kind of prayer countless times myself), prayer is about more than asking God to fill our requests and expressing thanks when our requests are fulfilled (when some good thing that happens is described as "an answer to prayer"). Prayer is a vulnerable, naked openness on our part to the divine indwelling in our spirits.

Prayer is therefore not even necessarily always an act of talking on our part. Indeed, I have come to believe that we talk too much in our prayers. Prayer should be more an act of listening, of shedding our heavy garments of self-defense so that we can no longer hide from or avoid the truth we are afraid or loath to hear. Prayer is radically open listening, anticipatory waiting, attuning all of our senses to the ways in which the divine Spirit that dwells within us is offering us insight, wisdom, strength, and guidance. Intercessory prayer, as the Quakers so beautifully put it, is "holding the other in the light," trusting in and calling forth the divine Spirit's abiding presence with the other.

When I meditate on prayer, I am reminded of the intense spiritual awakening I experienced during a week I spent many years ago living with the ecumenical Iona Community on the island of Iona in the Inner Hebrides, off the west coast of Scotland.[5] There the resident community lives (while other members live in small communities across the UK and in other parts of the world) and offers weekly themed retreats open to the public

---

5. The Iona Community describes itself as "an international, ecumenical Christian movement working for justice and peace, the rebuilding of community and the renewal of worship. Our Community was founded in Glasgow in 1938 by Rev George MacLeod. A visionary and social reformer, MacLeod was driven by a belief that faith is grounded in action. In rebuilding the ancient ruined Iona Abbey, trainee ministers and unemployed workers lived, worked, and worshipped together. We are now 280 Members and more than 2,000 Associate Members, Young Adults and Friends across the world. We remain true to that founding vision—sharing common work and community as we pursue justice and peace, in Scotland and beyond." https://iona.org.uk/.

during the summers (or at least this was the case when I was there in the mid-1980s). Everyone who takes part in these retreats lives in community with the resident members for the week, helping with cooking and cleaning and daily life in the ancient restored abbey.

There is also a daily rhythm of prayer, music, silence, and reflection in the old stone sanctuary at the heart of the abbey. And one day each week, a pilgrimage takes place around the island, guided by one of the community members. This entails hiking up and down hills, stopping at pivotal points of interest in Iona's storied history. Silent prayer accompanies each stop, where participants are invited to allow the sounds of birdsong, crashing waves, and wind to penetrate their very beings.

Two of these stops remain etched in my memory. One was the spot where the monk Columba (later beatified as Saint Columba) and twelve of his companions landed on the shores of Iona in 563 CE in their small boat. He and his small band of fellow monks had rowed their boat from their native Ireland, having felt the call to bring the gospel to Britain. There is a raised mound on this pebbly beach even today, and legend has it that when Columba came ashore he buried his boat there so that he would not be tempted to return to the safety and familiarity of his home.

This was a sign of his radical commitment to live out and share his faith in a strange place, a new and unfamiliar landscape. He was shaking off the safety net of his old, secure way of doing things and opening himself to a new way of living, one in which his old comforts were peeled away and shredded. This was an act of prayer, for in burying his boat he was opening himself to divine indwelling in a radical act of faith.

The other memory from my pilgrimage on Iona that has stayed with me over many years is sitting for a time beside one of the ruins of the small stone cells of these early monks, scattered along the hilltops across the island. Here the monks would periodically leave the abbey they had built and come to stay for a period of time in order to pray and restore their faith, so that they would have the strength and wisdom to move across the British Isles, sharing their Celtic form of Christianity.[6] In these tiny stone houses

---

6. The Celtic spirituality I inherited from my Scottish ancestors is a distinctive indigenous form of interrelational theology. The Celtic Center summarizes Celtic spirituality as follows: "Because the Celtic people of northwestern Europe were out of the reach of the Roman Empire and its Roman Church, . . . this allowed them to maintain their ancient spiritual practices regarding the dignity of nature and community, the equality of men and women, and their vibrant poetic imaginations as portals to understanding humans and God. When Christianity arrived, Celtic communities were able, for many centuries, to find a beautiful synthesis of this ancient spirituality and the Christian understanding of God's divine presence and belonging for everyone . . . The Christian Celts saw the presence of the Divine in a relationship with creation that

of prayer, the monks brought nothing with them. They fasted and opened themselves to the divine indwelling they needed in order to live out their faith.

Such times apart are not an end in themselves; this is not an escape *from* the world. Rather, this is a prayerful opening to the consciousness needed to live faithfully *in* the world. In this stark, empty space, all distractions fade away, so that illumination can make its way to the surface of consciousness. This stripping away of our familiar habits, our propensity to rationalize and to cling to our habitual ways of putting our needs and desires first—this is prayer.

We need this prayerful predisposition at all times but perhaps most of all during the times when we have been stung by thorns, our "dark nights of the soul." In such times of stress, trauma, hurt, or conflict, our X Parts go into overdrive. Our reserves of insight and patience get depleted. We fall back on our customary ways of reacting to stress rather than opening ourselves to divine indwelling, whether this habitual response means complaining, raging, accusing, condemning, worrying, rationalizing, or withdrawing and feeling sorry for ourselves.

The cure for our stings does not lie in such un-prayerful behaviors. It resides in our divinely given capacity to overturn what has stung us, to see what lies beneath, within the thorns that have stung us, and to apply the salve of healing which comes from the wisdom that is embedded in the stings of life. The practical question we are left with concerns *how* we can, in actual situations, use the thorns that hurt us to heal us. Doing this sounds counterintuitive. How can something life-giving be embedded in the very thing that has stung us? This is not an easy question. But prayerful attentiveness can in fact reveal this to us. Let us imagine.

One possible path might be to prayerfully invite into our consciousness a "flip side" response to things that harm us, rather than our habitual response. I offer an example well known to me, that of worry. I would need to start by asking what lies beneath my ingrained worry that my children and grandchildren may come to harm. If they are late returning home, the X Part embedded in my brain tells me that they must have been in a car crash and are dead at the bottom of a ravine! If they get a bad headache, what if it's a brain tumor? (Of course these are ludicrous thoughts, but worry is not about rational thought.)

---

stressed humility, the dignity of all things, and God's presence in and through all of creation. They maintained rich spiritual practices through prayer, meditation, communing with nature, care for those in need, hospitality, and poetic use of the imagination and art. They saw the presence of the Spirit in all experiences, and were skilled at seeking encounter with God in all of life." https://www.thecelticcenter.org/celtic-center/.

But what if I overturned this worry, allowing what lies beneath the toxin of worry to heal the toxin of worry? I would see that what lies beneath the sting of my worry for my loved ones is, in fact, my love for them. I worry because I want no harm to come to them, because I value their lives unconditionally. And so a prayerful response to the sting of my worry-thorn would be to give voice to that love rather than to its unfaithful flip side. When my worries assail me, I can therefore proclaim, "God is with them, no matter where they are or what they are facing." I can turn my faithless worry into its faithful opposite and proclaim the divine love that always seeks their wellbeing and sustains them in the midst of their struggles.

This may sound like some pop-psychology "positive affirmation" exercise, but it is much more than that. Because it is grounded in the attentive listening and radical openness of prayer, there is an added element, and that is the surprise of discovering previously unknown divine intentions embedded in the thorns of life. These revelations may come in the most unexpected, unimagined ways.

In imitation of the liturgical call to "hear what the Spirit is saying to the church," in our everyday struggles we can also ask prayerfully, "What is the Spirit saying to me? Where is the Spirit in the depths of this thorn that is stinging me?" The answers can be astonishing at times. I invite you to examine your own life and see what these questions provoke in you. For example, what can the loss of a relationship reveal to you about how you can more wisely navigate the complexities of other relationships? What can your physical dis-ease show you about how to correct your bodily and emotional imbalances that contribute to disease? What cleansing may be flowing through your rivers of tears? If you habitually react to conflict by retreating, or by lashing out, or by arguing, what might be opened up to you if you allow prayer to empower you to make a different response? For starters, responding in a non-habitual way will startle your sparring partner and jolt the relationship into a new way of relating.

The key to turning the thorns of the *alamea* that sting us upside down and placing their undersides on our wounded selves to release our toxins is *listening* for the divine presence that empowers us to do what we have assumed was impossible. This is a very special kind of listening, a profoundly transparent, non-defensive listening. It is not an anxious or desperate pleading with God to "save us from the time of trial." Sometimes we *need* the time of trial to teach us, to strengthen us, to transform us. Prayerful listening is an intense openness to "what the Spirit is saying" to us in whatever situations we face. It is an affirmation that there is in fact a divine indwelling within us, which is always *for life*. It is the only way to counter our self-absorbed "human natures."

FAITH OR FEAR

Living as a person of faith is not easy. Even if one has a born-again conversion experience that transforms one's outlook and mindset forever, life still intrudes. There is in every life, at times, hurt, disappointment, failure, betrayal, conflict, loss, grief. These realities impinge upon everyone, the faithful and the faithless alike. In the light of such challenges, confessing faith is not the same as living in faith. When I look back upon my own life, which has been a genuine effort to put my faith into practice, what has most consistently challenged or stymied my efforts to do that has been fear.

Living in faith requires an active decision to surrender fear and to live in the assurance that divinely permeated life can prevail in the midst of trials, tribulation, travail, doubts, and dangers. Faith is the only thing that can overcome fear. As Heb 11:1 reminds us, faith is "the assurance of things hoped for, the conviction of things not seen." Most of us live with some underlying fears that threaten such assurance and conviction, even though we may not acknowledge this to others. I share the essence of my own fear only as a point of reference, or as a pinprick to remind readers of your own relationship to fear.

I learned fear as a young child because of my father's vulnerability due to his Type 1 diabetes and periodic insulin reactions, which left him impaired and me terrified. The insulin reaction episodes turned this quiet, saintly person whom I adored into someone else, someone who could not be more different than who he really was. I learned fear because of my love for him and my anxiety about his wellbeing. His vulnerability created my own vulnerability. When he went away, usually for the many church meetings he had to attend as a minister, I would stand at the window and anxiously await his return, fearful that he might have an insulin reaction while driving and die. (He lived to 96, so I wasted a lot of time being fearful.)

The uncertainty created by my father's condition left me with a deep-seated fear that I could not trust that love would endure. Growing up, I wanted more than anything to live in the assurance of God's abiding love, but I battled against the alternative reality that bad things happen to good people. Faithful people I knew prayed for their loved ones to be healed from disease or adversity, but it did not always happen.

My fear that one could not always rely on security and safety also rippled outward to envelop how I related to the wider world. When I was a child in the 1950s, Americans were constantly made afraid of communism, of the Soviet Union, of nuclear war. They built bomb shelters in which to hide should the nuclear war we all feared come to pass. I became afraid of war, of nuclear annihilation, at a very young age. As I grew older and began to see what the American Empire was capable of (think Korea, Vietnam, interventions all over the globe), I became afraid of my own country. When my awareness of the climate crisis grew, I became afraid that life on earth would become unsustainable.

Whenever I succumbed to my fears, this diminished my capacity for living a life of faith. From a young age, that affected my bodily life. At the age of eight, my blood sugar levels were suddenly elevated, and it was feared that I had inherited my father's diabetes. I was physically strong in certain ways, and grew up loving hiking and playing baseball, but I became afraid that I would die before my time. As an adult, I inherited several health challenges, many of them caused or exacerbated by stress.

The Hungarian-Canadian psychotherapist Gabor Maté has spent many years researching and writing extensively about the connection between trauma and physical-emotional wellbeing. His preoccupation is the result of his own personal experience of being separated from his mother as an infant while his Hungarian Jewish family was fleeing from the Nazis. Embedded trauma, associated in his case with extreme feelings of abandonment, or, in my case, with fear of losing those whom one loves, becomes rooted in our bodies.

Maté has investigated how the entrenched trauma which is evident today in American life—aggravated by the breakdown of social cohesion and the social safety nets necessary to protect the vulnerable—manifests itself in our epidemics of drug addiction, suicide, heart disease, cancer, sexual abuse, criminal and self-destructive behaviors, and more. Because Western medicine fails to treat the whole person, it ignores how the toxicity of our social existence places a terrible burden on our immune systems and undermines the balance between body, mind, and spirit which we need to survive and thrive. The publicity blurb for Maté's book *The Myth of Normal* states that he "brings his perspective to the great untangling of common myths about what makes us sick, and connects the dots between the maladies of individuals and the declining soundness of society."[7]

Maté makes these connections between trauma and wellbeing from a scientific perspective. I add the spiritual dimension, which is more than a dimension—it is the heart of interrelationality. It is the divine spark of life and love that interpenetrates everything. It is what enables us to discover in our traumas the underlying life and love which God gives us as a gift (remember the *alamea*). God has always been the "something stronger than fear" in my own life that has enabled me to cling to faith or to return to faith

---

7. See Maté, *Myth of Normal* and *When the Body Says No*.

during times of tribulation and despair—not just faith confessed, but faith lived.

This last sentence is the affirmation I proclaim as an act of faith today. To the extent that I nurture the inner balance of mind, body, and spirit which faith enables, I am able to live a life of wellbeing, regardless of what physical or other challenges I may face. As a *for-life* interrelational being, I affirm that there is an (at times hidden) inner balance that never ceases desiring to become a reality in one's body-mind-psyche.

It is faith that enables me to make this claim, and to live it out. I will always be a flawed human, living as a creature who is confined in certain respects in my "human nature." We might call the ways we give in to our human natures *sin*, as we remember that human nature is about self-centeredness and self-promotion. Sin is whatever keeps us trapped in our preoccupation with our own desires and our fears that they won't be met. When our faith is strong, we can embrace the divine abundant life offered to us. When our faith is weak, we succumb to the fear that only worsens our loss of balance and integration.

Ideally, our faith community ought to be a source of strength, guidance, and solidarity as we struggle with our battles between faith and fear. The church should exist in part to support and equip its members to cultivate the faith that frees us from fear and empowers us to act in our own lives, with our loved ones, in our communities, and in the world by living out a *for-life* ethic. I fleshed out what this interrelational theology of church means in chapter 2.

Unfortunately, this way of being church is not what some of our churches tend to do. They are all too often the last place we would normally go to open up with others in vulnerability, daring to be honest about the fears that undermine our faith. In many of the churches with which I am familiar, people step through the front door on Sundays with smiles on their faces, and it is assumed that these are faithful people because they are there in church.

But our established churches are not always well-equipped to cultivate the *kinship* that binds the kindom of God together, and therefore these churches struggle to be a sanctuary of honest, compassionate, gently challenging, Christ-like love. The common rituals of worship must still sustain the members of these churches in some way, for they continue to show up on Sunday mornings. But the truth is that we don't come to church as spiritual giants; we come as persons grappling with our "human natures." I remember my father once telling me as I was growing up that the difference between Christians and atheists is that we know we are broken, we know we are sinners—sin being that which defines our brokenness, our disconnection from our interrelational *for-life* divine design. I keep searching for faith communities that address that brokenness.

I affirm here that faith is the antidote to fear and the way to abundant life in the interwoven tapestry of life. Faith is what empowers us to cast aside and reject everything that harms us in our bodies-minds-spirits. The task of cultivating this faith is what we are called to do as Christ-followers, not only within ourselves but in our relationships with others and with creation. This is the meaning of salvation for us as interrelated persons.

FINDING OUR PLACE IN THE BIG PICTURE

I have been thinking about jigsaw puzzles, having just finally completed a very difficult one. I prefer puzzles with a lot of contrast in colors and shapes, which makes it easier to identify pieces that fit together. This one was different. It was mostly trees, mountains, sky, and water. It was daunting. I left the trees for last, as they covered a good deal of the surface of the puzzle and were very similar in detail and color. Some days I could only fit a handful of pieces. It came to seem almost impossible, but I persisted and finally the whole picture was complete.

We humans want to see things and people as discrete, easily identifiable entities. But life is often messier than that: occluded, unclear, muddied and muddled. Sometimes the relational pieces just do not seem to fit together. We try to force them to fit when they do not. We want to convince ourselves that this or that person is a "fit" with who we are. We push and push and push, but the two pieces of ourself and the other just do not fit.

Some people choose to focus on one small portion of the whole, a "safe space" of predictability, where little like-minded pieces (our family, our ethnic group, our religious group, our clan, our peers, those who share our political orientation) make a comfortable fit. But if we stay in that small frame, we can never see the larger picture. We cannot orient ourselves in relation to the larger world in which we live. When we persist in facing inward, toward what is familiar, this shrinks our minds and spirits. Our worldview becomes closed and atrophies over time.

As a result, we are unprepared to face the realities of the larger world which impinge on us. In the numerous interviews I have seen with Holocaust survivors (to which I return in chapter 12), many of them said that their families did not leave Europe as Nazism took hold because their parents were confined within their comfortable, tight-knit Jewish communities. Their lives revolved around their closed circle of relatives, friends, and synagogue. This meant that even when they could no longer avoid confronting the onslaught of Nazism, they tended to think that they could still somehow remain safe within their own small enclaves. But by then it was too late to escape. This *complacency of the familiar* is our common human predicament.

And yet the larger truth is that we are all connected to a myriad of other parts of the larger picture, regardless of how uncomfortable this makes us, or how ignorant we may be of what is going on in the big picture. A jigsaw puzzle is not the best analogy in this regard, for it has edges and corners. There is an end to the picture. In real life, however, we are part of the whole universe, and there is no end to it. We fit within the endless panoply of creation. In a practical sense, of course, our big picture as humans takes the form of our life on planet Earth. This means that we are not immune from the climate disaster humans have caused, whether we believe it is real or not. We are not detached from the wars and senseless acts of violence that are ripping human societies to shreds. We are impacted by and impact life on this planet in many ways.

And so, even while I may gaze daily in pleasure at the small veggie garden I have planted on the balcony of my apartment, as I greet my bird friends that hop onto my balcony railing and my grandchildren who exuberantly appear at my door, I am connected not just to my familiar adjacent puzzle pieces but to pieces that are some distance from me. My gaze must also extend to the children wailing for their dead parents in Gaza and the parents wailing for their dead children in Gaza. I am linked to the suffering of the victims of the war in Ukraine, both Russian and Ukrainian. The drug cartels that terrorize citizens in Mexico and Central America, sending them fleeing northward in fear for their lives, are my concern; both they and their victims are members of my human family. My humanity connects me with the thousands of people dying from opioid addiction in towns and communities in places like West Virginia and Ohio, and to the citizens of the Pasifika nation of Kiribati whose taro plants are inundated with rising seawater.

My mind cannot process and analyze every reality in the world, but I nonetheless have a moral responsibility to open my eyes to the big picture with intentionality, openness, and compassion. I must take time to stand back from my own life's small part of the picture and look at the whole picture as it truly is. Where there are missing pieces, rips and tears, horrific images, I must open my eyes and see them for what they are. And I must keep plodding and probing to fit the pieces together as best I can. Fitting together the pieces of a jigsaw puzzle is an exercise in patience and attentiveness. It requires a sharpness of eye to discover what goes where. When I keep making mistakes, I must not give up, and this requires persistence.

I have often stood back and marveled that, after the passing of time and effort, I suddenly discover a sense of clarity and completeness in certain aspects of my life. As one example, I have had to move many times due to the living out of my vocation in several countries around the world. Each time I have moved to a new place, often a new country, I have worked until I dropped with exhaustion to create a home out of the chaos of random stacks of boxes, at times in sub-standard housing inundated with cockroaches, ants, mosquitoes, and mice.

In the end, after several days of unpacking and arranging, finding just the right place for this and for that, I always have a home. It is complete. Everything is in its rightful place. And I often ask in wonder, "how did I make another home?" Every time I have moved, across oceans and continents, I have had to start the process anew of making a home in a strange place. There are always obstacles, headaches, and snags, but in the end I always say in awe, "how did I make a home?" It is as though the picture was already complete in its divine design, and its component parts only needed to be revealed to me.

I work on jigsaw puzzles as a hobby, for it is both challenging and, in the end, satisfying. Fortunately, they come in boxes whose covers show a model of what the final picture is meant to look like. Without these examples, I would be lost. I would have no idea where to begin. Perhaps, over a very long time and with suffocating frustration, I might eventually be able to sort out what the whole picture was meant to be. But thankfully I have a picture on the box to guide me.

I also have a guide in life, which is faith. The picture of the intended wholeness of life is expressed to me in the wisdom of sages, sacred texts, saints, the canvas of creation's majesty, and demonstrations of unconditional love. I am not lost, staggering in the dark to wade through confusion in an impossible struggle to fit the pieces together. There is an image before me to which I can turn as I search for the connecting pieces from day to day and year to year.

That is the image of the God who is *for life*—which is the same as saying *for love*. At times this image bursts forth in moments of sublime clarity, in revelations that take my breath away. In such moments, I am able to take a step back and take in the awe-inspiring beauty of the wholeness of life. In those rare moments, I can see myself, my own rightful place, in the divine tapestry. I am a tiny, infinitesimal speck of uniqueness in the big picture, but I do belong. I have a place which is needed to make the tapestry whole. In that space, I want to shine forth with light.

5

Lifting the Mat of Forgiveness

I LEARNED FROM MY parents, from Sunday school and church, and from the whole of my moral instruction as a Christian, that I had no choice but to forgive others. I did not have to like everyone, but I did have to love them. Whenever I had a falling out with my sister or brother as a child, we all had to say "I'm sorry" for any harsh words spoken, no matter who "started it." When my best friend and I had our first (and only) falling-out, at age eight, both of our mothers made us apologize to each other after a week during which each of us cried daily in misery at being estranged from each other. These kinds of apologies, and the forgiveness thereby given and received, did by and large bring peace of mind and restoration of wholeness to my small circle of relationships that mattered most.

FORGIVENESS OR JUSTICE?

My first serious conflict occurred in fourth grade (year four) and involved the class bully, Nancy Gail Campbell.[1] I was a shy, diffident child who strove at all costs to be well-behaved, to be a "good child." But I must have already been unconsciously nurturing my budding instincts as a fighter for justice by age nine, because I reached the tipping point of righteous anger when Nancy Gail went on the attack. One day in the playground she opined loudly that anyone who drove a black car was a criminal. Since at that time my father still drove our old 1949 black Chevrolet, I felt compelled to take exception.

1. Americans from the South often call people by their first and middle names.

"No," I timidly rejoined, "not everyone who drives a black car is a criminal, because my father drives a black car and he is a saint." I probably didn't use the word "saint," but I knew that was what my father was, and I tried to give voice to that. No one could be a better person than he, and he was not to be lumped in with bad guys. When Nancy Gail persisted in her preposterous assertion, moving more and more in my face as she did so, at a certain point something snapped. I honestly cannot remember who struck first, but to my utter astonishment I landed a punch somewhere on Nancy Gail's person. (My grandchildren like to say I punched her in the nose, but it was more like an arm; they want my gravestone to read, "Here lies Nanna; she punched a bully in the nose.")

Most of our class got involved at that point, taking sides or perhaps simply enjoying an opportunity for a fight. Some of the boys were in Nancy Gail's camp, as they were somewhat in awe of her bullying prowess. Suddenly there was a gaggle of nine-year-olds (except for me; I had sat down on the ground and was crying), wrestling, poking, shoving, hair-pulling, dragging, punching, and name-calling, and the entire class was made to stay in the classroom during the afternoon break. The teacher made both Nancy Gail and me stand before the class and apologize to each other.

In that moment, I was humiliated publicly for the first time in my life, but something in me was inwardly rebelling at being forced to "make peace" with a bully the likes of Nancy Gail. I was sorry that I had hit her, but I was not sorry for standing up for my father's good character. This was one time I felt certain that I was right and the other party was wrong. And thus my apology to her was only partially heartfelt.

I never again engaged in fisticuffs with anyone, and I remained, for the most part, someone who tried with all my heart and will to emulate the way of peace embodied by Jesus. No matter how often I failed, I nonetheless held this Way before me as the ideal I sought to follow. But there was this persistent stubbornness in me when it came to forgiving injustices—or those who perpetrated them. More accurately, there was confusion within me about the whole issue of mercy vs. justice, tolerance vs. the righting of wrongs.

Here's the rub: our Christian faith asks us to pardon those who hurt us, to turn the other cheek, to walk the extra mile, to forgive seventy times seventy. At the same time, our faith also calls us to stand on the side of the oppressed, to turn the world order of the powers and principalities upside down (their manipulation, domination, and power-mongering), to come down on the side of the last, the lost, and the least. Kindom life demands that we right wrongs, that we take an active stance in mending the brokenness of creation. The highest good is to give our lives in solidarity with the oppressed, as Jesus did. We cannot stand by idly and watch acts of cruelty and hatred take place.

PEACEMAKING OR PLACATING?

How do we reconcile these two undeniable demands of our faith, when at times they seem to be contradictory? This is a particularly compelling question for women, because it is deeply engrained in us that we are to be the peacemakers in whatever context we find ourselves—in our families, churches, workplaces, communities, and in the world. We instinctively feel it is up to us to see that things run smoothly, that frayed tempers are soothed, that harmony prevails—and this is our job especially in relation to husbands.

Why is this? Perhaps this inbred propensity to placate demanding men harks back to the dim and distant past in human history, when women, as the "weaker sex" (physically), depended on men for their survival. Ancient women were more the "gatherers" and men more the "hunters" because of their physical strength. If men as the primary providers got fed up and left, how would the abandoned women manage? This is not in any way to characterize women as weak but to acknowledge differences in biology. These differences have largely been overcome, in terms of physicality, as we have evolved as a species, but they still persist as latent DNA in our subconscious self-perceptions.

I give you the story of a woman I know who wore the mantle of peacemaker in her marriage for many years, who took it upon herself to knit together the fraying and torn fabric of her marriage through endless acts of forgiveness of her husband, letting things go, letting things slide, in an effort to maintain a semblance of peace for the sake of her children. She placated her unfaithful and emotionally abusive husband for nearly a quarter of a century, even though she was a feminist who always stood up for the equality of women. In the end, after what felt like an eternity of being on the receiving end of betrayal and abuse, she finally realized, "God does not ask me to endure this any longer; I am empty," and she left with her teenage children. Her leaving was a cry for survival, but beneath that was a cry for justice.

How are we supposed to reconcile our calling to practice mercy and forgiveness with our equally compelling calling to stand up for the cause of justice? Everyone has to address this question, but I voice it here especially as a woman. If we practice the former to the neglect of the latter, we place our very souls in peril. But what does it mean that, as Christians, we are asked to forgive those who have harmed us? The woman whose story I have shared could do nothing to change her husband's character or his actions. He caused great harm; it was not a *for-life* relationship. What should forgiveness mean in such situations?

WIDENING THE CIRCLE OF JUSTICE

Perhaps the heart of forgiveness in such relationships, in a *for-life* ethical perspective, is the desire for the wholeness of those who have harmed us, alongside our commitment to our own wholeness. That desire allows us to let go of anger, and that frees us to let the other person go from our consciousness, along with our hurt. But because we still long for justice—the other side of the coin of our Christian embrace of mercy—we must find a way to transform the hurt we have felt in the face of personal injustice into a wider channel of justice-making.

This is to say that even when there can be no righting of wrongs, no mending of the torn fabric of a particular relationship, we can nonetheless channel our desire for justice into more promising arenas. Instead of holding on to the searing memories of the particular wrongs done to us, we can hold on to a vision of "right relationships"—relationships of equality, compassion, and mutual respect. We can allow our own experience of injustice to be transformed into an alternative vision in which justice prevails. This alternative vision, which flows through and is scarred by our pain, impels us into loving action on behalf of others who suffer injustice. It is faith that enables us to turn our own desolation into empathy for others, as well as ourselves.

In this process, "my" suffering becomes "our" suffering, and "your" struggle becomes "my" struggle. Hence the plight of mistreated women everywhere has become my struggle. I have found that such women seem to sense an ally in me. Their healing is advanced to the extent that they come to better understand the forces which led their spouses or partners to control them, and that led them to respond as they did. That understanding can, in turn, lead to a kind of forgiveness, as they come to see their abusers as damaged human beings in need of their own healing.

But this forgiveness cannot mean "Because I love him, I must stay with him and subject myself to more of the same abuse." A *for-life* God does not ask that of us. God does not desire that we participate in any relationship that undermines our wellbeing. Instead, women who have suffered at the hands of controlling men can find healing by joining in the larger struggle for justice—not only for mistreated women but for all who are subjugated and abused by others. This solidarity makes us whole, even when the struggle seems endless and at times overwhelming.

We do not have the power to right every injustice, for we cannot change the attitudes and actions of others. But we do have the power to stand alongside the downtrodden and the vulnerable and to walk together with them toward the light. That walk, in itself, recreates the world, even while the world remains imperfect and injustice persists all around us. It is this calling to *walk alongside* that is most compelling for me in my *for-life* faith journey. The solidarity of accompaniment enables us to walk this walk with dignity and strength, which grows as we hold our walking companions upright and are held upright in turn.

And when we encounter along the road those who have perpetrated injustice—including those who have done so to us personally—we can, walking in our strength together, extend the hand of mercy even to them. We can invite them to walk with us, to choose a different path; and if they are not ready or able, we can say with force, "then we will walk this path without you, hoping that in time you will join us." This is an inner reconciliation which is not dependent on the mindsets or actions of the perpetrators of injustice. Our salvation is that, as interconnected beings who are part of a *for-life* kindom community, we do not walk this path alone. We journey together.

RECONCILIATION THROUGH "LIFTING THE MAT"

Every culture has an innate longing for reconciliation. Although, steeped in our human natures as we are, we tend toward conflict and contention, we also have a deep yearning for reconciliation. In my work in cross-cultural theology, I have been drawn to study the varied ways in which different cultures deal with conflict and practice forgiveness and reconciliation.[2] Although these customary practices vary in nuance and emphasis across diverse cultures, underlying them all is a sense that conflict should not be allowed to become toxic, and that pathways toward reconciliation must be nurtured. From a Christocentric perspective, such reconciliation cannot be separated from justice, for we are called to cultivate "right relationships"— relationships in which each person or group is valued as having the same inherent value and worth.

One such cultural ritual of reconciliation which has had a profound impact on me as the result of my years in Pasifika is the *ifoga* ritual in Samoan culture. The *ifoga* is a public act of apology by a family for a family

---

2. See Johnson, *Drinking from the Same Well.*

member's transgression against someone from another family. Marie Ropeti-Apisaloma writes that the *ifoga* ritual

> ... entails the *matai* (chief) of the offending family, accompanied by family members, covering himself with an *'ie toga* ('fine mat'), and sitting in silence in front of the house of the offended party until such time as the offended person removes the mat as a sign of forgiveness, and invites the offending family into his or her home for an exchange of words of repentance and forgiveness, food, and gifts.... It is a way to mend broken relationships.[3]

This dramatic act of movement toward reconciliation has affinities with Christian understandings of reconciliation, which are also about restoring relationships. I was living in South Africa during the time of the Truth and Reconciliation Commission following the end of apartheid. Archbishop Desmond Tutu was chair of the commission, and his statements during the months of testimony were theologically rich. Over and over, he stated that there could be reconciliation between black and white South Africans when acts of repentance and restoration of trust were seen to be done.

Although the *ifoga* ritual is enacted in the Samoan culture, and thus I cannot claim to understand it from an insider perspective, it does trigger certain imaginings when I hear about it. Having lived in a similar tropical climate in Fiji, I can imagine what it must feel like to be the person sitting under the mat in the heat and humidity. The mosquitoes would be relentless. There might be periods of rain. Sweating would be profuse.

I imagine that the *matai* under the mat must have had consultations with his family in advance to discern whether or not the family member responsible for the offense was genuinely ready to apologize and take concrete steps toward reconciliation. An acknowledgement of one's wrongdoing, and how this has shamed one's entire family, would have to precede any decision to bring family members along to sit in discomfort for potentially a long period of time, until the offended family is ready to forgive.

In other words, taking this step of confession and atonement would not be easy. It would be costly and require humility. Likewise, the offended family must also be prepared to undergo its own time of uncomfortable waiting. They would be sitting in comfort in their house, knowing that the *matai* of the offending family was sitting in misery under the mat. There would be a powerful motivation to go outside of their comfort and remove the mat, for the very reason that the offending family has had the humility to take the first uncomfortable step toward reconciliation.

---

3. Ropeti-Apisaloma, *Nafanua Theology*, 135.

There is thus movement on both sides in this dance toward reconciliation. The offenders move from their home to the neutral space in front of the offended family's home. The offended family, in turn, eventually moves out of their own safe space toward those who are ready to ask for forgiveness for the harm they have caused. This is a mutual movement toward the restoration of relationship.

There are still protocols to observe once the mat is removed. When the mat is lifted and the offending family moves into the home of the offended family, its *matai* speaks on their behalf, offering a heartfelt apology for the wrong that has been done. The family presents gifts of *'ie toga* ("fine mats"), the highest form of gift-giving in Samoan culture. The *matai* of the host family then makes his own speech, accepting the apology and gifts on behalf of his family. Steps are taken to make amends for the damage that has been caused. And then, as in every Pasifika culture, the evening ends with the sharing of food.

I suppose one could question whether or not the *ifoga* ritual is always genuine, since there is huge cultural pressure to end conflicts and restore relationships. But whether fully genuine or not, once the ritual has taken place, it is binding. Whether or not one or more family members on either side still feel resentment and are not fully reconciled, there are obligations entailed in having engaged in this public act that removes the threat of further escalation, violence, or retribution. This, it seems to me, is a powerful depiction of what human relationship is all about. The thrust of the *for-life* ethic is always toward the mending of brokenness, the restoration of relationships.

Closer to home for me, having lived in Fiji and been immersed in Fijian culture, is the Fijian ritual gifting of a whale's tooth (*tabua*), the most highly valued object in the culture, in an effort to resolve conflicts. *Tabua* are given for other reasons as well, to honor someone or to show respect and gratitude for a particular relationship, but the most powerful ritual presentations of a *tabua* are those designed to bring about reconciliation.

I remember especially a time in the early 1990s when there was a near-split in the Methodist Church of Fiji and Rotuma, the largest church in the country. This happened because some in the church were in support of Fiji's military coups (whose purpose was to entrench indigenous Fijian political control over the large Indian minority), while others in the church felt the coups were wrong. It was the time of the Methodist Annual Conference, and some delegates were meeting in one Methodist church in Suva while opposing delegates were meeting in another church. The church was facing a possible formal split, described by some as a church coup. However, a group of women from both groups met separately and then marched together from one church to the other, presenting *tabua* to the leaders of both camps and pleading for reconciliation. A split was averted, and the conference came together.

A dear Fijian couple who were my colleagues at Pacific Theological College, and who remain treasured friends to this day, gave me a whale's tooth when I left Fiji, and they reminded me that this act entails obligations for the giver and the receiver. They said with a smile, "now you'll never be rid of us!" That was because their act of giving me the *tabua*, and my act of accepting it, meant that we were forever bound to one another. Nothing could come between us; our responsibility to care for one another was permanent and unbreakable.

RESTORATIVE JUSTICE

For-life relationality in the kindom of God is always about restorative justice, rather than the retributive justice upon which most societies' criminal justice systems are based. This is fleshed out in the insightful work of the Samoan theologian Selota Maliko, who has written about a restorative justice response to the problem of banishment in Samoan culture.[4] He draws on the work of Christopher Marshall, who defines Christian restorative justice as compassionate justice.[5] As Maliko explains, "Compassionate justice is more than just a feeling; it involves action—an urgent response of loving care, which entails leaving one's own comfortable position and moving forward to meet others, including those who have offended but seek forgiveness."[6]

In retributive justice, punitive retaliation against perpetrators is seen as necessary and deserved, and the more severe the crime, the harsher the punishment. Although most American prisons have some forms of rehabilitation, with provisions for education, some mental health programs, and at times job training, these are not an essential part of the prison sentence and are not related to the crime the offender has committed. They are about the rehabilitation of the prisoner but not about restoration of the damaged lives impacted by the crime, both perpetrators and victims.

This can be seen on a larger scale in the way the American Empire conducts foreign policy. At the time of this writing, it has placed draconian economic sanctions on at least twenty-six countries. This is collective punishment against innocent citizens of a country as an act of revenge against its leaders. Diplomacy is virtually dead as an element of American foreign

---

4. Maliko, "Restorative Justice."
5. Marshall, *Compassionate Justice*.
6. Maliko, "Restorative Justice," 154.

policy. Rather than any attempts to restore fractured relationships with other countries, the US prefers wars, threats of war, covert interventions, and endless sanctions. There is nothing *for life* about these policies of retribution.

What if our societies were to practice restorative justice? Many crimes would not require incarceration at all. In the restorative justice programs in some American towns and cities, perpetrators and victims of crimes are brought together to seek, through mediation, a way toward restitution and accountability. For example, if someone has robbed another person, ways are found to replace or compensate for what has been stolen. More importantly, perpetrators are made to listen not just to the material costs but the emotional costs of their crimes for their victims. Likewise, victims hear of the circumstances which have led their perpetrators to commit the crime. They must sit together, face to face, until they become human to one another. The goal is justice understood as the restoration of right relationships.

This is hard work. If we choose to remain trapped in our "human nature" mindset, we will either try to get away with whatever we can in order to have our way, or we will hate and seek to punish those who have hurt us. In contrast, interrelational life in the kindom of God calls us to chart another path, one in which we never lose sight of our shared humanity with the other. That is what it means to be *for life*, meaning *for love*.

Part 3

A Widening Spiral of Relatedness

6

All Lives Matter

CORE VALUES THAT CIRCUMSCRIBE "LIFE" FOR US

THE FUNDAMENTAL THEOLOGICAL CONUNDRUM that prompted me to write this book centers around the question "Does God call us to practice a consistent ethic?" As I noted in chapter 1, the more I have reflected on the ethical imperatives of God's *for-life* essence, the more I have had to grapple with the fact that our ethical choices are not always guided, first and foremost, by divine ethical imperatives. Although we may *proclaim* a certain theological ethic—e.g., "thou shalt not kill"—we do not always practice it; even if we have not personally killed, we may have supported armies and police forces and courts which do. There are countervailing belief systems that permeate our consciousness and predispose us to act in ways that run counter to a *for-life* ethic.

In other words, our actions are determined by a whole host of influences, not all of them divinely inspired. If we grow up in a family that tells us that a particular political party is superior to other political parties, that is the ideology we are likely to carry with us into adulthood. Even if the preferred political party shows itself over time to be antithetical to the ethical demands of a *for-life* God, our brains are conditioned to hold on to the belief inculcated in us that our political party is superior to others, or at least "the lesser of two evils."

Our familial influence is situated within a larger cultural worldview which is also "home," whether this is our ethnic, regional, or national culture. These cultural worldviews are grounded in their own value systems. I hail from Southern American culture and, within that, from Appalachian mountain culture. Both cultures have impacted the way I view the world, with Appalachian culture being particularly impactful. Some of these cultural values are complimentary to a Christocentric *for-life* ethic, and others are not.

It was only when I began living in very different cultures that I was able to take a step back from my own cultural rootedness and analyze my inherited cultural values in relation to other value systems and, most importantly, in relation to a divinely ordained *for-life* ethic. I discovered that unless something jolts us out of our entrenched cultural worldview, it remains taken-for-granted; we will never question it.

The overriding cultural influence for Americans, of course, is that of the myth of American greatness. There is much talk in our national discourse about "American values." These are centered in "freedom and democracy." Freedom is the most important value of all. It is ingrained in us that America is the uniquely wonderful "land of the free." The many Americans who hang American flags outside their houses would, if asked, no doubt say that these flags are a sign of their love of freedom.

But what does this mean? Freedom for what? Freedom from what? I have pondered this question for a long time. At the beginning of our history as a nation, freedom meant freedom from the yoke of British colonialism. But if we look carefully at the source of America's fight for freedom from the British, it was not that the early (white) American settlers did not like the British way of life—after all, most of them were British themselves. An important aspect of the rebellion of the early settlers was their desire for freedom from British economic control.

That is what the defining early moment of our revolution, the famous Boston Tea Party in 1773, was all about—dumping English tea into Boston Harbor because the taxes the British imposed on it were too high. The revolt against the British was to uphold the value that "what is mine is mine, and no colonizing force (and later, no government of our own) should be able to take very much of it away from me." (This observation is in no way to diminish the genuineness of the colonial American desire not to live under a monarchy but to create a more representative form of government.)

Within this foundational worldview lies the core underlying value that defines America, already identified earlier in this work—individualism. At the heart of the American identity is the concept of personal freedoms and rights. One should be free to live one's life as one sees fit, with the least amount of interference. Americans do organize themselves into collectives, but they are mostly for the purpose of safeguarding and championing this or that individual right. America has many groups that lobby the government for their pet causes (e.g., gun rights, reproductive rights, gender rights), but it has a weak concept of the common good. Americans seem to unite as a nation only in times of national crisis or war, when they join together to protect the nation's right to be an exceptional, superior nation in relation to the world (I discuss American exceptionalism in chapter 10).

From a theological perspective, the problem is that, if we subscribe to an underlying core value of individual rights, we will make ethical decisions that are guided by that value rather than the ethical imperatives of a *for-life-for-all* God. My reflections on this have exposed a number of striking inconsistencies that arise in our practice of ethics. The question these inconsistencies pose for those who seek to follow a *for-life* ethic is this: What if we were to consistently apply a *for-life* ethic across the board; what might that look like?

In this chapter, I will consider several ethical choices that confront American society today, all clustered around the questions *"what is interrelational life in this situation?"* and *"how should a for-life ethic be applied?"* My assertion is that, for many Americans, all of these "life and death" matters share the same underlying core belief in the sanctity of individual rights. Both gun rights advocates and abortion rights/pro-choice advocates, for example, appeal to this same core value, even though they are in opposing political camps. I examine this core value in relation to an interrelational ethic which is *for all life*.

THE BEGINNING OF LIFE

If God is, by definition, *for all life*, then we as divinely permeated, interrelated beings must also be for all life. But how far are we willing to go to put this ethic into practice with regard to human life? Do we really believe that all human life is *of God* and therefore to be treasured and protected? If we truly believe this, then how can we condone the abortion of a fetus in the womb? My reflection on this question has led me to the difficult conclusion that the "pro-choice" position I espoused for many years contradicts a *for-life* ethic. I have come to realize that my pro-choice position was the result of an "individual rights" ethic which I had inculcated as an American, rather than a *for-life* Christian ethic.

It is not easy for me to say this, because it puts me at odds with almost every American I know. I do not believe my parents would have been accepting of abortion, but from the time I left home and travelled along a path with open-minded "progressives," I agreed with the premise that a woman has the right to do with her body what she determines is best for her. Based on that rationale, the government should not deny her that inalienable right. Her personal autonomy over her body is sacrosanct.

I have known women who have had abortions, and I could not and do not sit in judgment over them for that difficult, often painful decision. From a legal perspective, I have come to question whether the issue of abortion should even be circumscribed by law. It is at heart an ethical issue, and perhaps it would be better fleshed out in faith communities, through prayerful discernment, rather than in courts of law. It is a slippery slope for governments and courts to make legal pronouncements about when human life begins and how far the law should go to protect it. Such pronouncements can change depending on the politics of those making or upholding the law, as we have seen in recent US Supreme Court reversals regarding the legal right to abortion.

I have been aided in my own thinking on this issue by Catholic theological positions on *the sanctity of life*. Catholic teaching asserts that abortion amounts to "attacking a being with a human destiny, being prepared by God to receive an immortal soul" (cf. Jer 1:5: "Before I formed you in the womb, I knew you").[1] What happens at conception is the creation of a new living being that is distinct from, if dependent upon, its mother. An embryo is not a person in the same sense as a child or adult, just as a seedling is not a full-blown tree, but if protected both will become the beings and have the life which has been divinely set in motion.

Even at the very beginning, therefore, Catholic theology asserts that an embryo is "distinctively human, with the inherent and active potential to mature into a human fetus, infant, child and adult. In addition to the scientific fact that a human life begins at conception, the only moral norm needed to understand the Church's opposition to abortion is the principle that *each and every human life has inherent dignity, and thus must be treated with the respect due to a human person*."[2] (Italics in original.) These assertions cohere with a *for-life* ethic, which goes further to assert that what happens at conception is the beginning of a human life that *partakes of God's very being*.

The decision for abortion is thus a decision to prioritize one human life over another. It is an implicit claim that the life of the mother has more value than the life of the child-to-be growing in her womb. When pro-choice adherents insist that "no one has the right to tell a woman what to do with her body," that is to ignore the fact that when a woman becomes pregnant, we are no longer speaking of *one* body but *two* bodies. For the pregnant woman, this is no longer about "my body" but about "our bodies."

1. US Conference of Catholic Bishops, "Respect for Unborn Human Life."
2. US Conference of Catholic Bishops, "Respect for Unborn Human Life."

If we are interrelational beings, imbued with the divine presence that is *for life*, on what moral basis can we say that the life of the mother is more important than the life of the human being growing in her womb? Perhaps if the embryo is doomed to an excruciatingly painful existence that will inevitably result in early death (such as cases where most of the brain is missing), it may be a loving and gracious act to save that embryonic life from future pain. If there is a medical crisis and the choice is between saving the life of the mother or saving the life of the child-to-be, an ethical case could be made that the mother's life must be saved as she already bears responsibilities in the world.

These are very difficult ethical quandaries. We should not be too self-assured about making blanket pronouncements about such life-and-death dilemmas. But these extreme situations are, in any event, only a tiny fraction of abortions. In most cases, the mother's life is not at stake, nor is the fetus doomed to certain death. Regardless of the circumstance, we should be gracious and loving as we navigate our way through the ethical implications of any woman's decision to terminate her pregnancy. (Anti-abortion activists who scream "Murderer!" at women entering abortion clinics are not practicing a *for-life* ethic.) What saddens me is that many women feel they have to make such decisions because they do not live in a *for-life* environment that would come to their aid and care for them and for the life they are carrying within them.

The reasons for abortion are many: a woman may not have the economic means to support a child. She may not have a spouse or loving partner to support her and their child. She may be the victim of incest. She may be a young teen who feels ashamed to have become pregnant out of wedlock, or who does not want to give up her education and future prospects by being tied down with a child. She may have become pregnant by accident and not want to face the inconvenience of an unwanted pregnancy. She may be traumatized by rape and want no future reminders of her rapist.

The point is that, in individualist societies, all of these scenarios exist within a societal framework which does not always provide adequate loving care for everyone, whether mothers or children. In an individualist culture, "we are not our sister's keeper." There is no reliable framework of care which would make abortion unnecessary.

I remember my surprise while living in Fiji to discover that abortions were extremely rare. This was also the case in the many other Pasifika cultures I encountered among my students and colleagues at Pacific Theological College. Abortion was legal in Fiji but only if the pregnancy "gravely endangers the mother's physical or mental health. The law does not allow voluntary abortion as it is against religious beliefs . . . Abortion in Fiji is a taboo."[3] At times, abortions did occur among unmarried teenage girls, but this was more typically in Fiji's Indian community, which did not have the same kind of communal support system as the indigenous Fijian communities.

That last phrase is crucial. It was not the case that there were no out-of-wedlock pregnancies in indigenous Fijian communities. Despite robust cultural mores surrounding sexuality, even virginity tests at marriage in traditional Fijian village customs, some unmarried girls did occasionally become pregnant. But when this happened, the child of such a union was welcomed into the families and communities concerned. The biological mother of this child did not "own" the child; it was therefore not up to her to decide if the child should live. The child belonged to everyone in its orbit. If the birth mother was unable to raise her child, that child still had a family—not just a nuclear family but a large extended family—and it would not occur to anyone to terminate this child's life.

Another facet of the notion of family in Pasifika cultures gradually became clear to me after getting to know my students and their families. Most of the students at Pacific Theological College came to the college as married students, often with children. They sometimes brought with them children who were not their biological offspring. A child may have been gifted to them by a relative who was unable to adequately care for the child. The wife of a colleague of mine gave birth to her eighth child at PTC, and when she and her family went back to their home island for the summer break, that child was gifted to a relative who had no children of her own.

I thought that was a very compassionate thing to do, but I remember thinking at the time, "I could never do that; I could never give my child to someone else." The key word in that sentence is "my." In individualist cultures, we tend to think that our children are our exclusive possession. If, on the other hand, our children belong to God and are only entrusted into our care—and the care of our families and community—that is something else. This question of the "ownership" of children relates to the issue of abortion, because if we have cultivated strong familial and communal bonds, a problematic pregnancy does not have to result in a death. The life of that child is protected by a much larger shroud of love and care than that of its biological mother.

One can argue for the legitimacy of abortion on the basis of the autonomous rights of the mother to determine what she does with her body. But we should then be clear that this is what we are doing, rather than basing our decision about the life of the unborn child on the faith assertion

---

3. "Global Abortion Policies Database."

that God is always *for life* and that therefore every human life has inherent worth, even the tiniest life. The emotional burden of bearing a child whom one is unable or unwilling to raise after birth can be borne if this burden is taken up by others who can provide the parenting one cannot give. A *for-life* society would remove any stigma attached to women who are unable, for whatever reason, to raise their biological child.

Unfortunately, the much-needed support system for pregnant girls and women is not always present in individualist societies. But what if it were? I have seen a few examples. I was privileged to know a Quaker woman many years ago in Asheville, North Carolina, who was the caregiver in a home for pregnant teenagers. They lived in a large house with her during their pregnancies and for some time afterward, as needed. She made sure they had the medical care they needed, that they ate healthily, exercised, and were homeschooled, and she helped them to make plans with their families and other support networks for their babies' futures.

Most gave them up for adoption. These girls were very young, some as young as thirteen, and completely ill-equipped to raise a child. Many came from dysfunctional families who were also unable to help raise the child to come. Sometimes these were blind adoptions, such that they would never know the parents who adopted their child. In other cases, they got to know the adoptive parents and were welcome to know their child as he or she grew older. These girls were surrounded by love and care. They did not have to feel that they had no alternative but to abort their pregnancies, because they had the support they needed to give their child the precious gift of *life*.

If our individualist-oriented societies gave families the support they needed to thrive, and encouraged a wider circle of communal support for every child and every parent, there would be no need for abortions. There might still be some exceptions, as outlined earlier, but these would be very rare. We would affirm, as a society, that every life has inherent sacred worth. We would affirm that human life of course begins at conception. We would do this as human beings grateful to be interrelated with a *for-life* God.

In a way, the moment of conception is an echo of the birth of the universe described at the beginning of this book. At conception, life miraculously bursts into being. The "stuff of life" is all there—the DNA, the genetic blueprint, the cells that are already multiplying from the first seconds of existence. There is nothing more sacred than that—the genesis of life. What happens after birth is the responsibility of many, and especially as faith communities we are mandated to help provide what every child needs. Likewise, what happens in the womb is the responsibility not just of the mother but of her community of love-givers.

"GOD DON'T MAKE NO JUNK"

I have a vivid memory from my childhood of being at a church picnic one summer when I witnessed something that became seared into my consciousness. I saw two girls who were seven or eight years old ostensibly taking a smaller Down Syndrome child, perhaps three years old, for a walk around the lovely picnic grounds by a river. The older girls would each reach out to hold a hand of the Down Syndrome child, only to then pinch her as they walked along, causing her to wail in pain. The older girls giggled as they did this. I was horrified but did not know what to do. Thankfully, an old man standing near me also saw what was happening and intervened, scolding the two older children and returning the wailing child to her parents. Afterwards, he stood shaking his head, and then he said, to no one in particular, "God don't make no junk!"

Although I was only twelve at the time, I grasped what he meant. The two bullying children treated this little "different" girl as though she were junk (defined in the *Oxford English Dictionary* as "something considered useless or of little value"). Even at their young age, they had already internalized the idea that the lives of those who are "different" from the norm do not have the same value as the lives of those who are "normal." Underlying this distinction between "normal" and "not normal" is the assumption that "normal" is better—after all, God designed humans to be "wonderfully made" (Ps 139), not damaged.

Using this logic, God would see to it that no one had any disabilities. Since clearly that is not the case, something must have gone wrong in God's plan. Although most would agree that mean-spirited people like the two girls at the church picnic wrongly make fun of disabled people, some Christians still believe that we should love disabled people *despite* the fact that a "mistake" has somehow been made; something has unfortunately gone awry in God's design.

Disabilities theology[4] throws such assumptions on their head. The boldest assertion is perhaps that made by Nancy Eisland, namely that God is a "disabled God."[5] This is shocking imagery for those accustomed to envisioning God as perfection. What I understand Eisland to be saying is that God is about multiplicity and inclusion, not about some arbitrary notion of human perfection, for who can even define what that perfection is? One person's perfection may be another person's flaw. Who is to say that those

---

4. In addition to Nancy Eisland's work, recent publications in disabilities theology include: Swinton, *Who is the God We Worship?*; Brock, *Wonderfully Wounded*; Gaventa, *Disability and Spirituality*; and Eilers, "Theology and the Experience of Disability."

5. See Eisland, *Disabled God*.

with obvious disabilities are less ideal than those who have less obvious disabilities? Don't we all have imperfections of some kind?

The notion of a "disabled God" is an acknowledgement that "nature" affects everyone and everything, and that nature, as I argued in chapter 1, does not always adhere to one "perfect" design but goes its own way and is multi-variegated. This means that we humans do not fit into one predetermined mold—as biological beings, we have differing abilities and attributes. It is the *for-life* God who makes us whole and one with all others, and who also shares in our diversity. This is vividly reenacted in the eucharist, where we partake of Christ's "broken" body, not his "perfect" body. We repeat Jesus' words at the Last Supper as we lift the bread—"this is my body, broken for you."

Disabilities theology challenges the ways in which our churches have at times seen the disabled not as whole persons but as flawed persons to be tolerated, or as "projects" to be "worked on" and hopefully made to "fit in" (with the normal people). A dark stain on the church's history is its past beliefs that disabled persons were more sinful than "normal" people, at times being thought to be possessed by evil spirits.

Thankfully, real strides have been made by some churches in recent decades in welcoming and accepting disabled people as valued members of the kindom community. Disabilities ministries in churches are increasingly "not program-based but relational-based; . . . this means recognizing that, for all people—no matter what combination of abilities or disabilities we possess—our deepest and common need is for God."[6] The practical dimension of disability ministry entails creating spaces and aids that cater to the needs of those with disabilities in the church; the spiritual dimension means encouraging and facilitating "access for all to the gospel."

Today some disabilities theologians focus in particular on how the church relates to those on the autism spectrum, the most rapidly growing disability in recent decades, at least in the West. David Fitch has called for a *faithful presence with the lived experiences of autism.*[7] He argues for a transformative process in our churches that begins with a "willingness to intentionally engage people with autism, recognizing them as siblings gifted by God and valuable parts of the Body of Christ."[8]

The disability of autism is especially near and dear to my heart, as I have a grandson who is on the autism spectrum, whom I love unconditionally. This brilliant, gifted child has endured bullying and avoidance because

6. Hubach, "Disability Ministry."
7. Fitch, *The Church of Us versus Them.*
8. Cited in Creamer, "Theological Accessibility."

of his "difference." Until very recently (changing now that his mother is his minister and his church a welcoming place of refuge), he has not always felt welcome in the church, where some seem to have wished that everyone there would just be "normal"—presumably meaning "the same." He told me once that he had never felt close to God in church. My daughter told me several years ago that when their family would have Sunday evening "chapel" at home, he would often walk to the window, look to the far horizon, feel God's presence, and express the most profound theological insights.

The old man's assertion that "God don't make no junk" is, I believe, an affirmation that God recognizes every human being as the opposite of junk—treasure. This is the case no matter what "other-than-the-norm" condition nature sometimes imposes on us. Since God is *for life*, God is for every human life.

WHEN "ALL LIVES MATTER" IS A SMOKESCREEN FOR RACISM

In 2013, three female black organizers initiated a movement in the United States to combat systemic racism, especially police violence against African Americans, called Black Lives Matter (BLM). It began in response to yet another acquittal of a white person for the murder of a black person, namely the acquittal of George Zimmerman in the shooting death of 17-year-old Trayvon Martin in 2012. The movement became a national movement in 2014 after the police killings of Michael Brown in Missouri and Eric Garner in New York and evolved into a worldwide movement against racism after the death of George Floyd in 2020 at the hands of police in Minneapolis, Minnesota.

Black Lives Matter's website states that its mission is "to eradicate white supremacy and build local power to intervene in violence inflicted on Black communities by the state and vigilantes. By combating and countering acts of violence, creating space for Black imagination and innovation, and centering Black joy, we are winning immediate improvements in our lives."[9] After being in the forefront of massive protests across the United States and in other countries following the George Floyd murder, BLM's influence has waned, but that is not the focus of this reflection. When movements become institutionalized, with paid staff and funding from think tanks and corporations, it is not unusual for them to lose grassroots momentum.

---

9. "Black Lives Matter." Among a number of prominent scholarly studies of the Black Lives Matter movement, see, for example, Ransby, *Making All Black Lives Matter*; and Lebron, *Making of Black Lives Matter*.

I would like to focus instead on the alternative catchphrase that was widely uttered by white Americans who did not like Black Lives Matter—namely, "all lives matter." This sentiment takes us to the heart of the problem with the continuing scourge of racism in America, in which some white Americans believe that it is unfair of blacks to keep bringing racism to the attention of the public because, they claim, America is not racist anymore.

The argument of the "all lives matter" voices is that, while slavery was wrong, it was over long ago. After the Civil Rights Act of 1964, all remaining vestiges of racism were legally vanquished once and for all: blacks could vote, share public spaces with whites, move into white neighborhoods, go to white schools and universities, and become politicians at the national level. There was lingering resentment among some whites about some of these changes, accompanied by the feeling that blacks had actually ended up getting preferential treatment—for example, through "affirmative action" laws designed to correct the discrimination of the past by allocating a certain percentage of admissions to colleges and universities to African Americans.

However, the majority of Americans came to accept that the time was past when one could openly admit to being racist; indeed, claiming not to be racist created a self-satisfying sense of righteousness. Some extremist racist groups, such as the Ku Klux Klan, Proud Boys, Patriot Front, and other white supremacy groups, still call for the separation of blacks and whites and overtly claim that the white race is superior, but most white Americans convinced themselves that they are not racist and that the country as a whole is not racist. Therefore, in their view, blacks should be happy with what they have been given and stop claiming that *their* lives "matter" in any distinguishing way. A pet peeve of these self-satisfied white Americans is the teaching of *critical race theory*[10] in American universities and colleges, since it unpacks the history and present structures of systemic racism which, their argument goes, no longer exist.

I want to acknowledge here that there are of course white Americans who are genuinely not racist and who have black and brown friends and relations; the American story is not hopelessly racist. However, overt and covert racism obviously still exists in America and other Eurocentric societies. America came to be a prosperous nation on the foundation of racism, first against the Native Americans and then through the institution of slavery (see chapter 10). The American myth of greatness was first articulated by white men, and despite the fact that, by the year 2045, whites

---

10. Critical Race Theory is "a set of ideas holding that racial bias is inherent in many parts of Western society, especially in its legal and social institutions, on the basis of their having been primarily designed for and implemented by white people." Jones, "Critical Race Theory."

will be outnumbered by blacks and Hispanics, the foundational worldview and resulting political and economic systems of the United States remain Eurocentric.

Overt racism can be seen today perhaps most prominently in the treatment of the black population by the American criminal justice system. Not only are blacks arrested disproportionately to their percentage of the population, they are convicted more often and given longer prison sentences than white people. And, as the Black Lives Matter movement has highlighted, blacks are murdered by police far more often than whites. The 1994 Violent Crime Control and Law Enforcement Act (known as "the Crime Bill"), put forward by none other than then-Senator Joe Biden, has had particularly disastrous results for the African American community. The Crime Bill has

> . . . contributed to ongoing rampant police misconduct and racial profiling by deploying hundreds of thousands of officers into neighborhoods of color; . . . it also expanded the use of the death penalty; imposed mandatory life sentences for individuals with three or more felony convictions; and levied harsh new penalties for justice system-involved youth. Many of these harmful provisions remain in effect today and continue to target and destabilize communities of color.[11]

In a way, these overt outworkings of systemic racism are more honest than the more covert ways in which racism works. Although being openly racist is not as permissible as it once was, and although insisting that one is not racist may assuage one's conscience, it can have its own insidious consequences. Shouting "all lives matter" is a subtle way of saying "my life matters (as a white person), and you need to quit belly-aching about yours (as a black person)." I know Americans who feel this way. They claim not to be racist but have no black friends; no black people ever visit in their homes; they never worship with black people; they would never want their children to marry a black person. They live in a white world, and they want black people to stay in their black world.

For these people, "all lives matter" is a hollow statement. Black lives or brown lives, or lives of any race other than the white race (Arabs, Asians, and so on), simply do not matter for them in the same way that their own white lives matter. This conviction is at the heart of racism. But what predisposes someone to believe that his or her race matters more than any other? Such a belief is completely antithetical to a *for-life* ethic, and to life in the kindom of God, where humans are gathered together like the diverse parts of a body, with each part, while different from the others, offering

---

11. "Three Ways the 1994 Crime Bill Continues."

something essential to the interconnected whole of life. Why would any one race come to think of itself as superior to any other, given the divine design for interrelatedness?

I have long struggled to answer this question. I was very fortunate that my parents somehow, for the most part, escaped the racism of their time and place in American history. I can remember riding in the car with my father as a child and his stopping the car to pick up blacks walking home from work. The children I went to primary school with (all white—this was before mandated racial integration of schools) never ventured into the black part of town—sadly named Stumptown. Yet my father took me with him into the muddy, rutted streets of Stumptown to take people who had no cars to their homes, and he talked with them in the same way he did with everyone else.

My mother grew up on a farm in a remote part of mountainous northwest North Carolina. There were few black people there, mostly only poor white farmers, but interestingly this area had been part of the Underground Railroad system of safe houses for runaway slaves during the period of slavery (Appalachian people did not own slaves; even if they had wanted to, they were too poor). A few of these former slaves settled in northwest North Carolina after the Civil War, and the farm next to my mother's family farm was inhabited by the descendants of one of these families. I remember my mother telling me that she was not really aware of racism until she left home to go to a church boarding school as a teenager. Her community's isolation from the outside world, and the shared experience of poverty, made it somehow possible for her black neighbors to be just that—neighbors.

As a minister, my father was instrumental in working with several black and white ministers to cultivate better race relations in the North Carolina town where I lived as a pre-teen and teenager. He took me with him to the home of a black minister to plan events for this interracial group. While I was in high school, the racial integration of schools became a legal requirement, and my high school went from having no black students in my first year to having one black student my second year, and then seventy-five black students my third year, in a school of around six hundred students.

These black students kept to themselves, ate lunch by themselves, and rarely talked to the white students, but as time went by the walls began to crumble bit by bit. This happened first for me when one of our teachers said something outrageous in class one day, and I made a funny remark under my breath to the black girl sitting next to me. She couldn't help but smile, and this led to further whispered conversations, until the time came that she and her friends asked me one day to sit with them at lunch. We were moving toward simply being fellow humans.

At its heart, racism stems from a deep-seated need to feel more secure by imagining that one's own race is better than others. The underlying assumption is that my race, my ethnic group, my culture—because it is the one that formed and nurtured me—must be the way life should be lived. My race is the norm, which makes others sub-normal. But this is not the way God created us to be.

As a human species, we did not start out as many races. We started out as an emergent human race in the depths of Africa. Over many thousands of years, we moved further and further away from our common place of origin. As time went on and we moved into different climates, we developed distinctive physical features, different skin tones and hair, different languages and customs, but our underlying humanness remained the same.

We forget this common humanness when we privilege our race over another. We forget that we are so much more alike than we are different. I heard about an episode of the famous American comedy television show *All in the Family* in which the racist Archie Bunker had to have a blood transfusion in the hospital. I'm not sure whether he received it from an Asian or an African American, but he was horrified that his blood would be forever tainted. It could not be. We all have the same blood.

All lives *do* matter, but not in the way the unconscious racists mean when they shout "All lives matter!" to drown out the shouts of "Black lives matter!" Black people shout that slogan not because they do not believe the white race or other races matter too but because black lives have not mattered in American history and still do not matter in equal measure today. They have to shout that their lives matter to remind the country that their lives *should* matter as much as white lives matter.

Because we are interrelated beings, the only cure for racism is *mutual encounter*. This is true in relation to all differing groups, whether racial, ethnic, socioeconomic, or religious. Abstract pronouncements about our equality will not convince us. Only actual encounters with others who are different from us will move us toward seeing one another as equally valuable human beings—as, in fact, our *kin* who share life with us in the kindom of God.

I was first pushed in that direction when my father took me into Stumptown. Barriers came down further when I began to chat with my black schoolmates in high school. In college, I became a close friend of the first African American in the school of music, a fellow piano performance major. During my summer living in a village in the Nicaraguan jungle, I came to know indigenous Mesquite Indians and the descendants of Afro-Caribbean slaves because I lived in a hut next to them and shared their daily struggles. During a summer cultural immersion experience in Japan, I lived with Japanese students and encountered their very distinctive way of life. As an adult, I have lived among Jamaicans, black South Africans, and the myriad peoples of Pasifika and Aotearoa (New Zealand). I am richly blessed to have a half-Belizean son-in-law and a British son-in-law.

It is when one sits with "different" others, eats with them, laughs with them, cries with them, listens to them, shares stories with them, debates with them, prays with them, and works with them that one is pushed out of any desire, however unconscious, to think of one's own race or "in-group" as in any way superior. The greatest privilege of my life has been the opportunities I have been given to be thrust into encounters, some of which became deep friendships, with racial and cultural "others." Such encounter is not always easy. We still like to do things the way we grew up doing them, to practice "our" customs, traditions, art forms, ways of speaking and acting.

God is not calling us to give up our distinctive ethnic and cultural identities. They are what makes the world interesting and stimulating, and our home culture gives us a sense of belonging. But God is calling us to intentionally encounter others whose ways of being in the world differ in certain respects from our own. In my work in cross-cultural theology, I have used as a metaphor to describe this intentionality the act of *crossing a bridge*.[12] My group (race, culture, religion) lives on one side of the bridge, yours on the other side. We each live in our own familiar enclaves. But we need to know one another. We may not live permanently on the other side of the bridge (although living for extended periods of time "in" other cultures has transformed my life for the better), but we need to be intentional about crossing back and forth over the bridge as neighbors.

Perhaps the most fertile space for transformative encounter is in the middle of the bridge, where both sides can come to sit on the mat of *talanoa*[13] and dialogue together in an open, uncluttered, liminal space that privileges our common humanity. There, as the cross-cultural theologian David Augsburger famously said, we celebrate that we are simultaneously "like no others, like some others, and like all others."[14] We need such encounters in order to jolt ourselves into new perceptions, new insights, new appreciations of the beautiful variety we find in human life. In such encounters, we come to learn what it really means that "all lives matter."

---

12. See Johnson, *Drinking from the Same Well*.

13. *Talanoa* is a distinctively Pasifika form of dialogue, in which people sit together and share their stories and ideas freely. In an unstructured way, this leads to mutual understanding, new insights, and at times collective decision-making, even reconciliation.

14. See Augsburger, *Pastoral Counseling across Cultures*.

GENDERED LIFE AND THE PROBLEM OF WOKE-ISM

Human life exists along a continuum of gender identifications. The vast majority of humans, in every race and culture, are situated in one of two biologically distinct genders, male and female, each of which is naturally attracted to the other. This is what has enabled procreation and the continuity of the human species since humans first walked the earth. At the same time, there are more diverse nuances of gender along the continuum. Gender is more fluid than we used to think.

Although heterosexual males and females are clustered along the broad middle of the continuum, farther along toward either end are those who are "gender-diverse." There are some who feel that they have been born into the wrong body and should be the opposite gender than the one their biology has assigned them. There are those who are attracted to their own gender, or to both males and females. There are some who are non-binary, who do not strongly identify as either male or female. There are those who feel so strongly that they are in the wrong body that they take the extreme step of hormonally and/or surgically changing their gender. The spectrum is complex and seems to have more permutations with every passing year, at least in the West.

From a biological perspective, gender may be influenced by several factors, from what happens to a fetus in the womb to cellular differences in a certain part of the brain, to environmental influences on the parents and the child. Psychologically, the influences on gender identity are not as "scientific," but they clearly exist. Some girls who have been sexually abused as children grow up to reject males, feeling safer expressing themselves sexually with other females. Some boys who have a weak father figure and a strong mother figure grow up to take on a feminine role in sexual relationships with other men. Some males and females even assume a particular gender identity as a form of protest against conventional gender roles. Where there are strong psychological and sociological factors at play, gender identity may be said to be more a choice than an inherent biological predisposition. As one example, some individuals engage in same-sex relationships as prisoners but revert to heterosexuality once they are released.

Since gender entails both biological and psychological determinism, along with some fluidity, we should not make judgments about how people see themselves as gendered beings. We most certainly need to reaffirm that "God don't make no junk" when it comes to gender. It is not a divine mistake that there is diversity and multiplicity in the ways human beings experience gendered life. This diversity is simply, once again, "nature" doing its thing. As a friend of mine used to say, "people are very varietal" (a wonderful word).

Our *for-life* God designed us to be human manifestations of divine Spirit, and this spiritual core of our humanness is more fundamental than anything else, including our gender. That said, it should be patently obvious that no one should be discriminated against for their gendered identity, which in any event may evolve and shift over their lifetimes. Those Christians who condemn gender diversity as sinful often base their arguments on obscure passages of Scripture, written many millennia ago by persons who were embedded in their own cultural mores. Many cultures throughout history (though not all) have been rigidly heterosexual in their prescriptions for human behavior, including the cultures we meet in Scripture. Such culture-laden views are not authoritative for us as faithful people seeking to emulate a *for-life* God.

Beyond their proof-texting appeals to Scripture, many Christians who condemn anyone who is not heterosexual are appealing to the same culturally-limited values highlighted in other sections of this chapter. The underlying problem is, again, the demeaning "othering" of those who are not like what some have decided is normative. Although in individualist cultures like the United States there may be greater leeway in accepting gender diversity, since the core value is "do your own thing" and "each to his own," there are still minorities within these cultures who struggle mightily to tolerate all kinds of "otherness"—other races, other cultures, other religions, and other gender orientations. Anyone who is different from whatever they deem to be normative is judged as inferior.

The social dynamic of antagonism between those who are tolerant and those who are intolerant of "difference" may actually be more pronounced in extremely individualist societies, because their "do your own thing" mindset threatens to remove the lingering vestiges of security amongst those who are clinging to the old certainties that used to ensure social cohesion. In American society, the "anything goes" mentality is experienced as morally bankrupt by those who see the old value system, in which "right and wrong" and "male and female" were clear categories, slipping away. They lash out in response.

I see this being played out today in American culture, which is fiercely divided between those who insist that everyone should be allowed to "do their own thing" as free individuals and those who desperately want to hold on to their old cast-iron verities. The animosity between these two opposing worldviews has coalesced in recent years around the phenomenon known as "woke-ism," and perhaps nowhere more so than in relation to gender.

We first need to rescue the term "woke" from its current aberration. The term "began appearing in the 1940s and was first used by African Americans to literally mean becoming woken up or sensitized to issues of justice . . . The word is rooted in African American Vernacular English (AAVE), and was used in African American street and youth culture for a long time."[15]

I would describe *woke* as an African American form of *conscientization*—critical consciousness of the sources of racist oppression and empowerment to resist such oppression. The term gained broader popularity with a line from a famous play about Marcus Garvey[16] by Barry Beckham which premiered in 1971, *Garvey Lives!*: "I been sleeping all my life. And now that Mr Garvey done woke me up, I'm gon' stay woke. And I'm gon' help him wake up other black folk."[17]

Unfortunately, in recent years the term "woke" was captured by white liberals and came to mean "political correctness" as they see it. It evolved into an all-encompassing term employed to describe liberal political positions on issues like racism, climate change, and, in particular, the gender rights of LGBTQ+ people. The white liberal embrace of woke-ism was accompanied by a sense of fragility, in which members of certain non-normative groups became emotionally "triggered" by the opinions of detractors or their use of certain language. Schools and universities had to create "safe spaces" to protect such aggrieved individuals and notify students at the beginning of classes that there may be triggering language in the lesson, in which case the affected students can leave class and receive counseling.

As a part of the rise of woke-ism, there is now a new insistence that people use the preferred pronouns asserted by the LGBTQ+ community, rather than the traditional "he/him" and "she/her."[18] Failure to address someone with the appropriate pronouns is known as "misgendering," a sign that the offender is definitely un-woke. All of this has come to be seen by the un-woke as a sign that the woke wrongly believe they are entitled to special deference because of their "difference."

For the un-woke, woke-ism has thus become a derisive term used to describe those who have weaponized their particular identities, especially

---

15. Ng, "History of the Word 'Woke.'"

16. Marcus Garvey was a Jamaican political activist who founded the Universal Negro Improvement Association (UNIA) in Jamaica in 1914, which sought to further black nationalism through the celebration of African history and culture. His influence spread far beyond Jamaica, including among African Americans in the United States.

17. Ng, "History of the Word 'Woke.'" See also Beckham, *Garvey Lives!*

18. Examples of recently preferred gender pronouns include *they-them-theirs, ze/hir/hir, per/per/pers*, and *it/it/its*.

in the LGBTQ+ community, to claim entitlement for their hyper-sensitivity. The English actor, screenwriter, and producer John Cleese once tweeted, "A lot of woke behaviours seem to me [to be] posturing, striking attitudes that allow them to experience the lovely, warm glow of moral superiority..."

The misappropriation and weaponization of the term *woke* has been a nail in the coffin of genuine interrelatedness between those in opposing ideological camps in the United States. Especially in relation to gender identity, it has created an intractable divide between those who claim their right to their own niche along the gender continuum and those who long for the good old days, when men were men and women were women, and families consisted of mother, father, and their biological children. These traditionalists also hurl the label of woke-ism against those attempting to combat the climate crisis (a familiar epithet being, "the woke are going to force us to eat bugs!") and against the "social justice warriors" (a very pejorative term) who joined in Black Lives Matter protests.

Woke-ism is detrimental to the cause of bringing everyone together as divinely imbued humans. It has not helped the cause of those gender-diverse people who actually have to contend with serious discrimination at times, even violence or threats of violence. When one's own sense of vulnerability (because one lives on the periphery of normative life) becomes all-consuming, this can lead to the inverse of vulnerability—an elevation of one's special identity to a position of righteous superiority over one's detractors, leading to the normalization of a sense of victimhood.

I see this inversion in "woke" politics, in which appointments or elections to positions of power are lauded *because* of one's gender or other "special identity"—as though one is innately superior *because* one is black, brown, female, gay, or transgendered. That is absurd. I can easily name names of those in positions of power who, as people of color, or female, or gender-diverse, do terrible things. They may be warmongers; they may be corrupt; they may be empire-apologists. No one is ethically superior *because of* their group identity, whatever it may be.

This is the irrational end game of individualism gone mad. It is *me-ism*. It is a false elevation of one's in-group above others. Woke-ism is a reflection of the extremes to which individualism as an ideology can go to undermine the divine intention for interrelationality, in which all of God's creatures are lovingly interconnected and mutually respected. The divisive extremes of woke-ism are not what it means to be interrelated beings who practice a *for-life* ethic. May we be saved from this twisted subversion of *woke*.

THE END OF LIFE

We move, finally, to the end of life, the bookend to our opening discussion in this chapter of the beginning of life. This is an exploration of the ethical implications of our relationship with death. I will focus only at the end of this section on "natural" death from disease or old age. I want to reflect first on how we appear to view death in mainstream American culture, for this reveals much about how we value life. I will mention several facets of our societal relationship with death.

In a *for-life* ethic, there is no justification for causing death to occur unnaturally, through acts of violence. This taboo is enshrined in the biblical commandment "thou shalt not kill"[19] (Exod 20:13, Deut 5:17) and in Jesus' commandments to love our enemies and to treat others as we would like to be treated. Unfortunately, as we will see in chapter 12, the Old Testament is replete with killing, especially the mass killings entailed in the Israelites' conquest of the promised land. Biblical killing, in fact, harks all the way back to the beginning of Scripture, when Cain, a son of Adam and Eve, the original humans in the Gen 2 creation story, murdered his brother Abel (Gen 3:4–9).

Jesus' ethic, in contrast, is one of compassionate and abundant life for all and does not therefore sanction the arbitrary ending of life for some. But if a *for-life* ethic really does mean that we should not kill others, this challenges the very foundations of the American way of life and the way of life of many other societies as well—although America is a particularly death-dealing society. In the discussion of the American Empire in chapter 10, we will be reminded of the violent origins and underbelly of the American nation, from its violence against Native Americans to its wars against the British, its civil war, its Spanish-American war, wars with Mexico, two world wars, and wars in Korea, Vietnam, Iraq, Afghanistan, and many other countries, including its present participation in the wars in Ukraine and Palestine. America has been at war somewhere throughout most of its history, and many Americans seem to idolize those who kill in our name, our soldiers and police.

This can only mean that, as a society, Americans actually believe that killing is justified and can be condoned and even celebrated, despite our attestations in our churches that "thou shalt not kill." Many of our best-selling movies are about war or gratuitous violence. The online and video games to which many of our youth (and some adults) are addicted glorify the most

---

19. I generally use the NRSV for scriptural citations, but somehow its "You shall not murder" does not have the same ring to it as the much more familiar King James Version's "Thou shalt not kill."

vile forms of killing. By the time American children reach the age of 18, they have witnessed over 16,000 murders and 200,000 acts of violence on television or the internet.[20]

America has a very high rate of deaths from gun violence compared to other countries. In 2021, this was more than seven times as high as the rate in Canada and 340 times higher than in the United Kingdom.[21] The US also has by far the highest rate of mass shootings; no other country comes close. In 2022, the US had 647 mass shooting incidents; the country which came second was Russia, with 21 mass shootings, while countries such as China, the United Kingdom, Australia, and the Netherlands had only one such incident.[22] The vast majority of countries had no mass shootings.

Yet despite this alarming record, it has been impossible for the United States to enact any meaningful gun control legislation, even though countries with stricter gun regulations statistically have fewer deaths from gun violence. America is awash with guns. Forty-five percent of Americans live in a household with guns, many with multiple guns. Forty percent of white Americans own a gun, compared with 24 percent of blacks, 20 percent of Hispanics, and 10 percent of Asian Americans.[23]

The National Rifle Association (NRA) is one of the most powerful political lobbies in the United States, and it has successfully prevented the passage of any efficacious gun control laws by donating millions of dollars to politicians. Those who resist any gun control legislation, even laws to outlaw the private ownership of automatic assault weapons, argue that it is their "Second Amendment constitutional right" to own guns, and they fear that gun control laws will mean the confiscation of their guns. The Second Amendment of the US Constitution actually says this: "A well-regulated Militia being necessary to the security of a free State, the right of the people to keep and bear Arms shall not be infringed."[24]

Many constitutional experts point out that this amendment was intended to provide for situations in which the government might be unable to maintain law and order, presumably in a time of civil war, invasion, or armed insurrection. At such times, armed militias (provided they are "well regulated") could be formed to protect communities. However, for gun enthusiasts, this amendment is personally sacred; it is like an Eleventh Commandment that almost obligates them to own guns, and the more the better.

20. Muscan, "Media Violence: Advice for Parents," 585.
21. Aizenman, "How the US Gun Violence Death Rate Compares."
22. "Mass Shootings by Country."
23. Schaeffer, "Key Facts About Americans and Guns."
24. Second Amendment, *Constitution of the United States.*

They often say they need guns to protect their families, an argument that has led to various states enacting "Stand Your Ground" laws which entitle individuals to legally shoot and kill intruders, or anyone who approaches their property and makes them feel threatened.

America's epidemic of deaths from gun violence tells us that life is actually fairly cheap for many Americans. The life of an intruder, gang member, enemy, or random stranger whom we want to get rid of is worth very little, or nothing. The lives of those we kill in our many wars mean nothing. This means that many American Christians do not really believe the sacred commandment "thou shalt not kill," even though they recite this commandment and some lobby to have sculptures of the Ten Commandments placed in the rotundas of state capitol buildings. The love of guns is a *for-death* ideology, not a *for-life* ethic. Guns are instruments of death, nothing else, and therefore, from a *for-life* perspective, there should be no guns. Let police use non-lethal tasers to stop violent offenders in their tracks, rather than shooting them with guns meant to kill.

I remember when I was studying ethics with the renowned Christian ethicist Stanley Hauerwas, and a student asked him one day in class, "Why are you a pacifist?" He answered immediately, "to stop myself from being violent." His Christian *for-life* ethic was needed as a form of restraint, to counter his (and our) natural human instinct to do violence. Recall again that "human nature" is about self-preservation and self-promotion. There is nothing inherently ethical about this. If we give ourselves permission to take a life, we do not value that life.

The argument I often hear to justify taking another's life goes like this: "But what if someone broke into your house and pointed a gun at you or your family? Shouldn't you kill him first?" I usually respond by telling the following true story: In the village where I lived in Jamaica, violence was rife. It was during a period of virtual civil war in the early 1980s, and there were daily gun battles and an epidemic of violent home invasions, as poverty was endemic and the country was inundated with weapons. For months, I heard gunshots every night.

One night, the home of the Church of God minister and his wife who lived down the road from me was broken into. The husband was away, and the wife was awakened with a gun pressing into her temple. The gunman said some version of "your money or your life." But the wife had something else in mind. She sat up in bed, looked the gunman in the eye, and said in a clear, ringing voice, "In the name of Jesus, I cast out your demons! You do not want to kill me. God loves you and will forgive you. You can have our money, but there will be no killing in this house!" And then she began to pray loudly. She told me that the gunman began to weep and fled from the house, without even taking the money she offered.

It is certainly the case that not every such scenario would turn out as this one did. But I have never forgotten that this woman, in the midst of the most dire threat to her life, relied on the *for-life* God whom she worshiped. She addressed the gunman as a fellow human being—"you do not really want to kill me." She appealed to his humanity. If confronted with a similar situation, I might well have instead fainted in terror, but I hope that I could be as brave as this faithful woman, who lived out her faith when it mattered most.

There are other ethical aspects related to the end of life, and these have to do with the extent to which we are legally entitled to determine when life ends for an individual. I am thinking first of legal executions by means of the death penalty. In the United States, some states permit the death penalty while others do not. When a jury decides that the death penalty should be applied because a crime is particularly egregious, its members are agreeing that this criminal's life has no value. It deserves to be snuffed out.

It is argued that because this criminal has taken the life of another, his or her own life should be taken as retaliation or compensation for the life lost. But this of course does not bring back the life of the person who has been murdered. Instead, two people are now dead. How does this square with a *for-life* ethic which values every life? It does not. Either every life has value, or we are taking life into our own hands and demeaning the value of human life based on our own desires or prejudices. Such action is a denial of "thou shalt not kill," "love your enemies," and "do unto others as you would have them do unto you."

Then there are the decisions we are legally allowed to make regarding when we want our own lives to end, or those of our loved ones. Suicide, of course, is self-murder. It is an epidemic in our crumbling empire, where there are so many economic, health, and other stresses. I feel only compassion for individuals whose lives are so loveless and hopeless that they no longer value them. Had they been surrounded by a *for-life* kindom community of love-givers, suicide would not have been the only path to take.

There are also thorny ethical questions surrounding euthanasia. I have empathy for those who are facing a slow, agonizing death and do not want to come to the end of their lives by hanging on in misery through the intrusive interventions of machines—misery for themselves and for their families. I also feel empathy for family members who find themselves in a situation in which their loved ones are hooked up to machines which are artificially keeping them alive, even though the medical advice is that they are not going to recover. In most American settings, families have the legal right in such situations to have these machines turned off, hastening their loved ones' death.

This is perhaps the most difficult ethical decision regarding the end of life. A divine *for-life* ethic calls us to fill our spirits with love and compassion as we face the end of life, whether our own or that of our loved ones. But knowing when and how to navigate through the process of dying while still honoring life is not always straightforward. There are cases in which someone who has been in a coma, sometimes for months or even years, presumably in a vegetative state, wakes up and returns to conscious life. There are cases where people who have a terminal disease, and have decided to forego further treatment and let themselves die, mysteriously begin to heal.

We should be cautious, therefore, about being overly proactive or presumptuous in hastening the end of life for ourselves or our loved ones. We do not want to prolong suffering, but we do not always know when it may be possible for life to continue *as life*. Most hospice providers have a compassionate way of helping patients and their loved ones to travel this journey toward the end of life. They understand that while the machines at the disposal of medical providers in "advanced" countries are able to prolong life almost indefinitely, machines are not life. They can support life (which is why they are literally called "life support"), but they are not the breath of God.

One of my favorite hymns has always been "Breathe on me, breath of God, fill me with life anew." I would only amend that slightly to "Breathe *in* me, breath of God." Life is the flow of divine breath through us from the beginning to the end of our earthly life. Our calling as *for-life* people is to honor that sacred rhythm of inbreath and outbreath in the most respectful of ways.

I have been around Fijian families at the time of death, and they believe that dying people will ideally complete everything that needs to be completed in their web of relatedness before they die. Often the dying tell stories or give wise instructions. They tie up any relational loose ends. Some of my Fijian friends have shared with me the stories their loved ones told as they were dying. No "life support" machines were involved, only human "life support" through the constant care and comfort of loved ones.

This is a good way to die. Fijians mourn for a hundred days following the death of a family member, wearing black every day and staying away from parties, sports, or frivolous activities. But on the hundredth day, the family hosts a magnificent feast for the whole village and for relatives and friends from far and wide. I have been to one of these feasts, and it was joyful and life-affirming. The black mourning clothes were cast aside. There was singing and laughter, along with more solemn expressions of respect and affection for the loved one who had died. The life of the deceased loved one had moved on into the next season of "eternal life." His or her life mattered in the way that *all lives matter* in the kindom of God.

The excursions throughout this chapter have been honest explorations of the mosaic that is *human life*, in all its complexity and variety. Our human natures, if unanchored in our divine *for-life* natures, can oh-so-easily veer off-course. Our human natures always want us to put ourselves and our in-group first. They lead us to make up stories to convince ourselves that we are better than "others" who are not like us, or who do not fit perfectly into the mold our societies have told us is normative. This "othering" creates divisions, estrangement, and even hatred and death. As *for-life* kindom persons and communities, we cannot indulge in such "othering."

7

"Blessed Are You Who Are Poor"

During my years living in rural Jamaica, I lived in a typical Jamaican village among the poor. This experience led me to ask many questions about poverty. Why is there so much poverty in the world? Is it simply the case that "the poor will always be with you," and therefore there is no way to eradicate poverty? How does that square with the core of the gospel, Jesus' proclamation that he had come to bring good news for the poor? If God is *for life* for all creatures and creation, does this not mean that poverty cannot be tolerated?

Before plunging into these questions, I will set the stage for our exploration by recalling an experience I had in Jamaica that had a profound effect on me. One day each week, I would "go visiting" with two or three elders from each of the four churches I pastored along with my husband. This meant meeting the elders at the church and then walking together up and down steep tracks to visit both church members and others who were in special need. The elders had their ears to the ground and knew a lot about people's circumstances.

On this particular day, two elders arrived at the church with a large basket of food and we set off. Because Jamaicans in rural villages live not so much in centralized areas (which typically consist only of a church or two, the village school, a few houses, and a couple of small shops) but spread out up and down the surrounding hills, pastoral visitation entailed a lot of walking in the tropical heat. This day, the elders informed me that one of our visits would be with an elderly man whose wife had recently died, and whose grown children had "gone foreign" (the Jamaican expression for migrating to the US, Canada, or the UK). The man was grieving alone and was too old to harvest crops to sell in the town markets, so we would bring him some non-perishable foodstuffs.

This elderly gentleman lived a long way from the village, up a very steep track. When we finally made it to his house, he came out and greeted us warmly. We expressed our condolences for the loss of his wife and offered him the basket of food. But he politely demurred. He thanked us sincerely but told us that there was a family further up the track which was in dire straits because the husband had left to try to find work in Kingston but never returned. The wife was left with several small children, and they were really hurting. He would take our basket of food to this family.

When I hear the phrase "Blessed are you who are poor" from the Beatitudes (Luke 6:20), I sometimes think of this old man. Here was someone who had almost nothing, and yet his heart was filled with generosity for others who had even less than him. I often felt, as a result of living in rural Jamaica, that the poor amongst whom I lived were the most generous people I had ever known. They were, in a sense, "blessed" because they were able to understand the experience of being in need. They had empathy with others because they knew the meaning of suffering.

But saying that the poor are "blessed" can be a slippery slope. Poverty is *not* a blessed state. There is nothing blessed about not having enough to live a life that ensures one's wellbeing. My daughter once lived for several months in the slums of Pune, India, volunteering at a creche for extremely poor babies and young children. What she witnessed there, not only in the creche but in her encounters with people on the streets, was shocking in the extreme. I remember her telling me, when she returned home, "there is absolutely nothing romantic about poverty; it is horrific through and through."

The elderly man in Jamaica who turned down a basket of food so that he could share it with his neighbors was, in my view, an exemplary human being. He lived an ethic of generosity and kindness. He was able to make ethical decisions even in the midst of his own need. I have witnessed this empathic capacity more so among the poor with whom I have lived than among the wealthy I have known. However, this does not mean that the poor are by default more morally righteous than others. The poor fall prey to the same kinds of temptations as other humans, for we all reside in our "human natures." Some who are poor become so desperate that they turn to violence and commit crimes. They may succumb to the stresses of poverty to the extent that they perpetrate domestic violence. The poor, like everyone else, are susceptible to all of the ethical challenges of being human.

Against this backdrop, we turn to the theological challenges entailed in our response as interrelational *for-life* people of faith to the reality of poverty. If all of God's creatures are equally valued, then it is an injustice when some of them do not have the means to live a daily life in which their material needs are met. As *for-life* kindom communities, we are called to respond to that injustice. This means that we must first have a clear understanding of what poverty consists of and what its causes are.

THE CAUSES OF POVERTY

More than 800 million people, 10 percent of the global population, live in what is defined as "extreme poverty," calculated as living on less than US$2 a day; many hundreds of millions more live "below the poverty line" and are "economically vulnerable" and "food insecure."[1] Among those who study the problem of global poverty, a number of key factors have been identified as leading contributors to poverty.

Inequality

Inequality in relation to poverty is about some people having more than they need and others not having enough. Poverty is often the result of larger social imbalances related to the marginalization of some groups in relation to other groups. (I will return to marginalization momentarily.) When social inequality is combined with enhanced risk factors, the resulting poverty is more extreme. Concern Worldwide gives an example of the poverty risks associated with gender inequality: "A widow raising a family of five will not have the same resources that were available to her husband."[2] Women who are already unequal in relation to men in their societies are more susceptible to risks to their security and access to resources. Other risk factors may include situations such as living in low-income neighborhoods, towns, or cities, or in countries with extreme wealth and income inequality.

Conflict

One of the leading causes of poverty worldwide is conflict. Large-scale, protracted periods of armed conflict create devastating poverty. One contemporary example is the poverty caused by the years of war in Syria, which "... ground an otherwise thriving economy to a halt. Millions have fled their

---

1. "Top Causes of Poverty Around the World." Information in this section is gleaned from this research on the causes of poverty conducted by Concern Worldwide.

2. "Top Causes of Poverty Around the World."

homes, often with nothing but the clothes on their backs. Prior to 2011, only 10% of Syrians lived below the poverty line. Now, more than 80% of Syrians live below the poverty line."[3] We see the same correlation between war and poverty today in Ukraine, Yemen, Palestine, Somalia, and other "hot spots" around the globe. War destroys not just militaries and soldiers but the livelihoods and wellbeing of those living in or displaced by the conflict zone.

Hunger and Malnutrition

Hunger, malnutrition, and resulting stunted growth are not only results of poverty; they are causes of poverty. Those who do not have sufficient food lack the strength to work productively. When people's immune systems are weakened by malnutrition, they are more susceptible to illnesses that prevent them from working, and unemployment leads to poverty. This is a vicious cycle, afflicting not just adults but children. Research shows that "For children born into low-income families, health is a key asset to their breaking the cycle of poverty. However, if a mother is malnourished during pregnancy, that is passed on to her children. Adults who were stunted as children earn, on average, 22% less than those who were not stunted."[4]

Inadequate Access to Healthcare

Inadequate healthcare is a significant contributing cause of poverty. When people have to travel long distances to see a physician or find medicines, this "drains vulnerable households of money . . . This can tip a family from poverty into extreme poverty."[5] Lack of access to maternal health care is particularly intertwined with poverty. In societies built on gender inequality, studies have shown that "New mothers and mothers-to-be are often barred from seeking [medical] care without their father's or husband's permission. Adolescent girls who are pregnant (especially out of wedlock) face even greater inequities and discrimination."[6] The lack of health care in such situations contributes to or exacerbates poverty.

---

3. "Top Causes of Poverty Around the World."
4. "Top Causes of Poverty Around the World."
5. "Top Causes of Poverty Around the World."
6. "Top Causes of Poverty Around the World."

Lack of Clean Water, Sanitation, and Hygiene

More than 2 billion people across the globe do not have access to clean water, which means that "people collectively spend 200 million hours every day walking long distances to fetch water,"[7] most of them women and children. That is time which cannot be spent gaining an education or earning a living. Contaminated water also causes waterborne diseases, further preventing people from working. Poor sanitation and hygiene compound this situation. One example is the millions of girls who cannot attend school during their menstrual cycles due to lack of access to hygiene supplies, lessening their chances of gaining an education that can lead to employment that could lift them out of poverty.

Climate Change

Climate change is a major contributing factor to rising global poverty. The World Bank estimates that the climate crisis will "push more than 100 million people into poverty over the next decade"[8] (by around 2030). This is related to growing disruptions in agriculture and fishing. In the many countries in the world that are still largely agrarian, most of their citizens survive on subsistence farming, with almost no reserves to fall back on if their crops fail. Because climate change is intensifying the damage to agriculture caused by droughts, wildfires, floods, and hurricanes, and because fish stocks are being decimated due to rising sea temperatures, millions of people have less and less access to food, pushing them further into poverty. As certain areas become unsustainable, people are forced to become climate refugees, who move from poverty into extreme poverty.

Lack of Education

I have already noted the correlation between the lack of education and poverty. Those with literacy and numeracy skills have a much better chance of finding paid employment that can prevent or alleviate poverty. Education has rightly been described as "the great equalizer," and "UNESCO estimates that 171 million people could be lifted out of extreme poverty if they left school with basic reading skills."[9] Failures to deliver education

---

7. "Top Causes of Poverty Around the World."
8. "Top Causes of Poverty Around the World."
9. "Top Causes of Poverty Around the World."

are often linked to other causal factors noted above, as situations such as armed conflict and disruptions caused by climate change negatively impact the ability of communities to keep their schools operating.

Poor Public Infrastructure

A lack of access to reliable public infrastructure—roads, bridges, transport, wells, sanitation, electricity, internet, and so on—isolates communities and inhibits their ability to engage in many activities that are necessary to live a productive life. Examples include not having public transport or navigable roads to take agricultural goods to market to sell, to get to schools or workplaces, or to receive medical attention. Having to travel long distances by foot, rather than by mechanized transport on reliable roads, takes up time that could be spent in industrious activities which would reduce the effects of poverty or lead families out of poverty. Lack of electricity or internet connectivity impedes the ability of youth to study and secure an education. Lack of water and sanitation infrastructure negatively impacts the basic health needed to move out of poverty.

Global Health Crises

The global COVID-19 pandemic is the most recent widespread public health crisis that has accelerated poverty. Other more regional epidemics, such as "Ebola in West Africa, cholera in Haiti, or malaria in Sierra Leone, have demonstrated how governments can grind to a halt while working to stop the spread of a disease."[10] The COVID pandemic created huge job losses, as millions of people were forced to stay home during lockdowns, not all of whom were able to work from home. Some of their jobs never returned. Education was disrupted. Farming and shipping were disrupted. Given the global mobility which characterizes contemporary life, epidemics and pandemics are likely to increase, and governments need to do much better planning and responding if the poverty induced by such events is to be mitigated.

POVERTY AND MARGINALIZATION

Jesus' announcement of the blueprint for his ministry in Luke 4:18, which thus becomes the blueprint for our own life of faith as *for-life* kindom

10. "Top Causes of Poverty Around the World."

communities, is a clarion call to eradicate all forms of injustice, including poverty. As those who emulate Jesus' ministry, we are mandated to bring *good news to the poor*, as well as release for captives, liberation of the oppressed, and "sight" (clarity, wisdom) for the "blind" (unaware, misguided).

Some people are thrust into poverty accidentally—for example, when a family's house and all their belongings are destroyed by fire, or when an earthquake, flood, or landslide destroys everything one owns. However, most of the interconnected causes of poverty highlighted above can be linked to social injustice. They are part of a web of injustices that rely on *marginalization*—the pushing of some to the periphery of existence, outside the reach of abundant life. Poverty associated with injustice results from the marginalization or "sidelining" of the most vulnerable by those at the center. Marginalization is the antithesis of a *for-life* ethic that welcomes everyone as equals around the table of fellowship and solidarity in the kindom. This is a round table, where everyone has equal value, not a sharp-edged table where some seats may be more privileged than others.

The theologian who has best articulated an ecclesiology centered in the metaphor of the "round table" is Letty Russell,[11] who saw round table imagery as a way of breaking down barriers between the center and the margins. What she calls the *round table principle* "... looks for ways that God reaches out to include all those whom society and the church have declared outsiders, and invites them to gather around God's table of hospitality."[12] At this round table, center and margins no longer exist. The "Church in the Round" is a "community of faith and struggle working to anticipate God's New Creation by becoming partners with those who have been at the margins of church and society, around a table of welcome."[13]

Further reflection on marginalization reveals how it creates the conditions that lead to poverty. The causes set forth in the previous section are objectively observable sociological realities, but we need to probe more deeply to explore what underlies and leads to the social inequities that make poverty possible. In her examination of the relationship between poverty and marginalization, Eunice Atwood writes that "To be marginalized . . . is to be excluded, distanced, and disconnected from the life of a community."[14]

We see this marginalization even in the biblical story. The Old Testament prophets recognized that the wealthy often became wealthy by taking advantage of others, pushing them to the margins of existence. This mindset

---

11. Russell, *Church in the Round*.
12. Russell, *Church in the Round*, 25.
13. Russell, *Church in the Round*, 12.
14. Atwood, "How Does Theology Call Us to Challenge Poverty?"

of exclusion—the antithesis of the inclusion God desires—lies behind acts of marginalization that leave the excluded struggling to survive in precarious circumstances.

The sin that lies at the heart of marginalization is captured in Upolu Vaai's distinction, noted in chapter 1, between a "we have" mindset and a "we are" mindset.[15] Those who believe that they are entitled to "have more" can only increase what they have by subtracting from others. Letty Russell contrasts what she calls the "bad math of subtraction" with the "gospel math of multiplication," which expands inclusion around the welcome table rather than subtracting some from participation in kindom life by removing them to the margins.[16]

In a subtraction mindset, the elites can only have more if everyone else has less. If an individual wants to become a business tycoon, he has to maximize his own profits by paying his workers low wages. If everyone in the business were to share the profits equally, the owner would have less than what he previously had acquired to maximize his wealth, but his workers' wellbeing would be multiplied—they would no longer be poor.

Atwood rightly observes that most societies indoctrinate their citizens to look to and listen to those who have wealth and power—the elites in the center who make our societies' rules and determine how distanced the marginalized will be forced to be from the center. In contrast, Jesus focused his gaze not on the powerful and wealthy but on those who were marginalized. Since our gaze must follow Jesus' gaze, Atwood concludes that "to abandon people experiencing poverty is to abandon the gospel."[17]

When we reflect on the experience of marginalization, we get to the crux of the injustice of poverty. Marginalization leads to isolation, separating the poor from God's desired kindom community, where everyone faces one another as equals around a round table. In *For the Least of These: A Biblical Answer to Poverty*, Peter Greer describes asking a group of poor people he encountered in Rwanda how they experienced poverty. Interestingly, they did not respond by talking about their lack of food, housing, or income. Instead, their responses can be summed up in the response of one woman who said, "Poverty is an empty heart."[18] Others spoke of their isolation from participation in community life, of not knowing what their

---

15. Vaai, "We Are, Therefore We Live."
16. Russell, *Future of Partnership*, especially chapter 1, "God's Arithmetic," 25–43.
17. Atwood, "How Does Theology Call Us to Challenge Poverty?"
18. Greer, "Stop Helping Us," 222.

real abilities and strengths were, of the isolation and hopelessness they experienced not knowing how to lift themselves out of poverty.[19]

This is an extremely telling finding. Pushing some to the margins so that others can be "we have" people is sinful because it robs the marginalized not only of the material necessities of life but of their full humanity. It robs them of their "we are" divine gift of *for-life* human existence. Because we are interrelated with all others, no one should be allowed to subsist on the margins of a life of wholeness. The wealthy should not be allowed to "have more" when the cost is an "empty heart" for those who have less.

I almost added a subtitle to this chapter—"Overeating in Eden." My reflections on poverty took me back to the story of Adam and Eve in the Garden of Eden which we explored in chapter 1. As I noted then, I came to see this story as, in part, a morality tale about the need for restraint. Adam and Eve wanted to be "we have" people rather than "we are" people. Since the fruit of the forbidden tree was within their reach, they wanted to eat it. This is what happens to greedy "we have" people. They always want more. They never feel they have enough, and so they have to bring about the poverty of others in order to achieve and safeguard their own wealth. Theirs is a problem of over-consuming, overeating. Their overeating not only denies the necessities of life to the poor, it makes themselves, the overeaters, sick in the long run. Not knowing when enough is enough can be fatal.

JESUS AND THE POOR

Before we delve into Jesus' understanding of poverty found in his Beatitudes affirmation, "Blessed are you who are poor" (Luke 6:20), we need to clear up something Jesus said about the poor which has often been misinterpreted to suggest that poverty is simply an inevitable aspect of life, which can perhaps be alleviated but never eradicated. This is, of course, Jesus' statement in Matt 26:11, "You always have the poor with you, but you will not always have me." This was in response to the disciples' chiding Jesus for allowing a woman to pour expensive ointment on his head, when the money used to buy this luxury item could have been given to the poor (Matt 26:6–13).

The first point to be made is that Jesus, in his statement in verse 11, was acknowledging that he and his disciples and friends were in the midst of an extraordinary circumstance, in which the woman's lavish act of pouring expensive ointment on his head flowed from her love for who he was. Because of her motivation and sincerity, her behavior should therefore be

---

19. Greer, "Stop Helping Us," 222ff.

allowed to stand. Her gesture was a sign that this woman knew that Jesus' days were numbered.

Indeed, when Jesus reminded the disciples in verse 11 that they would not always have him with them, he followed up in verse 12 with the statement "By pouring this ointment on my body, she has prepared me for burial." He was alerting his disciples that he was going to be arrested and sent to his death imminently, something that was in fact set in motion with Judas Iscariot's betrayal the very next day. The woman's extravagant gesture was a visible sign of her loving farewell for Jesus and a metaphor for the unreserved generosity we are all called to practice in our love for others.

Second, in telling his disciples that the poor would always be with them, Jesus was referencing a passage of Scripture which his disciples would likely have known well—God's instruction in Deut 15:11, "Since there will never cease to be some in need on the earth, I therefore command you, 'Open your hand to the poor and needy neighbor in your land.'" It was because poverty was a pervasive presence in ancient Israel that the Israelites were instructed to be "open-handed"—to show extraordinary generosity to the poor.

Jesus was speaking in this passage, therefore, in response to an existential set of circumstances, acknowledging that poverty was a "taken for granted" social reality which should be addressed, but also that allowances should be made for those who give lavishly out of the love in their hearts. This passage must be seen in light of the larger truth that everything about Jesus' ministry was a call to live in ways that would negate the social sins that cause poverty.

Jesus spoke many times about poverty, and several of his parables and teachings address our responsibility to come to the aid of those who are poor (e.g., Matt 25:40, Matt 11:4-6, Luke 8:43-47, Luke 14:12-14, Matt 19:21, Mark 10:21-22, Mark 12:41-44, Luke 11:39-42, Luke 12:16-21). I want to focus on perhaps the best-known declaration of Jesus about the poor, in the Beatitudes (his Sermon on the Mount), comparing the texts in Matthew and Luke.

In Matt 5:3, Jesus said, "Blessed are the poor in spirit, for theirs is the kingdom of heaven." This has often been the preferred Beatitudes text, rather than the passage in Luke 6:20, for the Matthew text appears to let us off the hook in terms of dealing with the actual poor. The "poor in spirit" are typically understood to refer to those who acknowledge their *spiritual* poverty. They are blessed to the extent that they come before God in humility, admitting that their spiritual life is in need of divine help. (This interpretation is, of course, only a conjecture, as we have no way of knowing the original intention of the phrase "poor in spirit," despite many interpretive efforts by New Testament scholars.)

Luke 6:20 differs substantially from the Matthew text, even though both are recitations of Jesus' Beatitudes, with essentially the same litany of blessings. Luke 6:20 says, "Blessed are you who are poor, for yours is the kingdom of God." The next two verses continue in the same vein—"Blessed are you who are hungry now, for you will be filled" and "Blessed are you who weep now, for you will laugh." The first obvious difference in the Matthew and Luke texts is that, in Matthew, Jesus is speaking *about* the poor, whereas, in Luke, Jesus is speaking *to* the poor. Some translations say, "Blessed are you who are poor," and others say simply, "Blessed are you poor."

Jesus draws a sharp contrast between the poor who are blessed and the rich who are condemned. In verses 24 and 25, he flips the script from blessings to curses and suddenly says, "Woe to you who are rich, for you have received your consolation. Woe to you who are full now, for you will be hungry. Woe to you who are laughing now, for you will mourn and weep." The central theological issue raised in the affirmation "Blessed are you poor" (and its inverse, "Woe to you rich") concerns what it means for the poor to be blessed and the rich to be cursed.

There are innumerable scholarly exegetical works on the Beatitudes, both in Matthew and Luke. I approach "Blessed are you poor" not as a biblical scholar but as someone vitally concerned about poverty and the poor as brothers and sisters in the kindom, which is always *for life*. I place greater emphasis on the Luke "Blessed are you poor" text precisely because here Jesus is directly engaged with the poor, relationally present with the poor. Especially in the context of the following verses, which bless those who are hungry and those who weep, I believe that "blessed are you poor" is, in the first instance, an expression of compassionate care and comfort. They may be poor, hungry, and in despair in the present moment, but that is not the end of their story. Because they are a part of the kindom of God, a life of justice and wholeness is coming.

This is a concrete hope, not simply hope that at the end of time the poor will find relief from their poverty in heaven. Their blessing is an affirmation that they are no longer to live on the margins but seated around a round table where everyone's resources are shared equitably. This kindom table is not for "rich" and "poor," because sharing equitably will mean that the rich give up their excesses so that all may have enough. Distinctions between rich and poor will then vanish.

Upolu Vaai's comments about "enoughness" are relevant here. We recall that "enoughness" means that wealth is shared in such a way that everyone has "enough," which means that the "more is better" value system of the greedy is overturned.[20] The truth is that there is "enough" to go around on our planet. The only reason that billions of people do not have enough is because the wealthy have too much. The poor will experience the blessing Jesus promises when the rich let go of their excess wealth and share it with the poor. Then there will be no more poverty. Everyone will have "enough" to live an abundant life filled not just with food, clean water, and housing, but with relational richness and creativity, an abundant life of music, dancing, arts, and crafts. Those who were weeping will find joy in their fellowship around the round table.

Jesus' blessing, then, is both a promise and a call to action. The poor, the hungry, those who weep, can only experience the blessing of wholeness of life when the injustice of their marginalization has been addressed. Who brings to life the blessing of the poor? *We do.* It is a charge Jesus issues to us as interrelated beings who practice a *for-life* ethic. The poor will only be blessed when *we* bless them with both physical and spiritual sustenance. This is a blessing that will fill "the empty heart" of poverty.

I return, finally, to the scene at the opening of this chapter, the elderly man in the Jamaican hills who was poor but passed on the gift of food to those whose needs were greater than his. I said when I shared this story that I believed this man was blessed. He was blessed not because of his poverty but because he knew how to bless others. He knew how to practice wholehearted hospitality and generosity. That is the joy we discover when we live as interrelated human beings who are always *for life*—especially life for those who need to be moved from the margins of isolation and rejection to the communion of the round table in the kindom.

---

20. Vaai, "We Are, Therefore We Live."

8

This Land Is Our Land

THE EVOLUTION OF BORDERS

I SOMETIMES PONDER HOW planet Earth ended up carved into hundreds of nations, each with its own borders and border crossings, with checkpoints and officers who check passports and visas, and who decide who is allowed to cross over these borders. How did we end up with the concept of *borders*—and its underlying assumption, *foreigners*? I think back to our origins as a human species, when our ancient ancestors roamed the land, whether in search of food, to avoid fighting or predatory animals, to escape droughts or floods, or simply because they were adventurous and wanted to explore new territory. In those early days, borders were non-existent.

For millennia, humans remained nomadic hunters and gatherers. They made seasonal migrations just as wildlife did, in search of water and food. Gradually they began to organize themselves into tribes or clans, whose members had kinship ties. Eventually, they became more settled and less nomadic. They began to grow crops, and the development of agriculture pushed them past their seasonal wanderings into more established settlements. As populations grew, homogenous communities began to protect the land on which they had settled from incursive animals or invading humans. They came to think of this land as "their" land, and they began demarcating their territory as a way of claiming it for their own use. Perhaps they began erecting stone walls or fences made from sticks and twigs. The first crude borders were coming into being.

Borders have always been at times flexible and at times arbitrary. The rise of large powerful nations with expansionist visions led to many changes in borders, as these nations became empires and conquered other peoples. The borders of the smaller, less powerful peoples whom they conquered were incorporated into the ever-expanding borders of empires. This pattern has been repeated many times in human history—from the Assyrian, Persian, or Babylonian Empires to the Roman Empire, and later the Holy Roman Empire, the Viking Empire, the Mongol Empire, the Ottoman Empire, eventually the British Empire, other powerful colonizing European states, and finally the American Empire. I am omitting other empires, but the point is this: conquest creates its own borders.

This has led to endless conflicts throughout human history, made worse because imperial powers have carved up the territories they conquered and arbitrarily created new nation-states or colonies. This has been perhaps most glaringly obvious on the continent of Africa, where boundaries were created indiscriminately by colonizing powers in ways that lumped together diverse peoples into "nations" in which they did not fit into a cohesive whole. When I lived in South Africa, I discovered that the country had twelve official languages, reflecting the diverse ethnic "nations" that had been subsumed within the borders of the nation-state called South Africa. Such arbitrary colonial demarcations of borders have led to a painful history of wars and squabbles over territory.

Many such border conflicts persist today—for example, between India and China, between Ireland and Northern Ireland, between North Korea and South Korea, between Armenia and Azerbaijan, between Sudan and South Sudan—the list is long. As I write this, Venezuela and Guyana are squabbling over a swath of territory which both nations claim as their own. Since it contains newly discovered oil reserves, the US is of course intervening on the side of Guyana, a former British colony that will give American oil companies concessions to extract the oil discovered in this territory. Ukrainians and Russians are fighting over borders, a clash dissected in chapter 11. The worst border disaster today is of course the long-standing one between Israelis and Palestinians in the monstrously carved-up ancient land of Palestine (see chapter 12).

I am not certain how human communities should most optimally organize themselves physically as people-groups, in ways that provide a sense of security and cohesion yet do not shut out those who are not native to their border designations. What I do know is that borders have been contentious constructions throughout history. Border lines all too often become pawns in the chess games which nations and empires play in their quests for dominance. At times they shift because of wars, internal and external, when a particular group gains the upper hand in campaigns for dominance.

The nations of Europe, for example, have been carved up and reshaped many times, creating permeable borders that have shifted back and forth. In the interviews I have listened to with European Jewish Holocaust survivors, they often said, in answer to questions about where they were born and raised, that their homes were once a part of one country but then became a part of another one—from Poland to Russia or Germany, or Lithuania or Slovakia, and so on. What is now a sizeable chunk of western Ukraine was, before World War II, part of Poland, Romania, and Hungary. With the demise of the Soviet Union, the countries of East Germany and West Germany became simply Germany. There was, at that time, a literal tearing down of the Berlin Wall border with pick axes and sledgehammers.

In what is now the United States, the flexible but discernible borders of the indigenous nations of this vast land were trampled on and destroyed by the incoming European settlers, and these indigenous peoples were herded into arbitrarily demarcated "reservations" designed to isolate them ("out of sight, out of mind"). Moreover, if it were not for the outcomes of wars and political deals, much of what is today the southwestern United States would have remained a part of Mexico. Louisiana would have been a territory of France. If not for American expansionism in the Pacific, Hawaii would not be a US state but its own Polynesian nation. American Samoa would not be a US territory but reunited with the rest of Samoa.

Because our human natures are geared toward self-preservation, we have become, it seems to me, ever more inflexible and contentious about borders. We have used them to close ourselves off from "others" we dislike or fear, or we have smashed through them as conquerors and colonizers in order to take over others' lands and make them our own. Borders have become over time all about *"what is mine"* (my nation, my people, my empire). Borders define the lands and waters we have told ourselves we own, and that we can therefore do with as we will.

In the American context, the "what is mine" mindset can be detected in the classic American folk song "This Land is Your Land," by the iconic folksinger-songwriter Woodie Guthrie.[1] Americans came to love this song in the same way that they love "America the Beautiful"—as an anthem to the land we claim as ours. We learn in Guthrie's song that America was created for Americans; we own it. It exists to promote *our* interests.

Most of the verses of this song extol the beauties of this land between our American borders, but a verse near the end of the song indicates that in this land we love, there are also barriers, meant to keep some people out.

---

1. Guthrie, "This Land is Your Land." As this song was copyrighted by Ludlow Music Co. in New York in 1940, I am not quoting any of its lyrics, other than the song title, which does not require permission.

Woodie Guthrie grasped something that was quite revelatory when he added this verse: it turns out that some are not welcome in our land. This applies not only to our physical borders but to the invisible borders we have erected that keep poor people, people of color, and various unwelcome interlopers outside the comforts of the homeland we "insiders" think is ours.

A CASE IN POINT: THE US SOUTHERN BORDER

America has had a vexing problem at its southern border with Mexico for a long time. There is a crisis at this border today because thousands of people arrive there every day from Mexico and the rest of Central America, and to a much lesser extent from South America. The resources of border states attempting to cope with this influx have been stretched to the limit, and the national government has been ill-prepared and incompetent in handling the crisis. This situation is one of the central issues dominating national politics. The fact that so many brown-skinned people are coming over our southern border infuriates a good number of Americans.

In the minds of these Americans, these so-called "illegals" crossing the southern border are extremely undesirable. This trope was repeated by Donald Trump from the very beginning of his campaign for the US presidency, when he rode down the escalator at Trump Tower in New York City to announce his candidacy on June 15, 2015, and said, referring to the refugees and immigrants coming into the US through Mexico, "They are not our friends, believe me. They're bringing drugs. They're bringing crime. They're rapists."[2]

This stereotypical depiction of the Mexicans and other Central Americans coming across the border is a portrayal that bears almost no resemblance to the truth. Even the US government body responsible for protecting the southern border, Customs and Border Protection (CBP), admits that criminality among undocumented immigrants and asylum seekers (refugees) is strikingly low.[3] In 2021, only 1.9 percent of illegal immigrants crossing the border had any criminal record, and although "the

---

2. Reilly, "Times Donald Trump Insulted Mexico."

3. It is acknowledged that there are distressing cases of sexual assault against women waiting in Mexico to enter the US. Some of these assaults are by Mexicans who enter these holding camps and others are by migrants in the camps. It is difficult to find reliable statistics about this alarming situation in the temporary holding areas, which have been described by many as "hell-holes."

number of illegal immigrants encountered by CBP increased by 236 percent [in 2021], the number of criminals *fell* by over 27 percent."[4]

The reality versus the stereotype regarding undocumented individuals crossing over the southern border into the US is even more glaring once crime statistics are compared between these border-crossers once they are living in the US and native-born Americans. A study by the Texas Department of Public Safety, comparing the criminality of Hispanic immigrants residing in Texas to that of native-born US citizens between 2012 and 2018, found that "Undocumented immigrants have substantially lower crime rates than native-born citizens across a range of felony offenses. Relative to undocumented immigrants, US-born citizens are over 2 times more likely to be arrested for violent crimes, 2.5 times more likely to be arrested for drug crimes, and over 4 times more likely to be arrested for property crimes."[5]

Research has also demonstrated that "areas with more immigrants experience no more crime than places with fewer of them, and immigration surges do not lead to increases in illegal activity."[6] These studies have been described by Charis Kubrin, professor of criminology, law, and society at the University of California-Irvine, as "another nail in the coffin of what we have been told about the link between immigration and crime."[7]

One can draw several conclusions about why the border-crossers at the southern border are less likely to commit crimes in the United States. First, the vast majority did not start out as criminals in the first place. Second, once they are living in the United States, they are extremely vigilant about obeying the law because they do not want to do anything to jeopardize their legal process of securing refugee status or work visas; they do not want to call attention to themselves by getting arrested and deported to their home country. Third, they are attempting to earn an income in the US so that they can remit funds to their relatives in their home country, and do not want to risk incarceration that would impede their ability to help their families.

Although it is true that drug cartels are a serious problem in Mexico and Central America, and that they are heavily involved in the movement of illegal drugs into the United States through the southern border, this is a problem of organized crime, with willing participants on both sides of the border. If there were no customers in the United States, the drug cartels would cease to exist. The average Hispanic attempting to cross the border into the US is not involved in these cartels, most of whose drugs enter the

---

4. Nowrasteh, "Criminal Illegal Immigration Rates Fall."
5. Light, He, and Robey, "Comparing Crime Rates."
6. Moyer, "Undocumented Immigrants."
7. Moyer, "Undocumented Immigrants."

US by plane or concealed in vehicles, though some migrants are used as drug traffickers by the cartels. Nor are there any significant numbers of international "terrorists" coming into the US through the southern border, or border-crossers from designated American enemy nations (Chinese, Russians, Iranians, Middle Eastern Muslims), as claimed in propaganda about the border crisis.

Why are so many people from Mexico and Central America crossing the southern border? Their detractors argue that they are coming to the US because they want free handouts—they want to "live off our government." This demonstrates a startling ignorance of US law, because as long as they remain undocumented or their legal status is in process (which can take years), they are not eligible for benefits accruing to US citizens, such as food stamps, Medicaid, or unemployment benefits.

The vast majority of these immigrants make the treacherous journey to the US because, quite simply, they are desperate. The sources of this desperation are several, but, as one recent study succinctly puts it, "The root causes of migration [at the southern border] are the same, regardless of where the point of origin is: extreme poverty, food insecurity, violence due to a dominating drug trade, and the impacts of climate change on extreme weather, agriculture, and livelihoods."[8]

All of these reasons for migration are interconnected, and many of them have been furthered or exacerbated by the imperial foreign policies of the United States. The US has interfered in Central America for a very long time, being responsible for numerous coups, destabilization tactics, and coercive attempts to take control of the resources of these countries. American interventions have enabled US corporations to "set up shop" throughout the region, extracting natural resources and using neoliberal policies to maximize profits through the abuse of workers by way of low wages, unsafe working conditions, and environmental deregulation that has caused ecological devastation.

The United States, in short, has been and continues to be actively involved in overt and covert interventions, exploitation, and regime change operations in various Central American countries, including Nicaragua, Guatemala, Honduras, and El Salvador, in league with corrupt right-wing governments and their cronies in the drug cartels. Only in Nicaragua have the citizens and government been able to resist US interventionism and cling to their own sovereignty and vision for lifting their people out of poverty.

The criminal gangs operating in concert with right-wing governments in Honduras and El Salvador have extorted the poor and threatened their

---

8. Latifi, "Five Things to Know."

lives if they do not pay bribes to the cartels in order to operate their subsistence businesses (such as setting up a fruit stand by the roadside). The US has enabled the coups or fraudulent elections which have brought these governments to power, and has undermined all grassroots populist movements for reform.[9] Why does the US hate these movements? Because they demand their own sovereignty rather than American domination, as Nicaragua has managed to assert despite many acts of US intervention. Many innocent people have been killed by the criminal elements that control these countries, and it is their surviving family members, whose lives are still under threat, who escape to the southern US border to apply for asylum.

The Americans who despise those attempting to cross the southern border make no distinction between illegal immigrants, who attempt to cross into the US for economic reasons—fleeing poverty in the hope of helping their families to survive—and asylum seekers. The latter are in no sense illegal; they have the right, backed by international and US law, to seek asylum because of threats to their safety. For the thousands of people fleeing the violence that permeates Central American countries like El Salvador and Honduras, the threats to their safety are very real, and they have been made worse by US collusion with their corrupt governments to further American imperial aims.

To summarize, the vast majority of undocumented immigrants and asylum seekers at the southern border of the United States are people who, like those Americans who hate them, love their families and simply want to live in security and peace. Their circumstances are so untenable in their home countries that they feel they have no choice but to flee northward in the hope of finding sanctuary in the much wealthier country of the United States. If most of us were in their situation, struggling to survive amidst hunger, crime, poverty, violence, environmental degradation, and criminal threats, we too would do everything possible to flee. If we had to walk a thousand miles carrying our children on our backs to escape these conditions, we would. We would do so because we are *for life*.

---

9. Secretary of State Hillary Clinton vigorously supported the CIA-backed coup which removed the progressive elected president of Honduras, Manuel Zelaya, in 2009, ushering in an era of horrific repression by the incoming right-wing regime and its affiliated drug warlords, whose campaign of terror led to a dramatic increase in asylum seekers from Honduras at the southern border. The US has supported repressive governments in El Salvador since the 1960s, including both overt (military, financial) and covert (CIA) backing for the right-wing military and its death squads during the civil war from 1980 to 1992. Although El Salvador today has a popular elected president, Nayib Bukele, human rights abuses and military/gang-related violence continue. The young charismatic Bukele gleefully describes himself as "the world's coolest dictator."

WHO'S IN AND WHO'S OUT?

I have provided the background information above in order to offer a contextual backdrop to the current impasse in American politics and American life over the influx of border-crossers at our southern border. I will not delve into the various immigration policies which have been put forward over the past few decades. None of them have solved the problem or eased the situation at the border, regardless of which political party is in power. They have been piecemeal steps at best, often to appeal to certain voting blocs in US elections. A case in point is Trump's efforts to "build a big beautiful wall" at the US-Mexico border. Only a small portion of this wall was built during his tenure and, in any event, there is no wall which desperate people cannot find a way over or under. A border wall cannot solve the underlying problem.

At the heart of the problem—not just for Americans but for people of faith everywhere—is how we ought to feel, as ethical beings, about borders in the first place. Borders are set up to keep outsiders out and insiders in. Borders are about exclusion. It is understandable that nations need practical but humane ways to protect themselves from being overrun by incomers. If too many immigrants flock into a country, it may be overwhelmed and not have sufficient resources or space to care for everyone.

However, if these are incomers about whom a country is positively disposed, ways are always found to accommodate them. After World War II, millions of displaced people made their way across the length and breadth of Europe and to other countries around the world, where they were largely made to feel at home. When dissidents in Fidel Castro's Cuba migrated to the US in the famous Mariel Boatlift between April and October, 1980, 125,000 were warmly welcomed into Florida. They were our friends because they hated Castro and so did America—a perfect example of "my enemy's enemy is my friend."

Similarly, European nations willingly opened their borders to six million Ukrainians in the early days of the war with Russia in 2022. Americans also have no problem with border-crossers at their northern border with Canada, because whoever is crossing that border is almost certain to be white. They are easy to welcome. But the brown-skinned poor people crossing the southern border are not the kinds of people some Americans want to live alongside. They do not meet the criteria of "acceptable" citizens. The hatred and fear of southern border-crossers is, at heart, a manifestation of America's ingrained racism and ethno-nationalism.

A THEOLOGY OF BORDERS

The problem, in other words, is not really that most countries do not have the space or the means to welcome outsiders within their borders, within reason. The problem is a nation's attitude toward those who seek to enter. And this raises a theological problem which is related to a core concern of this work: *Whose lives are valuable?* Can we be *for life* for some but not for all? Or are we called as interrelational beings who practice a *for-life* ethic to welcome all strangers as a sign of our affirmation that God's love is for everyone?

Let us recall that what characterized Jesus more than anything else was that he reached out intentionally to those who were the unwelcome "others" in his society—the outcasts, those rejected by the majority, the unclean. Even before the life and witness of Jesus, there was a thread running through Scripture which was a call to welcome strangers. This will seem like a contradiction to the biblical revelations highlighted in chapter 12, where we find the Israelites smashing through borders left and right to conquer the people-groups inhabiting the land of Canaan, which God had given as a promised land to his chosen people. That was the flip side of border cruelty—instead of keeping people out, the Israelites forced their way in.

But that is only one part of the biblical story. There are counter-narratives to the colonizing practices of the chosen people of Israel. A persistent counter-thread which runs through Scripture is the injunction to *welcome the stranger*. Once the chosen people were settled in Canaan, they had to encounter outsiders because of their promised land's strategic position along important trade routes in the Ancient Near East. People traveled from near and far through the promised land, and the Israelites had to find a way to relate to them. There is considerable biblical evidence of attempts to find an ethical way to relate to the "strangers" or "aliens" who found their way into the promised land. Here are just a few examples:

Lev 19:33–34: "When an alien resides with you in your land, you shall not oppress the alien. The alien who resides with you shall be to you as the native-born among you; you shall love the alien as yourself, for you were aliens in the land of Egypt."

Lev 23:22: "When you reap the harvest of your land, you shall not reap to the very edges of your field or gather the gleanings of your harvest; you shall leave them for the poor and for the alien."

Ezek 47:22: "You shall allot it [your land] as an inheritance for yourselves and for the aliens who reside among you. . . They shall be to you as native-born of Israel; with you they shall be allotted an inheritance among the tribes of Israel."

Moving to the New Testament, we hear in Heb 13:1–2: "Do not neglect to show hospitality to strangers, for by doing that some have entertained angels without knowing it." And Jesus speaks in Matt 25:35, 38, 40, saying, "'I was a stranger and you welcomed me.' The righteous then asked, 'When was it that we saw you a stranger and welcomed you?' . . . [Jesus replied,] 'Truly I tell you, just as you did it to one of the least of these brothers and sisters of mine, you did it to me.'"

These ethical imperatives present a daunting challenge to people who believe their borders are hallowed and not to be violated in any way. We are not "naturally" (in our human natures) predisposed to want to welcome aliens. Are these aliens trustworthy? Are they entering our territory with malign intentions? Will they be a threat to our way of life? Our 'natural' instinct may be to talk back to God about these intruders: "Seriously, God, do we *really* have to welcome aliens?"

But, in fact, this is what a *for-life* ethic asks us to do. We are not asked to have no borders. Most people-groups wish to identify themselves as nations or territories, and to have oversight over the lands in which they live, although they should be accommodating and flexible about who can live within their borders. The most critical ethical issue is how we treat those who cross over our borders. Leviticus 19:33–34 instructs us to "do no wrong" to such aliens, treating them in the same way we would our native-born citizens. Leviticus 23:22 tells us we must share the necessities of life with aliens. Ezekiel 47:22–23 repeats the injunction to treat aliens as native-born citizens and goes a step further, stating that we must even share our inheritances with them. Hebrews 13:1–2 tells us that we must treat them with utmost hospitality because they may be angels! Jesus associates welcoming the stranger with offering them sustenance and spending time with them.

I personally know people who are staunchly opposed to what they call the "illegal aliens" crossing the southern border of the United States. They buy into all the tropes mentioned earlier about these "illegals" being criminals, rapists, and drug traffickers; often they describe them as dirty and coming to infect us with nasty diseases. Yet these acquaintances of mine also self-identify as devout Christians. They are in church every Sunday, and they read their Bibles faithfully. I wonder what happens when they read passages of Scripture like the ones I have mentioned above. The thought of treating southern border-crossers as native-born Americans, sharing resources and inheritances with them, and even viewing them as possible angels, is anathema to these immigrant-averse Americans.

This is not to suggest that these people are bad people. On the contrary, they are in other respects caring people who love their families and friends and are generous to others in times of need. But perhaps they are reading their Bibles through the lens or filter of American core values, as discussed in the opening section of chapter 6. Let us remind ourselves that core values run very deep in every culture. They define our beliefs, customs, practices, and social behaviors; they are in some ways more ingrained in us than our religious values. The individualist core value of personal rights and freedoms in American culture puts "me and mine" first—not just *myself* but *my* in-group. This worldview is very protective of insiders, who, in the American context, believe themselves to be God's present-day (white) chosen people.

Because this is the case, we need to take a step back and ask ourselves certain questions: *What if* we were to practice an interrelational *for-life* ethic in relation to our borders? *What if* we were to welcome the exhausted, hungry, often traumatized people at the US southern border, who have often been walking for months? *What if* we were to welcome these "aliens" as *family*—not only as fellow citizens but as brothers and sisters, our *kin* in the kindom? *What if* we treated them as we would like to be treated? *What if* we gave them food, drink, clothing, shelter, and genuine relationship, as Jesus asked us to do?

(I do need to pause here and acknowledge the growing resentment of many African American and poor communities in the American cities where the current surge of asylum seekers are being dumped and put up in hotels and other accommodations, at taxpayers' expense. There is resentment because our own poorest citizens, including our growing homeless population, are not taken care of in the same way. They are not given shelter, food, and medical care. This is a problem caused by systemic racism and social inequality, and this disparity urgently needs to be addressed. However, the answer is not to deny sustenance to asylum seekers but to make sure that all communities have what they need to live.)

It is true that there might not be adequate space in the US if the majority of the citizens of Mexico and Central America crossed our border, although we do have vast amounts of empty space. That would certainly strain our resources to the breaking point. But the vast majority of those populations do not wish to do that. They would rather live in their own homelands, which they love precisely because they are "home." If a way could be found for them to live safely in their home countries, free from violence, free from poverty and oppression, free from ecological collapse, most would rather do that. I have seen documentaries in which some of these immigrants and refugees speak longingly, often tearfully, of their home villages, their mountains and rivers, their banana plantations, their native parrots perched in their trees, the tamales and tortillas roasting in their outdoor ovens.

Part of the way we might love these "strangers," in addition to welcoming them at the border, would be to work to help bring about transformation in their home countries so that they are no longer mired in violence, poverty, and insecurity, thereby enabling their migrating citizens to return home. This would mean, in the first instance, insisting that the American government stop its arrogant and greedy policies of interventionism in the countries of Central America, policies which have worsened poverty and systemic injustice. Instead, our government and our citizens should be joining hands with those who struggle for justice in these countries, working toward the day when their citizens can live in peace and prosperity. In the meantime, we must welcome them within our own borders as family members in a shared kindom of God.

The discussion in this chapter has focused on the ethics of borders in the country I know best, the United States. But today, when there are so many national and regional conflicts, and when the climate crisis is creating growing numbers of climate refugees, every country in the world needs to engage in ethical reflection on how they understand borders and "strangers." Should their borders be only walls, metaphorically built higher and higher, ever more rigid and impenetrable, to keep out outsiders who are different from their insiders? Or should their borders be flexible and welcoming?

In other words, shouldn't all of us, as *for-life* interrelated beings, intentionally be building *gates* in our metaphorical border walls, openings that we leave ajar for those who come to us seeking refuge from danger and distress? I believe our *for-life* God asks us to construct such gates—points of opening—and to welcome those who need to enter, for we are all related. We are all kin in the kindom of God.

9

Lawn Transformations— Oddly Satisfying?

HOW MUCH IS TOO MUCH INTERVENTION?

Since I rely on independent sources of news and commentary online, all kinds of channels pop up on my computer screen, at times with strange thumbnails. One day my attention was drawn to a thumbnail entitled "Lawn Transformation: Oddly Satisfying." That piqued my curiosity, and I had to see what this was that was so oddly satisfying. It turns out that there is a whole community of lawn care professionals who devote one day each week to "transforming" overgrown and neglected lawns, at no cost to the homeowner or resident. In return, the transformations are filmed and shown on the lawn care providers' online channels. As I researched further, I found that many of these individuals provide this service as an act of faith, to be a blessing to those who, for whatever reasons, are unable to take care of their lawns.

And so, somewhat sheepishly, I opened one of these channels. The video had an almost dreamlike quality. Because a day's worth of work mowing, trimming, edging, and chopping has to be compressed into approximately a half-hour video, the recording is sped up, so that the mowers appear to fly through the tall grass. The trimming next to fence lines, houses, porches, and sidewalks zips along, magically creating clean edges and revealing long-buried pathways.

I was mesmerized as chaos was transformed into order. I was reminded of Isa 40:4, "The crooked shall be made straight, and the rough places plain."

Houses and outbuildings that were obscured behind years of overgrowth suddenly revealed themselves. Vines were peeled from the walls of houses, and hedges that hid windows were cut back and reshaped. Watching all this, I fell into a kind of reverie. The experience was, in a nutshell, oddly satisfying. It was "odd" because it was an unusual, speeded-up way of watching order emerge from disorder.

But upon further reflection, I experienced a sense of disquietude. Something was wrong with some of these beautiful displays. The effort to undo the excesses of Mother Nature entailed all sorts of intrusive actions. I began to wince as some trees were cut down entirely and most trees had some of their branches lopped off. Many bushes and plants were uprooted and chopped to pieces with the most amazing pieces of machinery. The "before" and "after" clips at the end of the videos contrasted the wildness of unrestrained nature with clean, orderly, minimalist expanses of closely cropped grass and carefully shaped plants.

Now the word "oddly" took on a new meaning. These vistas were not odd simply because it was unusual to see chaos replaced by order in fast motion but because there was something unsettling about the whole premise behind such activity. This is in no way to disparage the individuals whose profession is lawn care, or anyone reading this who takes pride in caring for your lawn. The people transforming lawns for free seem to be kind and caring human beings. The only problem with their profession, viewed in the context of divine *for-life* interrelatedness, is our human propensity to want to control everything, including creation itself.

It is certainly human nature to want to create our own human constructions of order. But what is the right ethical balance between human control of nature and respect for our ecosystems' need for balance and sustainability? In relation to lawns *per se*, why is the American ideal an insistence on making the natural spaces around our places of residence so pared, clipped, and trimmed? We seem to think that the closer our grass is cut to the ground, the better this is. Neighbors are tut-tutted when their grass is "too high" or their shrubbery "out of control." Sometimes local code enforcement officials are called, and they may slap a fine on the offending homeowners. The goal seems to be to create lawns of emptiness, blank green slates upon which our edifices can impose their presence, even if this degrades biodiversity.

It is not this way everywhere in the world, of course. In the tropics where I have spent most of my adult life, one does not have a "lawn" so much as a "garden." This is not the American concept of garden as a plot on which to grow vegetables. Pacific Islanders traditionally find spots to grow food some distance from their houses and call these plots of land, usually quite small, "plantations." A garden is the plant life that surrounds one's house. This is also true in Aotearoa New Zealand, where I have lived for some time.

In the tropics, one's garden is a riot of color, and I remember fondly the ever-spreading, glorious bougainvillea and hibiscus, along with the many enormous ferns and flowering plants. The staff house where I lived on the campus of Pacific Theological College in Fiji was also surrounded by banana plants, a coconut tree, a breadfruit tree, a paw paw (papaya) tree, a guava tree, and other trees from which some of the students used to remove bark or leaves to make medicinal teas. The Pacific Islanders I lived with trimmed their plant life back regularly, but this was necessary because everything grew so quickly in the tropical climate that it could easily completely take over the space, even making it hard to enter one's home. (I remember a house near the village where I lived in Jamaica which had vines growing all around its outer walls. When someone got the bright idea of pulling the vines down, the house collapsed; the vines were holding the house together.)

In Aotearoa New Zealand, there is not much empty space in one's garden for grass that has to be mowed. There are plants of all kinds, which are carefully tended. Tending one's garden is in fact a favorite pastime of most New Zealanders. This seems to me to be evidence of a much better sense of balance than the American notion of the expanse of carefully manicured lawns that showcase mastery over Mother Nature.

There is a theological lesson to be learned here. It is unnaturally "odd" to want to control nature to the extent that some seem to feel is necessary. In an "odd" way, this propensity for control lies at the heart of the climate crisis. It demonstrates our human desire to bend the natural world to our will. Of course, maintaining one's lawn through intense mowing, pruning, trimming, and cutting is largely a benign activity. There is nothing malevolent about it, and it can be a way of creating a sense of beauty in one's immediate surroundings.

However, when it comes to felling trees unnecessarily and diminishing the natural life that seeks to flourish around us, this control can steer us into an imbalance that has larger implications. Recognizing this, there is now a move in some sectors of the lawn care industry to moderate the American insistence on enormous, closely cropped lawns. Some are now advocating for leaving sections of grass uncut, and I have seen the most beautiful pictures of what happens in these set-apart spaces: wildflowers begin to grow; bees, birds, and butterflies return. The inherent desire for balance in nature reasserts itself in a short period of time.

RESTORING BALANCE—REWILDING AND *VANUA SAUVI*

This impulse is also seen in the rewilding movement that is expanding across the globe, which has grown in response to the climate crisis. There are manifold organizations involved in rewilding rivers, lakes, streams, and land habitats, replenishing fish stocks and animal life, removing invasive plant species, and planting native trees and plants, in an effort to recreate a healthy ecosystem in particular habitats. These projects are most effective when they also involve and benefit the human communities who live in or near these habitats.

I offer one such example which is personally known to me, as it is located in what I consider my second home, the Pasifika nation of Fiji. In many ways, Pasifika communities are in the forefront of efforts to rewild or return the land and sea to spheres of balance and sustainability. The case I reference here took place several years ago in the village of Rukuruku on the Fijian island of Ovalau, a village I visited many years ago, whose rewilding has been detailed by Rosiana Lagi.[1]

As in other intact indigenous cultures, in the Fijian context one cannot envision or discuss issues of environmental balance and sustainability without understanding the interconnectedness of all things. In Fiji, this interconnectedness is encapsulated in the concept of *vanua*. *Vanua* has at times wrongly been translated into English as "the land." But *vanua* is much more than the visible manifestations of creation. It is the essence of inter-relationship. In Lagi's framing, *vanua*

> ... encompasses the land, the sea, the cosmos, the people—all living things, including spirits, in a specific 'place'—and how each of them is related to and responsible for each other. It also includes the culture, traditions, knowledge, skills, ways of knowing, love, peace, prosperity, and communalism. In the indigenous Fijian psyche, vanua also embodies the social institutions responsible for the management of the vanua.[2]

The Fijian theologian who is best known for articulating a theology of the *vanua* is Sevati Tuwere, most prominently in his seminal work *Vanua: A Fijian Theology of Place*.[3] He insists that it is the spiritual essence of well-being in the concept of *vanua* that defines how Fijians relate to the physical

---

1. Lagi, "Vanua Sauvi."
2. Lagi, "Vanua Sauvi," 187.
3. Tuwere, *Vanua*.

world in which they live. This understanding is echoed by Sereima Nasilisili, who writes that *vanua*

> ... is the delicate balance between the sacred and the secular, the physical and the spiritual, that has been traditionally understood and expressed in the way Fijians look after their environment, their language, their culture and traditional practices. Living in the *vanua* and preserving harmony and balance within its mutually interactive systems is the heartbeat of life and requires a deep understanding of all the parts of the interrelated systems. It is the upholding and maintenance of this balance that leads to *sautu* (wellbeing, harmony), the life goal of people in the *vanua*.[4]

In other words, *vanua* is the all-encompassing ethical lifeworld which holds together the material, spiritual, personal, and communal aspects of existence. This includes placing limits on humans' use of the physical environments in which they live. When the intimate relationship between persons and creation becomes imbalanced, restrictions are placed on human activity in order to restore balance and sustainability.

In Fijian culture, such acts of restriction—the placing of temporary bans or taboos on certain activities—are known as *vanua sauvi*. As Lagi explains, *vanua sauvi* entails the temporary closure of sections of land or sea which have become compromised and degraded by human overuse or abuse. This taboo is interwoven with customary law to ensure the sustainability of resources that will make possible the wellbeing of both the physical environment and the human communities who inhabit that environment.

Rukuruku, the village in Lagi's study, like many other Fijian coastal villages, has been adversely affected by the sea level rise associated with global warming, causing significant "coastal erosion and the depletion of land and sea resources."[5] Therefore, in 2011 a *vanua sauvi* restriction on the use of land and sea resources in part of Rukuruku was decreed: "No one was allowed to cut trees, plant, or use resources from the specified land and sea areas. A traditional protocol was followed to ensure that all the members of the community were informed of the restriction and would respect it."[6]

The results of this action have been remarkable. During the several years of the *vanua sauvi*, the villagers of Rukuruku witnessed a "vast change" in the area that had been placed under restriction:

---

4. Nasilisili, "Custodianship," 75.
5. Lagi, "Vanua Sauvi," 193.
6. Lagi, "Vanua Sauvi," 193–94.

> Lost plant and fish species have been restored and have had spillover effects. Surplus fish and sea resources from the *Vanua Sauvi* have spilled over to the non-restricted areas, providing food for the villagers and a source of income as the surplus fish and sea resources are sold. Moreover, the re-growth mangrove forest has acted as a nursery, producing more fish and sea resource species, at the same time acting as a barrier slowing coastal erosion... In the forest area, lost plant species have re-grown, and the forest cover now provides foliage that contributes to the growth of new plants and supplies nutrients for plants in non-restricted areas. In addition, endemic fruits... that were believed to have become extinct began to bear fruit again, and crops... that were planted in nearby farms began to have a higher yield. Landslides that used to occur in this area have been prevented due to the re-growth of plants. Moreover, the forest now acts as a reservoir, producing water in the river that is a source of water for the villagers, which for the previous five years had been drying up.[7]

Anecdotal evidence even suggests that the overall temperatures surrounding the village, which had been increasing due to global warming, have moderated as forest areas have been replenished and have grown, creating a significant carbon sink.

This is only one of many examples of indigenous peoples taking decisive action to restore their environments to a life that balances the natural processes of land and water with human needs. In these actions, humans' desire to control and optimize their extraction and exploitation of natural resources for their own ends takes a back seat to their humble partnership with nature. They do not prioritize their own desires at the expense of the health of the things and beings of creation which sustain them.

In chapter 1, I spoke of "nature" as being about self-promotion. Because human beings are part of nature, they share this inbuilt desire. We humans struggle with this mightily. This "natural" instinct to put ourselves first runs counter to our spiritual calling to live ethical lives as interconnected beings, interwoven strands in the tapestry of creation. In order to be such ethical beings, we must intentionally discern when to place a *vanua sauvi* on our acts of individual or collective self-centeredness.

The world at large needs a massive *vanua sauvi* if it is to survive the climate catastrophe which is unfolding before our eyes. We have to stop ourselves from our excessive exploitation of creation if we are to survive as a species, and if our earthly home is to be habitable. There are innumerable scientific studies that remind us starkly of the dangers in which we have

---

7. Lagi, "Vanua Sauvi," 194.

placed the planet we call home.⁸ There should be no debate about this. Even for those who do not want to listen to the science, the evidence can no longer be ignored.

"Once-in-a-century" storms now occur every few years. Temperature rise is, in every scientific study, worse than predicted in previous studies. The intensity of massive hurricanes and cyclones, wildfires, droughts, and floods increases every year, with devastating impacts on the land and sea, flora and fauna, and human communities. The polar icecaps and glaciers are rapidly melting, and sea level rise can no longer be ignored. Growing numbers of low-lying atoll islands in Pasifika have disappeared beneath the sea or become uninhabitable and continue to do so at an alarming rate. Climate refugees are already a reality in the region, with inhabitants of some low-lying islands, especially in the Micronesian island groups, having to flee what had been their ancestral homes for many centuries. Some of these small island nations may no longer exist in the near future. This is not hyperbole.⁹

I give these examples because they are close to home and to my heart. Those needing further evidence can read hundreds of studies which validate and explain the climate disaster in which we are living. Our only hope lies in our recognition of our place in the interconnected world in which we live. Do we have the ethical consciousness necessary to place a *vanua sauvi* on ourselves? Or do we want to continue our global equivalent of lawn transformations gone mad, extracting and chopping away at everything in order to fulfill our desires?

---

8. Among the hundreds of scientific studies of the climate crisis, I mention only a few: See all of the "Annual Reports" of the IPCC (Intergovernmental Panel on Climate Change) for the past quarter century or more, outlining the latest research by climate scientists (though it should be noted that some scientists consider these to be incomplete assessments, watered down due to the need for consensus among UN member nations); Cochard, *Consequences of Deforestation and Climate Change*; and UN Trust Fund for Human Security, *Climate Change*. For a theological response to climate change, see, for example, Schaefer, "Environmental Degradation, Social Sin, and the Common Good;" Conradie and Hoster, eds., *T&T Clark Handbook of Christian Theology and Climate Change*; Waqainabete, *Christian Environmentalism*; and Brotton, ed., *Ecotheology in the Humanities*.

9. It is perplexing and extremely troubling to observe the current trend of some influential commentators on the Left, who previously made the climate crisis a priority in their concerns, now adopting the assertions on the Right that climate change is a hoax. They have gravitated to the view that efforts to combat the climate crisis are a plot by "the globalists" (the neoliberal Western elites who dominate bodies like the World Economic Forum) to accelerate the dismantling of individual rights through the adoption of policies that reduce reliance on fossil fuels. This abandonment of the realities of the climate crisis demonstrates a loss of critical thinking which is frightening. It may be left to grassroots communities to fight for the survival of the planet.

THE PROBLEM WITH "BIG GREEN"

One of the problems with the environmental "green" movement, which has in the West increasingly become "Big Green"—the eco-industries controlled by capitalist (profit-driven) corporations—is that it separates scientific efforts to curb CO_2 levels from a holistic understanding of our divinely ordained place in creation. It sees technology as the sole answer to the climate crisis, largely defined by scientists from the West.[10] But there are problems with this "answer." All too often, Western efforts to combat the climate crisis make the false assumption that eco-technologies can allow those in the so-called "developed" world to continue to maintain their accustomed high standard of living, only in a more eco-friendly way that nonetheless leaves intact capitalism's excesses.

In this view, if only we switch to electric cars, use more solar panels and wind turbines, and commit to certain mitigation policies, we can continue to live the same materialistic, wasteful, profligate lifestyles to which we have become accustomed in the West and in other industrialized countries such as Japan, Australia, and oil-rich Middle Eastern nations like the United Arab Emirates. But that is to ignore the lesson of the Garden of Eden. Let us recall that the reason for the expulsion of Adam and Eve from the garden was that they did not practice restraint. They chose to eat whatever fruit they wanted, with no restrictions.

This mindset of limitless consumerism and self-gratification is destroying us. Earth inhabitants are created by a *for-life* God to live modestly, simply, with a light touch upon the earth, sharing equitably with all others and with all created things. We should remember Upolu Vaai's distinction between a "we have" mindset and a "we are" mindset. At the heart of the climate crisis which is endangering our planet is not simply the overuse of fossil fuels. It is that some humans (the minority, those with means) have far more than they need in order to live a meaningful life. They are addicted to having more and more—the capitalist motto being "more is better"—rather than simply being "we are" creatures. (We have seen how this is also the source of the problem of poverty.)

Our focus should be on what is needed to combat climate collapse in a serious and committed way, not solely through Big Green profit-driven businesses but through locally-based acts of *vanua sauvi* stewardship. Those who have more than they need must not only switch to electric cars (while continuing to drive "hither and yon" on a whim) but reflect through the lens

---

10. For an excellent critique of Western elites' control over the climate change narrative from a Pasifika perspective, along with a proposal for an alternative Pasifika eco-theology, see Lusama, "*Vaa Fesokotaki*."

of a *for-life* ethic on what they actually need, and how they can share more equitably with those who have too little. Far too much unnecessary "stuff" is made in the industrialized world, excesses whose production unjustifiably pads our human carbon footprint to the point of unsustainability. All this "stuff" does not even bring happiness, just clutter. We have very little time to correct this. We need to listen to indigenous cultures regarding how to correct this imbalance, as partners with creation.

SINS OF EXCESS

One essential and urgent aspect of correcting this imbalance has to do with the ethics of water use. As the planet heats up, there are increasing droughts, which are more widespread and last longer than in the past, leading to rivers drying up along with the underground water tables that supply water to billions of people. Yet, while this dire situation cries out for the conservation of water, industrialized countries, especially in the West, continue to overuse water at an alarming rate.

The United States is the worst offender. Statistics show that "Every day, the average American family uses about 552 gallons of water. Compare this to the average African family, which uses about 5 gallons of water a day."[11] Americans waste water at a rate that far exceeds any other country in the world. But water is finite; we only have what is in our oceans, rivers, and streams, and we have to share that finite amount with every human, every animal, and every plant.

This same disparity can be seen in a comparison of per capita energy usage in the United States versus other countries. This includes electricity, heating, air conditioning, vehicle use, machinery use, etc. Comparing a sampling of countries, using Energy Use Per Capita (MMBtu) data, in 2021 Afghanistan's per capita energy use was 2, Bangladesh's was 10, Bolivia's was 24, Ghana's was 11, Iraq's was 48, Lebanon's was 64, Denmark's was 108, China's was 115, and Russia's was 214, while the United States' per capita energy consumption was a whopping 295.[12] Something is very wrong with this picture.

Regarding energy usage by countries as a whole, in 2021 the United States' total energy usage was 98 quadrillion British thermal units (Btu), just over 16 percent of total world energy consumption, even though the United States' percentage of the world population is only 4 percent.[13] Since

---

11. Weil, "How Does Water Use in the United States Compare."
12. "Energy Usage Per Capita by Country."
13. "Energy Usage Per Capita by Country."

most of this energy is still derived from fossil fuels, it is clear that America is contributing disproportionately to the climate crisis, which, if the present pattern continues, will make life on earth unsustainable for both humans and creation itself. Most climate scientists give us a decade at most to remedy this.

These examples of the sins of excess are indicators of a failure of interrelationality. All human beings share our earthly home, and none of us are entitled to use more than our just share of the world's finite resources. If we live a *for-life* ethic, we cannot privilege ourselves and our own wants and desires at the expense of others.

HONORING THE LIVING WOMB

This reflection leads me back to the Maohi theologian Marc Pohue and his ôpü-eco-theology—*ôpü* being the Maohi word for creation or the universe, depicted by Pohue as "the living womb." In theological terms, the *ôpü* is the divinely created living womb which encompasses the land, the ocean, the atmosphere, flora, fauna, and what Pohue calls the "luminaries of the sky." The living womb of creation is a dynamic living being of "diverse, pluralistic, interconnected and interdependent networks. These networks are imbued with *mana* (sacred power) and the divine *Mëhoi* (Spirit), which gives them life, energy, being, values, capacities, and particularities."[14]

Creation in ôpü-eco-theology is a welcoming and protected home for all offspring and things of the living womb. Creation is a home that is "worth caring for, nurturing and sustaining, because humankind depends heavily on it to survive and flourish."[15] Creation in this sense is best understood as our divine mother. The original divine resolve to create the living womb entailed "bestowing upon her the qualities of birthing, growing, evolving and multiplying."[16] Creation can therefore never be an object to control because, as the maternal living womb, she is the giver of knowledge, wisdom, connectedness, and identity. Creation is the birth-giver of life.

In ôpü-eco-theology, therefore, God "indwells" and "works with" all of creation. God embraces the living womb. As Pohue writes, "This embrace is not a passive presence with the suffering living womb but a compassionate and resilient presence, which empowers the living womb to recover, restore, and continue the co-creation of the world."[17] This is a dynamic God who

---

14. Pohue, "Navigating with the Womb of Life," 55.
15. Pohue, "Navigating with the Womb of Life," 55.
16. Pohue, "Navigating with the Womb of Life," 55.
17. Pohue, "Navigating with the Womb of Life," 56.

interpenetrates all of life and infuses every living thing and being with an ethic that is *for life*. Pohue relates his ōpü-eco-theology to the ecological and human devastation caused by years of French nuclear testing in Maohi Nui and the response of Maohi Christians to this disregard for the womb of life.

Returning to the opening story in this chapter, I want to reiterate that the intent of this reflection has in no way been to cast aspersions on those who love to mow their lawns and trim their hedges. The ethical questions that emerge from this reflection, now more than ever given the unfolding ecological collapse, are these: How much control over nature is too much? What limits should we place on our desires to shape and reshape our earthly home? Most importantly, what are our intentions when we act as masters over our environment? Do we simply want to manage creation to protect our communities and enhance their wellbeing, in cooperation with nature (perhaps building sea walls, or constructing fire walls to stop larger wildfires)? Or do we tear up the earth and pollute our rivers, streams, and oceans because we are greedy and want to extract nature's resources to boost the profit margins of our neoliberal capitalist enterprises?

By "we" I mean, of course, not just individuals but nations. In my native United States, this means not only the elected government but the entire military-industrial-corporatist-national security state complex, sometimes known as "the deep state." Those who make up this complex are not elected; they are not accountable to the people and act with impunity. This complex of power rules the world and is destroying the world. It is the antithesis of the godly desire for a *for-life* ethic.

A TREE, A ROOF, AND A KINDOM INTERVENTION

I end this chapter with a story about a tree. It is not the tree of the knowledge of good and evil in the garden of Eden, but it is a tale of human interrelatedness with creation. It is also a story about kindom life. When I was the co-pastor of a circuit of four rural churches in the interior of Jamaica, the practice was to hold a "members' meeting" once a month after worship, on the Sunday when the pastor was present. (I led worship in each of the four churches one Sunday every month, rotating from church to church through the month, and the entire day was filled with worship, members' meeting, youth group meeting, and a more informal evening service replete with tambourines, guitars, soulful singing, foot-stomping, clapping, and dancing.)

Members' meetings were astonishing occasions, where parishioners voiced their hopes and suggestions for the congregation, and also their personal problems and complaints. Given Jamaicans' superb oratorical skills, these could be entertaining, captivating, or inspiring monologues by anyone who wished to speak. The congregation as a whole responded to the issues presented in the meetings and came to decisions about how to move forward and remedy problems.

In the members' meeting that has particular relevance for this chapter, it came to light that Brother[18] Ainslee had allowed his dying coconut tree to fall over the hedge onto the roof of Brother Gon's house, damaging the roof. We are speaking here of extremely poor people, who lived in small flimsy houses. They were subsistence farmers whose only income came from garden produce which the women in the family took to town markets to sell. Brother Gon had been warning Brother Ainslee for some time that his coconut tree was ailing, leaning, and needed to be cut down, otherwise it would fall on his house. But Brother Ainslee was old and infirm; he could barely walk, much less cut down a tree. So nothing was done.

During a particularly strong rainstorm, the inevitable happened: Brother Ainslee's coconut tree fell onto Brother Gon's roof. Brother Gon was now demanding that Brother Ainslee pay to have his roof repaired. These gentlemen had been good friends, but now their relationship was strained. What was to be done? Brother Ainslee needed a coconut tree, for coconuts are the essence of sustainable life for Jamaicans (and people of the tropics everywhere), providing nourishment, building materials, copra to sell, and fronds with which to weave baskets.

Brother Ainslee was now without a key means of sustenance. Even though his tree had been damaged by blight, it had still contributed to his family's wellbeing—and also to Brother Gon's family's wellbeing. When coconuts from Brother Ainslee's tree had fallen into Brother Gon's yard, he and his family had been free to eat and drink from them. Brother Ainslee did not "own" the tree, it just happened to be in his yard, however precariously. Both families now urgently needed help—a tree and a roof.

Clearly Brother Ainslee was not financially able to repair Brother Gon's roof, and clearly Brother Gon had no money of his own to repair his roof. And thus the member's meeting came up with a plan. When asked point blank how much each man could contribute weekly to buying the materials to repair the damaged roof, the answer was "ten cents." Then and there, the church treasurer agreed to receive and hold each of their ten-cent weekly contributions. Since twenty cents weekly would do very little toward fixing the problem, the congregation then agreed that each member would make a weekly contribution of whatever their families could afford until the roof

---

18. All members of Jamaican churches are referred to as "brother" and "sister."

was fixed. Able-bodied members agreed to donate their time to repair the roof when the materials were in hand. Brother Gon offered to help Brother Ainslee plant a new coconut tree, since Brother Ainslee was unable to do this on his own. The two men shook hands, prayer was called for (although, as their pastor, I was almost too overcome to speak), and their friendship was restored.

This is a living example of kindom life in the midst of the interwoven strands of human relationships and creation relationships. This story also has a connection to poverty, for poverty dictated many decisions and actions in the lives of Brother Ainslee and Brother Gon. Both of these neighbors were grateful for the divine gift of all that the coconut tree had to offer to enhance life on earth, including their own lives. They needed to share a coconut tree in a way that both protected the tree and was for their "common good." And their church needed to be a kindom community in which everyone played their part to bring about restored relationships—with one another and with creation—and even the restoration of a roof.

In the closing chapter of this book, which spins a practical "what if?" web of imagined ways of living in the world as interrelational *for-life* communities, I offer several suggestions for how we might address the climate crisis. I will end here simply by saying that there are ways to do this. If we work together, beyond our differences of race, culture, politics, class, and wealth, we can find tangible ways to save our planet and our human communities. We can metaphorically allow our earthly "lawns" to find the right balance between the order and aesthetics we seek and the need to let creation breathe in a way that places human needs alongside creation's needs. We must do this, for the sake of the survival of our earthly home. If we do so, it will no doubt be "oddly satisfying" in God's eyes. I end with a poem from Pasifika:

THE LANGUAGE OF TREES AND CLAMS

Wardley Barry-Igivisa[19]

> When my father cuts down trees to plant yams,
> he speaks to them. He summons their spirits
> and they reason beside the mumu pit.[20]
> At harvest he gets enough for a meal.

---

19. Barry-Igivisa, "Language of Trees and Clams," 49. Used with permission. Barry-Igivisa is originally from the Eastern Highlands of Papua New Guinea.

20 A pit dug in the ground for cooking food using hot stones

When my mother goes out to fish for clams,
she sings a song; she sings softly, sweetly.
Then she swims into the heart of the sea,
and brings back home just enough for a meal.

We have an understanding, us and them.
The land, the sea and our fathers are one.
We have farmed this land for a thousand suns,
and we harvest not to hoard but to heal.

But the spirits left when the machines came,
and with them the language of trees and clams.

Part 4

A *For-Life* Ethic Confronts a *For-Death* World

10

The Evil that is Empire

I HAVE ARGUED THROUGHOUT this work that if God is consistently *for life*, this has a direct bearing on the ethics we not only profess but are called to live out in every situation. If we honor the divine presence in our lives, we cannot be *for life* in some cases but not in others. We cannot be for the wellbeing of our own group, nation, or allies but against the wellbeing of peoples or nations we have designated as enemies. If my rights or the rights of my group or my nation are privileged over the wellbeing of all, that is a denial of a *for-life* ethic.

As I have worked through how such an ethic ought to be actualized in terms of specific social realities, I cannot ignore the reality of empire, for the empire which is my native country has dominated, at least until recently, what it has told itself was a unipolar world in which it was in control. That global dominance is diminishing rapidly, but dying empires are particularly dangerous because they become desperate to cling to their power. I will explore in this and the following chapter how that is so, but before I examine the evil of empire it is important to address a vitally important aspect of living under the sway of empire, namely, how we can know "what is going on."

STRUGGLING TO "KNOW" IN THE GRIP OF EMPIRE

In order to probe the evil of empire accurately and comprehensively, we must pay attention to how we access and interpret information. This is a huge challenge, because empires rely on the control of information in order to spin the narratives that sustain their evil work in the world. Empire—the compulsion of one country to control other countries through conquest, economic and political exploitation, or other forms of "power-over" tactics—succeeds in part by brainwashing its subjects. If we seek to practice a *for-life* ethic which insists on truth, we must therefore be extremely discerning in our quest for knowledge.

My sister once made this astute statement: "We can't know what we don't know." This may sound like an oxymoron, but if we dig beneath the surface of this pithy remark, we will unearth the reasons for a *for-life* approach to knowledge acquisition. My sister was making an epistemological point. Epistemology as a branch of philosophy is the study of theories of knowledge, especially the distinction between justified belief and opinion. It is, in simplest terms, the study of how we can reliably know something.

This is critically important for those who seek to follow a *for-life* ethic, because we cannot unearth the inner workings of empire, or any other manifestation of the social order, without raising honest questions regarding how we acquire knowledge about what is actually going on in the world and why. Empires want to keep that knowledge from us, and so they must maintain firm control over the dissemination of information. I will focus on this problem in relation to the empire whose policies and actions have had the most far-reaching consequences in the world for some time, the American Empire.

I grew up believing that the media played a positive role in informing Americans about the world. This first came to be relevant for me in relation to the great social upheavals of the 1960s, the decade in which I came of age, upheavals which spawned massive civil rights and anti-war activism. Journalists helped to expose the social injustices that underpinned both of those interconnected historical developments, and that is why I felt then that journalism was an honorable profession which could help me to better understand the complex realities of the world around me and thereby to know how best to respond as a person of faith.

But that journalistic ethic began to change. In part as a result of that period of social unrest, the resistance it spawned to America's unjust domestic and foreign policies, and the subsequent public questioning of America's empire narrative, the power brokers of empire became deeply annoyed by those in the media who asked too many questions, questions that threatened to expose their wrongdoings and ulterior motives.

A pivotal sea change occurred with the passage of President Bill Clinton's Telecommunications Act of 1996. It enabled and centralized large corporations' control of the media. The vast, diverse range of local newspapers and other forms of print media, and locally owned radio and television stations, had to be brought to heel. Only powerful corporations could be trusted to control the flow of information, because they have a cozy relationship with and benefit from empire's underlying agenda.

Thanks to the Telecommunications Act, today 95 percent of all media outlets in the United States are owned and controlled by just five large corporations. These corporations enjoy an incestuous relationship with the US government, regardless of which party is in power. News anchors and reporters in the corporate-owned media are thus now rightly labelled by independent journalists as nothing more than "stenographers" for empire. Their job, to use the philosopher Noam Chomsky's famous term, is the *manufacturing of consent*.[1]

The advent of 24-hour cable news corporations furthered the demise of independent investigative journalism in America. Cable television networks like CNN, MSNBC, and Fox News became not so much news as endless hours of listening to "talking heads" whose job is to propagandize the public by parroting the empire narrative. Although there are partisan divides among the networks on "culture war" and "woke" issues such as gender, abortion, and gun rights, they all support the ideology of empire. Prior to the corporate capture of the media, newspapers and television networks devoted considerable resources to actual investigative journalism. Reporters were "in the field," finding sources and digging up facts. They were given the resources they needed to find out what was happening and why. That era is now fading away.

The only antidote to the sanitized propaganda posing as news emerged on the internet. Journalists labeled as dissidents, who were no longer allowed in the corporate media space, had to create other platforms where they could engage in independent journalism, and they have done so against great odds and with huge risks to their careers and at times personal safety. Their critique of the mainstream (corporation-owned, empire-compliant) "legacy media" is twofold: its *sins of commission* and its *sins of omission*.

The mainstream media's *sins of commission* entail parroting the narratives of empire as if they were factual, without investigating in an objective way to find out what the actual facts are. "Fact-checking" has itself become controlled by the gatekeepers of empire, making it almost impossible to know what is, in fact, a fact.[2] Although Donald Trump popularized the term "fake news" as a way of describing any reporting unfavorable to him, it is

---

1. See Chomsky and Hermon, *Manufacturing Consent*.

2. Several recent studies have uncovered the extent to which fact-checking organizations like Politifact, Factcheck.org, and Snopes are themselves compromised. As Professor David Barker concluded in a 2017 study of fact-checking, "Fact-checkers cannot prevent the politicization of facts, because they themselves are evaluated through a political lens." Barker, "In American Politics Today."

ironic that so much fake news actually abounds. The major news networks have in recent years hired a whole host of "intelligence experts" with CIA backgrounds whose entire profession is based on subterfuge, propaganda, and outright lies.

A particularly striking recent example of the mainstream media's *sins of commission*—using propaganda to further the goals of empire—was its coverage of Russiagate, the manufactured scandal of purported Trump-Russia collusion that, the public was told, "undermined democracy" through the commission of nefarious acts to ensure Trump's win in the 2016 presidential election. For nearly four years, the mainstream media's breathless "coverage" of Russiagate was non-stop. Fortunately, by following the work of reputable independent investigative journalists,[3] especially the in-depth investigations of journalists like Aaron Maté and Matt Taibbi, I came to see what a hoax this story was, and how perfectly it served the aims of empire. The evidence which independent researchers provided to debunk the claims of Russiagate is irrefutable.[4]

The most ominous legacy of Russiagate has been that, in their obsession with destroying Trump, the spokespersons of empire (media, politicians, "think tanks," and the varied organs of the national security state) succeeded in their parallel aim of making Russia the enemy of all enemies, evil personified. Prior to Russiagate, Russia was not depicted in American

---

3. In addition to relying on primary sources, I include here some of the news organizations and journalists I follow in order to seek out accurate information: The Real News Network (in particular, the work of analysts Chris Hedges and Pepe Escobar); The Grayzone (especially the work of its editor-in-chief, Max Blumenthal, and its award-winning investigative journalist, Aaron Maté); BreakThrough News (especially the global coverage and analysis of its co-editors, Eugene Puryear and Rania Khalek), Mint Press News, Consortium News, ScheerPost, Telesur English, System Update (with Pulitzer Prize-winning journalist Glenn Greenwald), Democracy at Work (with Professor Richard Wolff), and the work of the independent investigative journalist Matt Taibbi.

4. Russiagate originated with the Hillary Clinton 2016 presidential campaign, which sought to "kill two birds with one stone" by dragging both Donald Trump and Russia through the mud. The Democratic National Committee (DNC), with Clinton's approval, hired Fusion GPS, a dubious "research and intelligence" firm, to dig up dirt on Trump-Russia ties, and it hired Chrisopher Steele, who had connections to British intelligence. He produced the infamous and completely debunked "Steele dossier," which alleged that Russia had salacious information on Trump. The Steele dossier became the basis for Russiagate. The DNC then accused Russia of hacking into their computer server and releasing e-mails unfavorable to Hillary Clinton, but it was proven forensically that there was no Russian (or any) "hack," as the e-mails were provided to Wikileaks via flash drive by a source within the DNC. Neither Trump nor his associates were found guilty of collusion with Russia.

public discourse as the embodiment of everything that is terrible in the world.

In fact, although Russia had been creeping up on America's "enemies list" in the years leading up to Russiagate, it was our friend following the dissolution of the Soviet Union in the early 1990s. President George W. Bush once invited President Putin to his family's vacation home in Kennebunkport, Maine, and famously said afterward that he had "looked into Putin's eyes and seen his soul."[5] The post-Russiagate quagmire of the demonization of Russia in which we now find ourselves shows all too starkly the dangers of the simplistic propagandizing upon which empire depends. Russiagate is just one of many such examples.

There is also the problem of the empire-acquiescent media's *sins of omission*. There is an impoverishment of comprehensive news coverage in the American mainstream media, which makes the majority of Americans woefully uninformed about the world. The mainstream media does not cover news which its imperial masters do not want the public to know about or think about. I have seen studies which measure the number of minutes in a given month or year that a particular topic is covered on US television news or the word count in print media. There is almost no coverage of the Global South (and America's interventions therein), the severity of the climate crisis, class struggle (including the causes and extent of America's economic decline), the growing efforts by many countries to create a multipolar world, and other empire-challenging realities—much less any dissenting perspectives regarding what the media does cover.

Perhaps the most troubling evidence of the American Empire's control over the dissemination of information is its shocking escalation of censorship of those who challenge the dominant narrative. The *sins of omission* in this regard can be seen in the failure of the mainstream media and politicians to protest this growing silencing of voices of dissent. Not only do they fail to protest the growing repression of dissent; they actively support it.

I have witnessed this firsthand because I glean information from anti-empire journalists whose platforms are routinely banned or shadow-banned (manipulating algorithms to steer viewers away from their online channels), and their sources of funding cut off. The scope of this growing censorship is chilling. Many who were affected by the so-called McCarthyite era of "red-baiting" (anti-communism/anti-USSR) in the US in the 1950s agree that what we are witnessing now surpasses what occurred then. This is

---

5. See the NBC News retrospective on this statement by President Bush in a 2001 press conference, "Flashback: President Bush on Putin's 'Soul.'"

so because today there are many more sophisticated and far-reaching forms of surveillance and censorship than what existed in the 1950s.

The silencing of dissent is the empire's way of putting its foot down and saying "there is only one acceptable narrative, and there can be no deviation from that narrative." This silencing expanded throughout the Trump presidency and accelerated during the Biden presidency. It worsened during the COVID-19 pandemic, when those raising questions about the efficacy and safety of vaccines or extended lockdowns, even reputable physicians and medical researchers, were defamed or de-platformed. The empire expects its subjects to believe what it tells them and not ask questions.

In this environment, "cancel culture" spread like a virus, and now those who disagree with the dominant empire narrative face cancellation of their online platforms or are otherwise suppressed. The mainstream media fully supports and furthers this cancel culture, calling for ever-expanding suppression of citizens deemed to be nonconformists (routinely branded as dangerous traitors).

Although cancel culture first attacked the populist/Trumpist Right, it soon began to come after the Left[6] with a vengeance. It has been establishment Democrats and their media allies who have been the loudest voices calling for increased censorship not only of those on the Right but, even more ferociously, those on the Left. Most independent journalists are seriously impacted by this censorship.

The propaganda and silencing of dissent soared into the stratosphere with the advent of the Russia-Ukraine war in 2022. It was deemed traitorous to bring any critical thinking, historical context, or questioning into any mainstream broadcast or print media reporting on this war. The US and Europe were instead gripped by war hysteria, with Ukraine's blue and yellow flag adorning housefronts, car bumpers, and social media profile pages (though this fervor has waned somewhat given the debacle of the war).

Chris Hedges describes the brainwashing in which the American Empire is engulfed today in this way: "Censorship is the last resort of desperate and unpopular regimes . . . It comforts the powerful with the narrative they want to hear, one fed back to them by courtiers in the media, government agencies, think tanks and academia."[7] What I have learned in my quest to find alternative conduits of information to those linked to the apparatus

---

6. There is no longer any genuine "Left" in the American Democratic Party. In most European countries, it would be considered centrist at best. As the Republican Party has moved further and further to the Right, so has the Democratic Party. Neither party challenges the ideology of empire. The "actual Left" has abandoned the Democratic Party.

7. Hedges, "American Commissars."

of empire is that seeking accurate information must be a very intentional, committed endeavor. It is not easy. What is easy is succumbing to the propagandizing which has penetrated every aspect of our lives. We are inundated daily by propaganda posing as fact, and because we grew up trusting the "established" media, it is extremely difficult to begin to question and mistrust it.

Yet mistrust it we must, if we seek to know the truth, which is a prerequisite of a *for-life* ethic. As people of faith, we cannot bury our heads in the sand. I am therefore compelled to seek out the truth from conveyors of information who are not under the spell of empire. We will never be able to resist the evils of empire unless we know what these evils are, where they come from, how they are being enacted, and where they seek to go. With this in mind, we turn our attention as truth-seekers to what empire is and to "what is going on" in the American Empire.

EMPIRE IN RELATIONAL AND THEOLOGICAL PERSPECTIVE

Empire is defined in the *World History Encyclopedia* in this way:

> An empire is an unequal relationship between a core state and a periphery of other states controlled from the core. On the simplest level, control means military control or occupation, or various forms of political intervention, but it can also cover economic or cultural influence. Economic pressure by itself has frequently been enough to manipulate peripheral states. Religion, ideology, and other cultural forces have habitually accompanied the political, military, and economic persuasion of empires.[8]

What is central to this understanding of empire is the notion of *unequal relationship*. I seek to explore what lies behind this unequal relationship. This leads me to attempt to unpack the hubris, greed, racism, and violence upon which empire is predicated and which it foments. I undertake this analysis not merely from a sociological, historical, and geopolitical perspective but, most importantly, from a theological perspective. I do so within the framework of the divine interrelatedness of all things and the *for-life* ethic implied therein.

In my examination of empire as a Christian who seeks to orient myself toward kindom life, my thinking has been enriched by a provocative

---

8. Davidson, "Empire."

publication by the South African liberation theologian Allan Boesak,[9] "Theological Reflections on Empire."[10] He begins by concurring with the 2004 *Accra Confession* of member churches of the World Alliance of Reformed Churches (now the World Communion of Reformed Churches), which laments that, in the present age, we are living in a world dominated by empire, specifically the American Empire. In that light, Boesak made this stark observation back in 2009:

> For the first time since the rise of human civilization, the history of which has to a large extent been the history of empires, one empire is now on the verge of becoming a truly global empire, an empire with no borders. For the first time as well, we are aware that even if the human race avoids self-annihilation through nuclear weapons, it is on a trajectory toward self-annihilation through human-caused climate change. These two crises are, moreover, closely related because the nation that is seeking to become the world's first borderless empire—the United States of America—is also the nation that, precisely through its imperialist policies, is the primary threat to the survival of the human species (along with that of other species as well).[11]

Here Boesak is asserting that the American Empire is unique in the history of empires because of its global reach (as a "borderless empire") and limitless range of mechanisms for asserting its power—all in the wider context of the potential for nuclear annihilation and climate catastrophe.

There is a religious veneer that covers the American Empire, namely its underlying premise that it is a good and moral nation representing Christian values of benevolence, however paternalistic they may be. Americans are constantly told that their nation's interventions in other countries are for the purpose of bringing "freedom and democracy" to these countries. Many Americans still believe this. They are convinced that they are blessed citizens of a Christian America, God's chosen people, and that this chosenness justifies America's actions around the world. Hence, as the theologian Rosemary Ruether writes, America's imperial crimes ". . . must be cloaked

---

9. Allan Boesak is a South African pastor and liberation theologian best known for his anti-apartheid activism. "With the 1977 publication of his doctoral dissertation, 'Farewell to Innocence: A Socio-Ethical Study of Black Theology and Black Power,' Boesak entered into the pantheon of Liberation Theologians who re-interpreted the principles of Christianity to apply to themes about justice and equality, in the midst of racial-based crises that took root in South Africa and abroad." "Biography of Allan Boesak."

10. Boesak, "Theological Reflections on Empire."

11. Boesak, "Theological Reflections on Empire," 292.

in the language of national values rooted in a belief that America is uniquely innocent and good, chosen by God to defend freedom and democracy around the world."[12]

Walter Herbert likewise makes a case for the American Empire's underlying ideology of religious nationalism and references the teary-eyed singing of what might be called America's national hymn, "America the Beautiful," at the prayer service in the National Cathedral in Washington, DC following the terrorist attacks on September 11, 2001. This singing "invoked the sacred America that was violated on 9/11 and defined the bond of shared belief through which the administration established justification for its war policy in the minds and hearts of the public."[13]

I grew up hearing (though not from my parents, thankfully) that America is a "Christian nation" which is "the greatest nation in the history of the world." Politicians still say the latter all the time. But when I began to live in other countries, I realized that America has no basis whatsoever to claim that it is either Christian or the greatest nation in the world. In every country where I have lived, its citizens love their country. No matter how serious its problems, it is the best country for them because it is their home. If they visit another country, they usually long to come home. They miss their favorite landscapes or seascapes, their families, friends, and communities, their native foods and festivals. Yet they do not call their country the "greatest nation in the history of the world" because, not being part of an empire, they do not have that kind of arrogance. They likewise do not claim that the religion they practice makes their country "the greatest nation in the world."

Religious nationalism is extremely dangerous. Boesak situates the religious underpinnings of the American Empire within the broader history of empires, in particular the Roman Empire. Imperial theology was "the unmissable foundation upon which it [the Roman Empire] rested. Basic to Roman imperial theology was the claim that Rome ruled its empire because the gods willed Rome to rule the world."[14] The Roman Empire, like the American Empire, was erected on the scaffolding of ". . . a religion that identifies and sanctions those who order, rule over and benefit from the empire, and creates and confirms the subordinate roles and compliant responses of those who are ruled."[15]

This imperial religion rests on idolatry—the deification and worship of empire—and it was precisely this heresy which the early Christians

---

12. Ruether, *America, Amerikka*, 1–2.
13. Herbert, "Faith-based War," 6.
14. Carter, *Matthew and Empire*, 20.
15. Carter, *Matthew and Empire*, 20.

> ... could not accept, and that so much of the New Testament so consistently resists. This [the Roman Empire] was the imperial reality in which first the Jesus movement and then the Christian church came into being, lived, worked, and testified... When they call the slaves and people from the lower classes who form the Christian communities a ... holy nation, God's own people (1 Peter 2:9), this is a direct correction of the empire's social-economic stratification and political hierarchy that places the aristocracy at the top and slaves at the bottom.[16]

Christians today are still called to resist the "powers and principalities"[17] associated with the American Empire, just as the first Christians felt compelled to do as they coped with the Roman Empire. As interrelated beings living a *for-life* ethic, we can never worship imperial idols that do not value all creatures and creation but only wish to exploit them. This is a huge challenge for American (or other empire-influenced) Christians today who have been propagandized by imperial lies. But it is a challenge we cannot ignore, for the survival of people and planet depend on our resistance.

ROOTS OF THE AMERICAN EMPIRE IN "AMERICAN EXCEPTIONALISM"

The American imperial narrative is premised on the myth of American superiority over other nations, peoples, and ideologies. This narrative is devoid of empathy for "the least of these"[18] because it is predicated upon the selfishness of powerful, entitled elites who have disdain for the powerless masses. In my exploration of empire, I have learned much from the work of Chris Hedges,[19] in my view one of the greatest social philosophers living today.

---

16. Boesak, "Theological Reflections on Empire," 295.

17. See Eph 6:12: "For our struggle is not against enemies of blood and flesh, but against the rulers, against the authorities, against the powers and principalities of this present darkness..." One of the most prominent theologians whose work critiques the "powers and principalities" is Bill Wylie-Kellermann. See especially his *Principalities in Particular*.

18. This is a reference to Jesus' explicit linkage between love of God and love of those who have been cast aside by the powerful. We recall that in Matt 25:40, Jesus says, "Just as you did it to one of *the least of these* brothers and sisters of mine, you did it to me."

19. Among Chris Hedges' many books, see, for example: *Empire of Illusion*; *America: The Farewell Tour*; *The Greatest Evil is War*; *Wages of Rebellion*; and *The World As It Is*.

In his many books, speeches, essays, and interviews, Hedges dissects the American Empire from an ethical perspective, situating it within the broad historical sweep of empires. He shows how empires always eventually fall because they are constructed on a foundation of insatiable greed. This cannot ultimately be sustained because it requires the rapacious hoarding of resources for the few at the top of the social pyramid, which eventually destroys the social bonds that hold societies together.

As empires begin to collapse under the unbearable weight of the greed of their powerful elites (in the American setting, the military-industrial-media-political complex), their military adventurism goes into overdrive. This has been witnessed time and time again in the history of the rise and fall of empires. They bloat their militaries to enable the theft of the resources of other nations and to maintain some level of popular support through appeals to patriotism, and often ethnocentrism, in the face of manufactured external enemies. Nowhere is this more on display in the world today than in the American Empire, but it has its limits. As the populations of declining empires experience rising levels of deprivation and systemic injustice, inevitably they rise up and resist. Then empires fall apart.

The American Empire is at the cusp of this collapse. Its imperial project has impoverished and sickened American society. For the price of just one of its multi-million-dollar fighter jets or weapons systems, child hunger in the US could be wiped out. If the grotesquely bloated military budget were cut in half, domestic and global poverty could be dramatically alleviated. Climate change could be tackled in a meaningful way. Everyone could have health care. The US pumps trillions of dollars into its military and national security state apparatus and then claims to have no money to provide a national health service, free education at all levels, climate crisis mitigation, prison and policing reform, a just immigration policy, the rebuilding of crumbling infrastructure, affordable housing—and the list goes on. The world's wealthiest nation cannot afford to do these things because it needs to maintain, at all costs, what it calls "American exceptionalism."

What is American exceptionalism? Are we exceptionally compassionate as a nation—to poor people, people of color, immigrants, prisoners, or other peoples around the world? Are we exceptional peacemakers, conflict mediators, and reconcilers? Are we exceptionally generous in sharing our wealth equitably among all people, at home and abroad? Are we exceptional in our welcoming of "others"—refugees, people from non-Eurocentric cultures, people whose political or religious views differ from our imperial myth of greatness?

No, we are exceptional in our violence, our warmongering, our exploitation of peoples and resources at home and across the globe. We are exceptional in our wasteful overuse of fossil fuels, making us the greatest contributor to the climate crisis that is destroying the earth. We are exceptional at bullying, meddling in other nations' affairs and bombing them at will, whenever we want to—international law be damned—or undermining them in more subtle ways through economic sanctions, CIA coups, and subversive agitation for "regime change."

We are exceptional in that we have over 900 military bases outside our borders (in addition to the 450+ bases in the United States), while Russia has 20 (mostly in the former Soviet republics, where it pays rent to maintain these bases), and China has one (a small naval base in Djibouti to protect its shipping).[20] We are exceptional because we spend more on the military than the next thirteen nations combined—we are responsible for nearly 40 percent of the world's total military expenditures.[21] We are exceptional in our willingness to militarily intervene or covertly interfere in other nations with impunity.

To name just some of these victims of our interventionism, we remember with shame Vietnam, Cambodia, Laos, Haiti, Grenada, Brazil, Venezuela, Chile, Bolivia, Honduras, El Salvador, Nicaragua, Guatemala, Cuba, Dominican Republic, Serbia, Bosnia, Ukraine, Iraq, Iran, Afghanistan, Syria, Indonesia, Congo, Somalia, Yemen, Libya, Niger, Ethiopia, Mozambique—among others. There are over a million dead in Iraq alone because of our exceptionalism.

This notion of exceptionalism is built into America's very DNA. It has a long history. It began with the concept of *manifest destiny*, the vision that the vast American continent was an empty land waiting to be filled with white European settlers who would inhabit, exploit, and control it from coast to coast, creating a prosperous *land of the free and home of the brave*. For some, this was a Christian project. They would build a great Christian nation, a *shining city set on a hill*. For others, this was a capitalist project. The elites would fill this land with ever-expanding agricultural and industrial wealth (wealth, that is, for the white male landowner class). They would become ever wealthier and more powerful; their wealth and power would be exceptional.

But for this project of exceptionalism to be successful, it needed a solid foundation to undergird it. Several obstacles needed to be overcome for that to happen. First, there were those inconvenient Native Americans. The

---

20. Herrera and Cicchini, "U.S. Military Bases and Personnel Abroad," 127. It is difficult to find comprehensive information about these foreign bases. The US government admitted to 920 in 2013, but the latest estimates by independent researchers are that, as of 2023, there may be closer to 1,000 US military bases on foreign soil.

21. Herrera and Cicchini, "U.S. Military Bases and Personnel Abroad," 127.

land was not empty after all. There were hundreds of cohesive indigenous nations with rich cultural traditions that had thrived for several thousand years before the white settlers arrived. We needed their land, so we had to annihilate them or push them onto "reservations," on the least productive lands we could find, and leave them there to become mired in poverty and powerlessness. We had to erase them from our consciousness in a project of cultural extermination. They were simply not a part of our exceptional nation, and still today they are completely missing from our public discourse and constructions of national identity.

We also needed a vast powerless, subjugated workforce in order to build our exceptional economic wealth, and that required slaves from Africa. They were less than us—"us" meaning not only our white male leaders who guided our exceptional project but all white people. They were nothing more than commodities in our capitalist economic project, commodities to be exploited. Even after slavery was abolished following the Civil War in the 1860s, their labor was still monopolized, first to continue to build America's agricultural base, which left African American communities in the South impoverished and disempowered through land alienation, sharecropping,[22] and Jim Crow laws.[23] In time, their labor was also needed to prop up America's manufacturing industries, and this necessitated population shifts to the north, where African Americans barely eked out a precarious existence in the ghettos of American cities, earning what came to be called "slave wages."

America's exceptional wealth, in other words, was built on the backs of poor black, brown, and, yes, poor white people. Efforts by workers of all races to come together to form unions were met with aggressive resistance. Especially in the 1930s, in the grip of the Great Depression, there were vibrant movements of socialist activism by workers who rose up against the injustices they were forced to endure—very low pay, long working hours, unsafe working conditions, and a perpetual debt trap through being forced

---

22. Sharecropping was a form of tenant farming set up in the rural South following the abolition of slavery, in which the landowner provided seeds, tools, and access to a plot of land for farming and the tenants contributed their labor and a share of the profits from the sale of their crops, the bulk of which went back to the landowner. This kept the farmers extremely poor and landless. Many former slaves continued to work for their previous owners, who simply shifted to managing their plantations through the work of sharecroppers. The practice of sharecropping soon extended to poor white farmers as well. "Sharecropping."

23. Jim Crow law refers to "any of the laws that enforced racial segregation in the South between the end of Reconstruction in 1877 and the beginning of the civil rights movement in the 1950s. Jim Crow was the name of a minstrel routine ("Jump Jim Crow"), performed beginning in 1828 by its author, Thomas ("Daddy") Rice and by many imitators... The term came to be a derogatory epithet for African Americans and a designation for their segregated life." Urofsky, "Jim Crow Law."

to live in company housing and buy food and supplies from company stores, on credit that could never be fully repaid.

These union movements, strikes, and acts of resistance by American workers resulted in extreme repression by owners, in collusion with police and governments, claimed by some historians to be the most violent repression of workers' movements anywhere in the industrialized world. This repression was so successful that union membership is now only 11 percent of the American workforce, down from its peak of 35 percent in 1954.[24] (It should be noted, however, that in the face of declining living standards and growing income inequality, union efforts are now on the rise again, with hundreds of strikes and union organizing efforts in recent years.)

Our founders saw the need for a legal framework to guide their exceptional nation, and designed a constitution which ostensibly guaranteed individual rights. But we often forget that the designers of this constitution were all white male landowners, some of them slaveowners. There were guaranteed rights for them, but initially not for everyone else. By 1828, white non-landowning males could vote in some states, but it was not until 1860 that all white males could vote. Women did not gain the right to vote until 1920. Enormous obstacles prevented most African Americans from voting until the Voting Rights Act was passed in 1964. Native Americans could only vote if they happened to be living outside of their reservations until the Snyder Act was passed at the end of World War I, granting all Native Americans the right to vote in appreciation for their service in the war.[25] America was built on a restricted notion of democracy.

And so this exceptional nation came into being and commenced its march toward empire. As with countries everywhere, the majority of its inhabitants were people who simply desired to live a life of security, stability, and hope for a better future for their children. But America as a nation, guided by the white male elites who sought to erase the indigenous Americans and who built their empire on the backs of slaves, was a nation whose exceptionalism was engendered and secured through violence, racism, and classism.

AMERICAN EXCEPTIONALISM AND CAPITALISM

The economic form of American exceptionalism was constructed on the basis of the ideology of capitalism. This is an inherently unequal system because it relies on the labor of the many to enhance the profits of the few.

24. "Union Membership of US Workforce."
25. "Right to Vote."

Capitalism cannot coexist with equality, which is why it is incompatible with a *for-life* ethic. It is incompatible with a Christocentric worldview, since Jesus explicitly elevated those who had the least power and status in his society as those especially beloved by God.

Liberation theology calls this Jesus' *preferential option for the poor*.[26] Jesus called us to show special love and care for those whom our societies tell us are expendable. The earliest followers of Jesus, as we have seen in our discussions of the kindom of God, lived a communistic life, not a capitalist life. They shared their worldly goods with each other and with the poor. This *for-life* ethic is the antithesis of capitalism.

Capitalism is also intrinsically unstable, because it is built on the false premise of limitless growth. Profit for the owners of wealth must, in a capitalistic system, increase endlessly. The catch-22 is that there must be customers to buy the goods that are being produced by capitalist enterprises, and yet the only way profits can be maximized is if the wages of workers are kept as low as possible. This leads to capitalism's ultimate downfall, because if workers are kept poor in order to ensure maximum profit for owners, they will not have the means to purchase what they have produced. The more wealth that is concentrated in the hands of owners, the less wealth there is for everyone else, and without consumers, capitalism cannot sustain itself.

Capitalism can best be sustained if a social contract exists between private enterprise and government which restrains capitalism through laws that restrict its overreach to some degree. Such a balance was achieved for a time in the United States through the efforts of President Franklin Delano Roosevelt (FDR) and his New Deal. He was no socialist; he was the quintessential capitalist. However, he became afraid that American capitalism was under threat, given the ravages of the Great Depression in the 1930s and the leftist, socialist, and communist parties and labor movements that were on the rise as a result. Labor unrest and union agitation were growing. Social upheaval was becoming endemic.

And so, in desperation, FDR called his capitalist allies together and told them that if capitalism was to be saved, they would have to make some

---

26. Gustavo Gutierrez was the first liberation theologian to argue for Jesus' "preferential option for the poor," in *A Theology of Liberation* (see my chapter 2). The "preferential option for the poor" refers, in the first instance, to the priority given in Jesus' teachings to those in greatest need, on the margins of society. Liberation theology highlights this focus by calling on Christians today to place the needs of the most vulnerable first. This has been wrongly critiqued by mainstream Eurocentric theology as asserting that God does not love the wealthy. This misses the point that the intent is simply to focus gospel life on those most in need of liberation from oppression. A helpful compendium of scholarship on Jesus' "preferential option for the poor" is Groody, ed., *Option for the Poor in Christian Theology*.

concessions. They would have to pay higher taxes and tolerate unions and a legal minimum wage. Fearing their own demise, they relented. FDR was then able to enact the New Deal and dramatically strengthen America's social safety net. In this project to "save capitalism" (his words), the American people did benefit through the introduction of a 40-hour work week, a minimum wage, a Social Security pension for retirees, unemployment insurance, and massive jobs programs.

This balance worked relatively well for a time. World War II created millions of new jobs to support the war effort. Manufacturing boomed. The US became known as a country that "made things." Growing numbers of the working class, especially those with union contracts, could afford to buy a car and a house. The GI Bill enabled millions of returning World War II veterans to gain a tertiary education. The decade of the 1950s was a time of social stability and relative prosperity. Capitalism seemed to be working.

But this prosperity was short-lived. The mavens of industry and business wanted more. Capitalists always want more. Following the tumultuous social upheavals of the 1960s, by the 1970s the ideology known as *globalization*[27] was on the rise. The owner class was already envisioning a profit bonanza from the technological advances that were making human workers increasingly expendable—robots are much cheaper than humans. But where humans were still required, it made capitalist sense to move factories and businesses overseas, to what were then called Third World countries, where workers could be paid a tiny fraction of what American workers were demanding for their work.

This shift was at the heart of globalization. And thus manufacturing in America began its slow death spiral, and the term "Rust Belt" was born—the former industrial hubs now littered with rusting shuttered factories, like the steel mills in Pennsylvania and Ohio, the derelict car factories in Michigan, and the crumbling textile mills in the South. As a result of globalization and the resulting shift from a manufacturing economy to a service economy,

---

27. Globalization has been defined generally as "the intensification of worldwide social relations which link distant localities in such a way that local happenings are shaped by events occurring many miles away." Giddens, *Consequences of Modernity*, 64. In economic terms, it is "the development of an increasingly integrated global economy marked by free trade, free flow of capital, and the tapping of cheaper foreign labor markets." "Globalization." As one non-Western example, globalization has been linked with "negative impacts experienced by small island states in the Pacific . . . ranging from environmental degradation due to resource extraction by foreign corporations to the pressures exerted on developing nations to accept the 'structural adjustment programs' of international institutions such as the International Monetary Fund and the World Bank in order to receive loans—a trade-off that only further impoverishes nations." Ah Siu-Maliko, *Embodying Aga Tausili*, 136.

American workers' livelihoods declined, while the capitalist owners' profits soared.

The *neoliberalism* that accompanied globalization called for collusion between the capitalist owner class and government based on the assurance of unfettered "free markets," minimal environmental and labor regulations, and maximum extraction of resources from other countries to enhance corporate profits. Here everyone and everything is a commodity to be exploited. This has appeared to work well for the American Empire over recent decades—that is, for its largest financial institutions and corporations, politicians, and oligarchs (the capitalist bosses). Recent decades in America have seen the greatest transfer of wealth from the bottom to the top in human history. The wealth of the top 1 percent has skyrocketed, while the wealth of the 99 percent has stagnated or declined.

Never in our history has there been greater income and wealth inequality. The number of American millionaires and billionaires has increased dramatically in the past few decades, while the standard of living for the majority of Americans has deteriorated. Billionaires like Jeff Bezos, Mark Zuckerberg, Elon Musk, Bill Gates, Warren Buffett, and the tech tycoons of Silicon Valley have become insanely wealthy. They own not two or three homes but six to ten homes, not a couple of luxury cars but dozens of luxury cars, not one yacht but multiple yachts. In a *for-life* ethical worldview which places the highest value on the common good, this is evil. It is unconscionable that anyone should be this wealthy while poverty grows exponentially and unabated.

It is because this dystopian capitalist nightmare is unsustainable that the American Empire is coming apart at the seams. As Chris Hedges puts it, in this late stage of declining empires, the "iconography" of social and political institutions may still remain—elections are still held (albeit severely flawed), and some semblance of law and order and social services are maintained (albeit increasingly dysfunctional). But the social bonds that sustain communities and the nation are hollowed out. There is an undercurrent of national despair, or what Hedges, following the sociologist Emile Durkheim, calls *anomie*, seen in the opioid addiction epidemic, the suicide epidemic, the homelessness epidemic, the decline in life expectancy, especially among working-class men, and the rise of mass shootings, domestic violence, and social unrest.[28]

Despite this stark social reality, the capitalist champions of American exceptionalism continue to cling to the myth of never-ending progress. In its most benign form, this created a society characterized in the past by

---

28. America's state of *anomie* is laid out starkly in Hedges, *America*.

optimism and a "can-do" spirit. Americans came to be known as pragmatic problem-solvers. They came to be known for their positivity and work ethic. In the varied countries in which I have lived, people have generally liked Americans as individuals, seeing them as approachable and friendly. They admire their industriousness. They enjoy American popular culture.

But this is not all that America is. In all of the countries where I have lived outside the United States, the optimistic American "can-do" spirit is virtually the only form of American exceptionalism which people have tended to admire. Most of the non-Americans with whom I have lived have had nothing good to say about America's global imperial projects. They consider America to be a global bully, arrogant, exploitative, heavy-handed, and dismissive of other cultures, especially non-white cultures.

The truth is that the global imperial manifestations of America's notion of its own exceptionalism are held in disdain by much of the world outside of its Western allies. The American Empire has demonstrated that it has no regard for other nations' sovereignty over their own resources or chosen economic and political systems. It believes that it has the right to control other countries all over the globe with impunity. No other nation in recent history has shown anything remotely akin to this level of hubris.

In enacting its imperial project abroad, the United States has broken almost every norm of international law, which mandates that a country has the right only to defend its own soil if attacked or to defend the sovereignty and survival of its allies when requested to do so. It does not have the right to make incursions into other countries simply because it does not like that country's leaders or positions, or because it wishes to lay claim to that country's resources, or because it sees that country as a rival.

America's imperial belief that it has the inherent right to take what it wants and do what it wants around the world can be traced back to its belief in its own *manifest destiny*. There were signs of an international expansion of the American imperial project early on, once America's capitalist successes were established. Examples include colonial projects and occupations in the Philippines (1898–1946), Nicaragua (1912–33), and Cuba (1898–1902), among others. The US continues to have colonial relationships with a number of territories where it has major military bases, such as Puerto Rico, Guam, and Okinawa. We need to understand the American Empire's expansionist ideology.

IMPERIAL EXPANSION THROUGH STEALING OTHERS' RESOURCES

America's early colonial exploits were about gaining control over other countries' resources in order to fuel its capitalist vision of ever-expanding progress. Examples included control over agricultural markets, secured at times through military interventions in support of American corporations like the United Fruit Company. The United Fruit Company's monopolistic and oppressive control of the banana industry in several Central American countries led to those countries, which found themselves in the clutches of this powerful US corporation, being labelled "banana republics."[29] This term is still employed today in a derogatory way to refer to countries deemed incapable of managing their own societies. Minerals and metals were similarly exploited by the US in countries such as Brazil, Venezuela, and the Congo, and there was a concerted grab for oil in the Middle East.

Ah yes, we come to oil. It was the extraction of fossil fuels that powered the Industrial Revolution. Although it was clear early on to scientists, and even to the fossil fuels industry itself, that the burning of fossil fuels released far more carbon and other gases into the atmosphere than could be absorbed in any sustainable way, the extractions continued unabated. Fossil fuels became commodities which the United States felt were theirs by divine right. And thus the US entered into the modern era of *wars for oil*.

America's insatiable greed for oil even became the linchpin of its financial system and the reason the US dollar became the world's most important currency. When it became clear how much oil lies under the sands of Saudi Arabia, a deal was struck. In 1945 the US agreed to protect Saudi Arabia and prop up its military as long as it would sell its oil—to the US and other countries—only in US dollars. This *petro-dollar* became the sole currency for the sale of oil, and the US dollar then became the currency for most international trade transactions. It became the world's *reserve currency*. This propped up the US dollar and strengthened American control over financial markets and global trade.

Many of our recent regime change operations have been linked to the need to preserve our hegemony over oil and currency. All one has to do to understand this is to look closely at our interventions in countries like Iraq, Libya, Iran, Syria, and Venezuela: they all have large oil reserves, and they all have sought at some point to find a way around the stranglehold of the petro-dollar.

---

29. The collusion of the United Fruit Company in the United States' imperial projects in Central America is spelled out in research by Morris, "Blood for Bananas."

Although the US has not recently militarily invaded Iran—though by the time anyone reads this, that may have happened—it has unleashed a devastating economic war against Iran. But this economic war, waged through the imposition of draconian sanctions, does not stem primarily from America's hatred of Iran's form of government (though it wrongly calls it a dictatorship; it has an elected government which defers to its Islamic religious authorities in certain respects). Even if it were a dictatorship, the US has no problem supporting thirty-six (73 percent) of the world's dictators.[30]

The US hates Iran because it claimed sovereignty over its own oil, refusing to let our oil companies control its oil industry, and because it claimed sovereignty over its own way of life. The CIA deposed the elected prime minister of Iran, Mohammad Mosaddegh, in 1953 precisely because he dared to espouse a counter-narrative to that of the American Empire. The US replaced him with the unelected Shah, Reza Pahlavi, who became the most corrupt, brutal ruler in Iran's history, and this ultimately led to the revolution that turned Iran into an Islamic theocracy in 1979.

The same narrative of American imperial expansion is painfully obvious in our relations with Venezuela. Yes, the US decries the fact that Venezuela has chosen a socialist path. But what has most irked the US is that Venezuela chose to nationalize its oil industry in order to use the proceeds to lift its people out of poverty rather than allowing US corporations to control the extraction of its resources and take the profits back to the US.

What the American Empire cannot tolerate, in a nutshell, is a country daring to stand up for itself and slip out of the empire's orbit of control. When this happens, the US has a playbook of revenge which it follows. If it is deemed too costly to wage outright military war, it wages economic war and other covert and overt forms of destabilization. And it always wages a propaganda war. It turns its citizens against the renegade nation by dehumanizing it and by not telling the whole story about the renegade nation. The long-term goal is *regime change*.

EMPIRE'S REGIME CHANGE PLAYBOOK: THE VENEZUELA EXAMPLE

In unraveling the machinations of empire, it is important to enflesh claims and assertions with real-life examples. Examples of the American Empire's heavy-handed expansionism are too numerous to reiterate here, but suffice it to say that its regime change playbook can clearly be discerned in many

---

30. Whitney, "US Provides Military Assistance."

different nations. I am aware of at least eighty-two documented cases[31] of US intervention in other countries from the mid-twentieth century up to 1989, ranging from covert CIA economic and political destabilization to outright coups, assassinations, and wars, hot and cold.

Venezuela is a typical example. As noted above, if Venezuela had not had the world's largest oil reserves, along with gold and other rare metals, the American Empire could perhaps have tolerated its socialist aspirations. It was when Venezuela took control of its own oil industry and reined in the US oil companies that had been given lucrative oil concessions that the US had to enact its imperial regime change playbook. The nationalization of Venezuela's oil industry had actually begun as early as 1976, but it was strengthened following the socialist Bolivarian revolution in 1999.

Venezuela was historically the victim of Spanish colonization, and when it achieved its independence in 1811, it inherited a grotesquely stratified society, with wealthy, lighter-skinned, Spanish-descended business owners controlling and discriminating against the darker-skinned African-descended and indigenous populations. Racism has been the underbelly of the Venezuelan colonial and postcolonial experience. After generations of subjugation of the darker-skinned masses by the ruling elites, a popular revolution occurred in 1999, named after the national hero Simón Bolivar, who had led the country to independence and had a vision of pan-Latin American solidarity.

Hugo Chavez, the leader of the Bolivarian revolution, who was elected as Venezuela's president in 1999 (and rescued by the Venezuelan people from an abortive CIA coup in 2002), was widely disparaged in the US and among the local Venezuelan elites for his indigenous and working-class background. But although most Venezuelans venerate Chavez, the Bolivarian revolution, popularly known as *Chavismo* and its supporters as *Chavistas*, was not about Chavez. It was a revolution for justice which had the broad and ardent support of the vast majority of Venezuela's poor.

The Bolivarian revolution ushered in a form of mixed socialism-capitalism, which allowed the wealthy to largely maintain their wealth while nationalizing certain sectors of the economy, especially the country's natural resources and basic services. It developed a vibrant direct democracy, which has thrived most remarkably at the local level. Venezuelan society was transformed in the Chavez years. GDP rose from US$4,105 in 1999 to $10,801 in 2011. In 1999, 24 percent of the population were living in

---

31. This figure of eighty-two countries that have been on the receiving end of American imperial interventionism has been verified in research by Yoon, "Explaining U.S. Intervention." However, since her research ended in 1989, the number of countries experiencing American interference has grown sharply in the intervening years.

extreme poverty, and this had fallen to 8 percent by 2011. Infant mortality fell from twenty per one thousand live births in 1999 to twelve per one thousand live births in 2011.[32]

Venezuela has held numerous elections since 1999, and every group of international election observers has deemed these elections to be free and fair, including former US President Jimmy Carter's Carter Center, considered by many to be the gold standard in election monitoring. Venezuela under Chavez developed cutting-edge electronic finger-printing technology and other safeguards to ensure that elections are fair. When Chavez died in office in 2013, Nicholas Maduro was elected to serve out his term and has been re-elected several times as Venezuela's president.

In the lead-up to the 2020 legislative election, the government met with opposition parties to urge them to take part in the election. (The CIA had been leading a destabilization campaign for some time, one of whose tactics was to discourage opposition parties from participating in elections, in an effort to delegitimize the electoral process; economic destabilization had already seriously undermined the economy.)

An agreement was reached on multi-party participation in the 2020 election, but just before the public announcement was to be made, the leader of the most right-wing opposition party made a phone call to his American overlords in the US State Department and was told that under no circumstances were they to take part in the election. The US then announced that the upcoming election was a fraud even before it had taken place. Several opposition parties contested this election anyway, won a small minority of seats, and have continued to serve as a loyal opposition.

But even before this election, in 2019 the leader of a very small right-wing party, Juan Guaidó, had proclaimed himself the president of Venezuela following a phone call with Vice President Mike Pence, who promised American support. Most Venezuelans had never heard of Juan Guaidó, and his party had miniscule electoral support, but he had been groomed by the US for his new role. As the investigative journalists Max Blumenthal and Dan Cohen wrote for *Telesur*,

> While Guaidó seemed to have materialized out of nowhere, he was, in fact, the product of more than a decade of assiduous grooming by the US government's elite regime change factories. Alongside a cadre of right-wing student activists, Guaidó was cultivated to undermine Venezuela's socialist-oriented government, destabilize the country, and one day seize power. He was trained at the US Center for Applied Non-Violent Action and

---

32. "Country Profile: Venezuela."

Strategies . . ., funded largely through the National Endowment for Democracy, a CIA cut-out that functions as the US government's main arm of promoting regime change.[33]

The US heralded Guaidó as the "real" president of Venezuela and gave him millions of dollars for his phony administration, even though he had never received a single vote for the presidency or even executed a successful coup. He was the guest of honor at Trump's State of the Union address in 2020, seated next to Melania Trump, and treated to a standing ovation by Congress. Guaidó's supporters were allowed to illegally take over the Venezuelan embassy in Washington, after the legitimate diplomats were shut out. This happened despite the fact that Venezuela had, and continues to have, an internationally recognized government, fully accredited by the United Nations. The assets of the US-based Venezuelan-owned oil company, Citgo, were illegally seized by the US government. Venezuela's gold reserves held in the Bank of England were frozen by America's loyal minion, the United Kingdom. All of these actions were clearly against US and international law.

The US under Obama had inexplicably declared Venezuela a "national security threat," even though it has never attacked or threatened the US in any way, and placed what became the world's most severe sanctions on Venezuela, since outstripped only by those imposed on Iran and Russia. These ongoing sanctions—including denying imports of food, medicine, COVID vaccines, medical equipment, spare parts, etc.—have been responsible for the deaths of over 40,000 Venezuelans,[34] with estimates that this figure is likely much higher.

The CIA has attempted several coups in Venezuela since the Bolivarian revolution, all unsuccessful. The aim of all of the American Empire's regime change operations in Venezuela—economic, political, and military—has been to overthrow the legitimate government of this sovereign nation and install a compliant US puppet state. President Trump's Secretary of State, Mike Pompeo, was up front about the reason for these operations: so that US companies could take charge of Venezuela's oil and precious metals.

None of America's destabilizing efforts, including its painful sanctions, have moved the majority of Venezuela's people to turn against their government and support the American regime change project. The cruelty visited upon them by the US has only made Venezuelans more defiant. Their solidarity and ingenuity have grown, not declined. Even in the face of the devastating sanctions, and the outflow of capital in the hands of the business elites, who have fled to Florida with their wealth since the Bolivarian

---

33. Cohen and Blumenthal, "Making of Juan Guaidó."
34. Weisbrot and Sachs, "Economic Sanctions as Collective Punishment."

revolution, the Venezuelan government has managed, just since 2020, to build 4 million new homes for its poorest citizens and to maintain its CLAP program, which provides monthly boxes of food and hygiene supplies for six million families.[35] Education at all levels and health care remain free for all.

The US government and its acquiescent media have characterized the right-wing opposition's resistance to the Venezuelan government as the valiant struggle of "freedom fighters" to "restore democracy" to Venezuela, ignoring the verifiable fact that Venezuela never lost its democracy. When Guaidó was attempting to turn his US-backed "presidency" into a public groundswell that would enable him to occupy the presidential palace, the US mainstream media dutifully showed up to film the "uprising." They gleefully filmed a Guaidó rally of several thousand opposition supporters and trumpeted it as the beginning of the end for Maduro and the *Chavistas*. What they failed to film were the several hundred thousand *Chavistas* massed in another part of Caracas at the same time.

The point in presenting this narrative in some detail has been to demonstrate how the American Empire's regime change playbook uses every means possible to achieve its goal of domination and control of countries it does not like, or which are friendly with the empire's enemies, or which have resources the empire wants for itself. In the Venezuelan case, this has included secret military interventions, CIA plots and attempted coups, defiance of the rule of law, dismissal of the results of fair elections, crowning an illegitimate lackey as a fake president, and cruel sanctions that have wreaked economic hardships and death upon the population.

This same playbook has been enacted in many other nations. This is systemic evil. It cannot be how a God who is *for life* desires us to relate to other nations. Empires are evil because they rest on the premise of "unequal relationships" in which those whom the empire seeks to exploit or destroy are not valued. A *for-life* ethic, in contrast, is at its heart a rejection of inequality in any relationship, including relationships among nations. The exposition of empire in this chapter leads us, in the following chapter, to the most dangerous and deadly manifestation of empire—conquest through war.

---

35. "Venezuela: 3m New Homes." Since this report in early 2020, another million houses had been built by 2023, and the target of 5 million new houses by 2025 is expected to be met. See Alava, "Army of Women."

11

Pacifism, Just War, and Empire Proxy War

IT IS CLEAR FROM the history of empires that, by definition, their insatiable appetite for power leads to the coercive control of other countries, and this often means outright war. We see this today in gruesome fashion on the blood-drenched steppes of Ukraine. We will come to the war in Ukraine as a case study later in this chapter, but first we need to ask difficult questions: What is a Christian response to war, as those who seek to practice a *for-life* ethic? And how far are we willing to go to love our enemies, as we have been mandated by Jesus to do?

THE CASE FOR PACIFISM

As a Christian who is called to be *for life*, I am compelled to be a pacifist, since war is, by its very nature, *for death*. Pacifism does not mean being passive; it is an activist position that entails acts of civil disobedience and non-violent resistance against systemic violence. It seeks to avoid violence through mediation that moves conflicting parties toward reconciliation. Pacifists see the weapons of war for what they are—agents of death. The theological underpinnings of my own Christian pacifism have been influenced significantly by the Christian ethicists John Howard Yoder and Stanley Hauerwas,[1] but in the current discussion I am drawing largely on the

---

1. See especially Yoder, *Original Revolution* and *The Politics of Jesus*; Hauerwas, *Dispatches from the Front* and *The Peaceable Kingdom*; and Early and Grimsrud, eds., *A Pacifist Way of Knowing*.

insights of David Hoekema.[2] I begin with the New Testament warrant for pacifism.

In the gospels, we consistently see that Jesus calls his followers to a way of life in which violence is overcome by love. We are called not to return evil for evil but to return evil with good (1 Pet 3:9: "Do not repay evil for evil or abuse for abuse but, on the contrary, repay with a blessing"). We are called to love our enemies and those who hate us (Matt 5:44: "Love your enemies and pray for those who persecute you"). If we take Jesus seriously, we must therefore "show love for all in our actions, and seek healing and reconciliation in every situation."[3]

Historical research tells us that the early Christian communities interpreted this radical *love-for-all* commandment of Jesus as "prohibiting the bearing of arms. Christians refused to join the military . . . Those who converted to Christianity while in military service were instructed to refrain from killing, to pray for forgiveness for past acts of violence, and to seek release from their military obligations."[4]

This pacifist stance was undermined in the aftermath of the emperor Constantine's proclamation of Christianity as the state religion of the Roman Empire in the fourth century, after which Christianity came to be incorporated into the framework and fabric of empire. Since empires are militaristic by nature and are often engaged in expansionist wars, pacifism in post-Constantinian Christianity became a diminishing minority position.

Hoekema helpfully summarizes the Christian pacifist response to the major critiques of pacifism. I will highlight four of these. First, there is the Christian pacifist rebuttal of the common critique that *pacifism means surrender* and that "capitulation to forces of evil is not moral." Returning to my claim above that pacifism is not passivism, this critique is incorrect in that it wrongly equates pacifism with non-resistance. As Hoekema reminds us, "The pacifist rejection of war is compatible with a great many active measures for defence against aggression."[5]

In other words, equating pacifism with passivism and capitulation reflects an ignorance of the historic successes which pacifist activism has achieved. One of the best-known examples is the non-violent campaign of Mahatma Gandhi to remove the British Empire, known in India as the Raj, from India following World War II. He did this by galvanizing millions of Indians to engage in sustained acts of non-violent civil disobedience. He

---

2. Hoekema, "Practical Christian Pacifism."
3. Hoekema, "Practical Christian Pacifism," 917.
4. Hoekema, "Practical Christian Pacifism," 918.
5. Hoekema, "Practical Christian Pacifism," 918.

also insisted on engaging in dialogue with the British officials who ruled India. In time, in concert with the massive public acts of resistance, they were won over. India's independence from Britain was the nail in the coffin of the already fading British Empire.

Although Gandhi had an over-optimistic view of the inherent goodness of people which Christians know is not the case (given our awareness of our self-centered "human nature"), his campaign for independence from Britain did demonstrate that pacifist social movements can succeed. Martin Luther King, Jr. attempted to emulate Gandhi's philosophy of non-violence in the American civil rights movement, filtered through a Christian lens. His Christian non-violent activism to reverse systemic racism had a momentous and far-reaching positive impact on American society and American history.

Second, there is the charge by non-pacifists that *pacifism rests on an unrealistic purity*. Pacifists are accused of placing a higher value on their own moral righteousness than on actually saving the lives of people who are being attacked by aggressors. Such purity seems to imply a lack of respect for those who fight in wars. But this is not the case. Pacifism is an objection to war itself, not a self-righteous judgment of soldiers who participate in war, some of whom have, in any event, been conscripted against their will or joined the military as their only means of livelihood. Pacifists refuse to participate in war not because they believe themselves to be morally superior, but because war is immoral in that it is *for death*.

Third, there is the charge that *pacifism confuses moral categories*. The basis of this argument is that pacifists are naïve to believe that the ethical principles we seek to follow in our personal lives can be applied to governments or nations. This critique assumes that because secular states are amoral (or immoral) by definition, we cannot apply the same moral standards to them that we would to individuals. The argument is that "Killing is wrong for individuals, but for states an entirely different standard must be applied."[6]

Christian pacifists respond that the idea that morality applies to individuals but not to societies is antithetical to the teachings of Jesus. Christocentric life in the kindom of God can never be restricted to private morality; Jesus' ethic was a direct challenge to "powers and principalities." Because the Christian faith is interrelational, it encompasses every aspect of life, including governments, nations, empires, and armies. Therefore, as Hoekema affirms,

---

6. Hoekema, "Practical Christian Pacifism," 919.

> There is no room in Christian social thought for excluding governments from the realm of morality. If Christian ethics permits killing in certain circumstances, then violence is legitimate as a last resort, both for individuals and for governments. But if, on the other hand, Jesus did in fact demand that the members of the new Kingdom [read: Kindom] he inaugurated renounce all killing, then we must restructure both our personal and our institutional lives to fulfill that demand.[7]

I would rephrase this rebuttal as follows: Since the gospel mandates that we love our enemies, it is clear that we cannot kill them.

Finally, there is the criticism levelled against pacifists that *pacifism takes too long to be effective*. It requires too much patience and forbearance to bear fruit. Especially in situations where violence has been inflicted on people for a long period of time, non-pacifists argue, they have no choice but to use violence in return. Pacifist activism seems inadequate in the face of such protracted crises. The pacifist rebuttal is that the problem with pacifism "taking too long" occurs not because of an inherent flaw in its non-violent forms of resistance but because there are too few pacifists. Pacifism is not a popular position, certainly in societies infected by an empire narrative.

Nonetheless, pacifists continue to agitate for peace, even when their influence may seem inadequate. And there are examples of non-violent resistance wearing down the powers-that-be. These include Gandhi's India and Martin Luther King's American South, and I would also argue that the sustained non-violent resistance to the war in Vietnam hastened the decision of the US government to end that war.

One argument that is commonly hurled at pacifists is that, without World War II, the Nazis would have controlled all of Europe and the Jewish race would have been obliterated. My response as a pacifist is that if the German Left, including its pacifist elements, had mobilized and not split following World War I, if they had collectively resisted Hitler through massive acts of non-violent civil disobedience in the early 1930s, Nazism would not have taken hold in Germany. If pacifists had begun their non-violent resistance to Nazism much earlier and more vigorously, the genocide and massive destruction of World War II could have been prevented. Hoekema likewise concludes that "Nazism would surely have been destroyed by sustained non-violent resistance had Christians and others not averted their gaze from its evil for so long."[8]

---

7. Hoekema, "Practical Christian Pacifism," 919.

8. Hoekema, "Practical Christian Pacifism," 919. It is important to remember that there was Christian non-violent resistance to Nazism in Germany, through the Confessing Church and its "underground seminary" movement, whose greatest spokesperson

I embrace pacifism not because it is "logical" within the framework of "human nature," with its underlying assumption that conflict, including violent conflict, is inevitable and that this inexorably leads to winners and losers. Within that rationality, a refusal to participate in violent conflict makes no sense, and pacifists are thus fools. However, as the apostle Paul reminds us, Christians must be willing to be "fools for the sake of Christ" (1 Cor 4:10)—misunderstood and even reviled for practicing a *for-life* ethic when the world's natural predisposition is to love self and tribe and hate enemies.

THE CASE FOR "JUST WAR"

Despite my pacifist perspective, I acknowledge that some people of faith support some wars on the basis of *just-war theory*. This is a well-established doctrine that attempts to ensure that a war is morally justifiable based on certain criteria, all of which must be met for a war to be considered just. The criteria are split into two categories: *jus ad bellum* ("the right to go to war") and *jus in bello* ("right conduct in war").

Just-war theory postulates that war, while it is a terrible thing, is sometimes morally justified in order to right a gross injustice being perpetrated against a nation or group of people. Just-war theory does not justify atrocities, targeting of civilians, inhumane treatment of prisoners of war, or an incursion into a country or territory for indefensible reasons. War that is solely for the sake of conquest is not considered a just war. The Geneva Conventions and the United Nations Charter, to which most countries are signatories, provide a legal framework to guide the practice of just war.

Christians who espouse just-war theory, as Hoekema points out, believe that "war is justified, according to just-war criteria, when its good result—the restoration of justice—outweighs the harm it will cause ... Just-war defenders argue that if all means short of violence have failed and organized violence promises to be a limited and effective means of reestablishing justice, Christians may participate in war."[9] This is an argument that "the end justifies the means," but it is an argument that is incompatible with a *for-life* ethic, since the "means" are not *for life*.

In the present age, in which the weapons of war can wreak unimaginable devastation, including nuclear annihilation, and when military activity is the greatest contributor to the climate crisis,[10] even some just-war

---

was the theologian Dietrich Bonhoeffer, killed by the Nazis in the dying days of World War II.

9. Hoekema, "Practical Christian Pacifism," 917.

10. It is now acknowledged by climate scientists that the US military is the single

apologists now concede that "... we do not know how to balance benefits against such costs. The just-war tradition cannot guide us in thinking about such a prospect"[11] (the end of sustainable life due to war). I accept this grim acknowledgement of the realities of war today.

I will nonetheless examine the American Empire's proxy war against Russia in Ukraine on the basis of the principles of just-war theory. Analyzing this war is a daunting task, because of the difficulties outlined earlier regarding knowledge acquisition in an empire setting.[12] Most of the information I will provide has not been reported in the empire-compliant US mainstream media, which has committed both *sins of commission* (telling blatant untruths) and *sins of omission* (ignoring inconvenient truths) in relation to this war.

I have taken the time to dig up the truth about the war in Ukraine because a *for-life* ethic insists on truth and because this war poses the greatest threat to world peace since World War II. What I have uncovered about this war puts me at odds with the views of some of my relatives and friends, but I have persisted because war has terrible consequences, both on and beyond the battlefield, and because we cannot challenge the evil of empire unless we understand what it is doing, and why. The Ukraine war can only accurately be understood in the context of America's imperial aims.

RUSSIA'S VULNERABILITY AND THE AMERICAN EMPIRE AGENDA

In order to begin to understand the war in Ukraine, some historical context is essential—something which has been absent from public discourse about this war in the United States and the West. As the American Empire narrative requires, this war has been framed in simplistic black and white terms as the good US and its European allies (plus Ukraine) versus the bad Russia. As a result, the public has not been informed about the larger contextual backdrop to the war. In order to appreciate the broader context that has shaped the war in Ukraine, it is important to have some awareness of Russia's history and national psyche, something that is completely ignored in

---

largest institutional fossil fuel user in the world, and thus the greatest contributor to CO_2 emissions. See Crawford, *Pentagon, Climate Change, and War.*

11. Hoekema, "Practical Christian Pacifism," 919.

12. Beyond the time and research efforts needed to ferret out the "actual facts" and historical context surrounding this war, there is a personal cost entailed in enduring the labeling and smearing that occurs when one voices a counter-narrative to that of the American Empire. One is labeled a "conspiracy theorist," "Putin puppet," "Russian asset," and "traitor." I stand by the truths I have uncovered and reject such labeling.

the American Empire's insistence only that this hated rival "must be weakened"—or, better yet, succumb to regime change with American help.

Russians have a very long national memory. Russia has been invaded many times and has suffered monumental losses in war. In World War II alone, Russia lost approximately 27 million of its citizens, far outstripping the losses of all the other nations embroiled in that war. That loss, and horrific tragedies during World War II such as the nine-hundred-day siege of Leningrad by the German army, which resulted in the deaths of a million people, remain very fresh in the minds of Russians. Their past history lives in their collective psyche in the present.

Russians have thus inculcated a deep sense of national vulnerability about being attacked by Europe from the west, and they have been attacked at least twice through Ukraine, including in World War II. The brilliant American historian of Russian history, Stephen Cohen, examined Russia's long history of uncertainty regarding whether it is part of Europe or part of Asia.[13] It spans both continents, although most of the country is geographically in Eurasia or the Far East. Russia's rulers were historically a part of an interconnected web of alliances and intermarriages with the royal families of Europe, but at times the Europeans treated Russia like a less sophisticated Slavic "country cousin"—as though Slavs are racially inferior to Europeans. This is ironic, since Russia has a rich repository of culture, fine arts, and literature, stretching back many centuries.

Russia has had a fraught relationship with democracy, with its longest governing tradition being that of the absolute rule of the tsars. The Russian Bolshevik Revolution of 1917 was its greatest historical pushback against that authoritarian past, but its lofty goal of a communist society of equals was ultimately undone by its state totalitarianism under Stalin. Gorbachev's vision of *perestroika* (restructuring) and *glasnost* (openness) in the early 1990s was a serious attempt to re-embrace democratic ideals. Unfortunately, when the Soviet Union collapsed in 1991, although democracy became a reality, chaos ensued, and the American Empire inserted itself into the thick of it, taking advantage of Russia's vulnerability in order to assert America's new role as the world's sole remaining superpower.

We cannot understand US-Russia relations today without acknowledging America's imperial interference in the internal affairs of Russia after the fall of the USSR. As Stephen Cohen describes this debacle, the American Empire's response to the collapse of the Soviet Union was nothing less than

---

13. See, for example, Cohen, *American Perceptions and Soviet Realities*; and *Rethinking the Soviet Experience*.

"missionary" in nature[14]—a crusade to transform post-communist Russia into a junior replica of the American capitalist system, which the US could then exploit for its own ends.

As soon as Bill Clinton assumed the presidency in 1993, his administration formulated an imperialist policy of "American tutelage" in Russia, which included unabashed support for the alcoholic, bumbling, but malleable President Boris Yeltsin. American "advisors" and business tycoons spread across Russia in the 1990s like invading locusts. Zbigniew Brzezinski, Clinton's national security adviser, described Russia as "passing into de facto American receivership."[15] That is classic imperialist rhetoric.

Life for Russians during this period was catastrophic. While it was a "get-rich-quick" time for the new Russian oligarchs and their American investor friends, poverty and unemployment surged, inflation soared, and communities were overwhelmed as the social safety net of the Soviet era was stripped away in the process of capitalist privatization. Between 1990 and 1994 alone, life expectancy for Russian men and women fell from sixty-four and seventy-four years respectively to fifty-eight and seventy-one years.[16]

There was direct US meddling in Russia's elections in this period. Just before the 1996 election, Russia was given a huge US-backed International Monetary Fund (IMF) loan that, as the *New York Times* reported, was "expected to be helpful to President Boris Yeltsin in the presidential election."[17] In his presidential campaigns, Yeltsin relied on US political strategists, including a former aide to Bill Clinton. When Yeltsin won the 1996 election, the cover of *Time Magazine* read, "Yanks to the Rescue: The Secret Story of How American Advisors Helped Yeltsin Win."[18] (The American Empire was proud of *this* election interference.)

Without the chaos of the US-backed Yeltsin era, when newly rich oligarchs and their American counterparts ran amok, Vladimir Putin would likely not have come to power. Yeltsin urged his US allies to back Putin as his successor because he was smart, level-headed, deemed best able to pull Russia out of its crisis, and—most importantly for the US—open to the West. The American Empire was all on board and embraced Putin's ascendancy. However, as Russia regained its footing under Putin's leadership and

---

14. This is laid out brilliantly in Cohen, *Failed Crusade*, and *Soviet Fates and Lost Alternatives*.

15. Brzezinski, "Cold War and its Aftermath," 41; see also his *Grand Chessboard*, chapter 4.

16. Notzon et al., "Causes of Declining Life Expectancy in Russia," 794.

17. Gordon, "Russia and IMF Agree on a Loan."

18. This appeared on the *Time Magazine* cover of its July 15, 1996 issue.

emerged as a strong, independent nation in its own right, the US began to see Russia and Putin himself as a threat.

Of course, America's characterization of Russia today as an imperial rival makes little sense, because Russia is not an empire and has shown no signs of wanting to be an empire that asserts its control all around the globe, as the American Empire does. It was never a global colonizer. The Soviet Union did aid liberation movements such as the anti-apartheid struggle in South Africa, but it never attempted to "take over" the countries involved in these struggles. It intervened militarily in Afghanistan in 1979 in support of its communist government, which was fighting extremist Muslim insurgents, but it regretted this move and left in defeat, hastening the end of the USSR.

Russia today is also not an imperial rival because it does not have the military and economic might of the United States. At the same time, it *is* a nation of significance. It is rich in natural resources such as grain, oil, natural gas, and precious metals. Under Putin, Russia's economy has recovered from the economic disaster of the Yeltsin years. In the ten years from 1999 to 2008, "Russian GDP grew by 94% and per capita GDP doubled."[19] Russia's poverty rate, which soared after the collapse of the USSR, is now lower than most European Union nations. Objective economists point out that, in many respects, Russia has a healthier and more resilient economy than the US because it produces commodities which its people need, while the US has become largely a service and financial instruments economy, rather than a manufacturing economy.

In short, although Russia is not an imperial rival, the US has badly misjudged its internal strength. US and NATO sanctions against Russia in the context of the war in Ukraine have thus backfired, depriving the West of the valuable things Russia produces while Russia has found alternative markets outside the West and reinforced its self-sustaining capacities and reserves. In this process, it has strengthened its relationships with many countries in the growing global *fair world order* movement for multipolarity—the distribution of power among many diverse nations.[20] This assessment is not to

19. Aris and Tkachev, "20 Years of Russia's Economy under Putin."

20. The most significant development in this movement away from the American Empire's unipolar dominance has been the growth and influence of BRICS (now BRICS+), the economic cooperation bloc started by Brazil, Russia, India, China, and South Africa which is rapidly expanding, with new countries signing on and a long queue of nations applying to join. BRICS+ is moving toward developing its own commodities-backed currency and already trades in member states' currencies, bypassing the US dollar. Russia plays a pivotal role in BRICS+, as well as in Eurasian alliances and cooperation initiatives with China. These developments are the biggest economic threat to the US Empire in its history.

paint Russia in glowing terms, or to downplay its internal imperfections (the corruption of the Yeltsin years has not yet been eradicated, for example), but only to state verifiable facts about Russian life, as a counterbalance to US propaganda and false portrayals of this country.

RUSSIA-UKRAINE TIES AND THE NAZI PROBLEM

We cannot understand the present conflict in Ukraine unless we appreciate the long and deep relationship between the two peoples directly engaged in this war. Russia and Ukraine have a shared history going back more than one thousand years. Their roots can both be traced to the first East Slavic state, Kievan Rus, which stretched from the Baltic Sea to the Black Sea and flourished from the ninth century to the thirteenth century CE.

Kievan Rus was established by Vikings who invaded in the ninth century, conquered the indigenous Slavic tribes, and established a kingdom whose capital was Kiev. The kingdom converted to Orthodox Christianity in 988 A.D., laying the foundations for the Russian Orthodox Church. In the thirteenth century, Kievan Rus was defeated by invading Mongols, the capital was moved north to Moscow, and the country came to be known as Russia. In the ensuing centuries, competing European powers sought to carve up the territory that is now Ukraine, but by the early eighteenth century it was once again firmly a part of Russia, which stretched all the way to Siberia in the Far East.

Following World War I, Ukrainian territory was first invaded by Poland and subsequently fought over by local forces loyal either to the deposed tsar or to Russia's new Bolshevik government, which came to power after the 1918 revolution. By the time Ukraine was fully re-incorporated into the expanded and renamed Soviet Union (USSR) in 1922, its economy was in ruins and its population starving due to a crippling drought. Over 25 percent of Ukraine's population were ethnic Russians (close Slavic cousins of ethnic Ukrainians), largely based in the eastern part of Ukraine. This demographic—Russian-Ukrainians concentrated in the east—helps to explain why the sense of Ukrainian nationalism was never as deep in the east as in the western part of the country.

World War II exacerbated the divide between eastern and western Ukraine. When the German army invaded Ukraine in 1941, many Ukrainians in the western part of the country welcomed them, and tens of thousands fought alongside them. Ukrainian Nazi collaborators became known as even more brutal than the German Nazis. They were so ruthless, in fact, in the ferocity with which they murdered Jews, Poles, and Romani that some German SS officers ordered them to moderate what they were doing. One of the few things I knew about Ukraine prior to the 2014 coup was that the most feared and cruel guards in the Nazi concentration camps were often Ukrainians.

I also knew about the infamous massacre of Jews at Babi Yar, but I was not aware of the role of Ukrainian Nazi collaborators in this defining moment of the early stages of the Nazis' Jewish genocide. On September 26, 1941, the day the Germans occupied Kiev, all Jews were ordered to assemble the following Monday at a Jewish cemetery. That morning over 33,000 Jews gathered—mostly women, children, and the elderly, as the men had been mobilized for the war effort. These thousands of unsuspecting Jews were marched under the guard of German Nazis and Ukrainian collaborators to Babi Yar, a scenic area on the outskirts of Kiev. Over the next thirty-six hours, 33,371 Jews were murdered and dumped into the ravines of Babi Yar. Over the next two years, until the Russians liberated Ukraine from the Germans in 1943, a further 70,000 Jews and Romani were murdered at Babi Yar, many by Ukrainian Nazi collaborators.[21]

These Nazi collaborators were led by Stefan Bandera, who in 2010 was posthumously awarded Ukraine's highest honor, "Hero of Ukraine." Bandera was the leader of the terrorist branch of the Organization of Ukrainian Nationalists before becoming a Nazi collaborator. By working with the Nazis, Bandera hoped to eventually sever Ukraine from the Soviet Union and establish his own Nazi state. Bandera held firmly to the Nazi belief that the Jews were an inferior race which must be annihilated. In a pamphlet he wrote for Ukrainian Jews, he said, "We will lay your heads at Hitler's feet."[22] With Bandera's help, over 1.5 million Ukrainian Jews were murdered.

It cannot be overstated that *Bandera is the national hero of Ukraine today*, still revered by many in western Ukraine. The present-day Nazis in the military, police, intelligence services, and government often refer to themselves as Banderites. Bandera features prominently in street names, statues, and huge posters in public squares throughout western Ukraine. In an interview on an American mainstream television network in early 2022 with one of President Zelensky's top deputies, a large portrait of Bandera can be seen on the wall behind him. In a piece by the reporter Richard Engel for NBC News in the lead-up to the war, in which a Ukrainian grandma is being taught how to use a machine gun, the soldier instructing the grandma clearly sports a swastika on his uniform. These American media reports did not mention the obvious Nazi affiliations.

---

21. Freel, "Ukrainian Role Admitted in 1941 Babi Yar Massacre."
22. Knaggs, "Ukraine Parliament Quotes Nazi Collaborator."

I have not yet been able to gain a deep historical understanding of why there has been such a continuing strain of Nazi sentiment among Ukrainians in the western part of the country. I know that there has been strong ethno-nationalism among western Ukrainians who look down on Russians as racially inferior, despite the fact that Ukrainians and Russians have shared Slavic roots. Other than this troubling aberration in the Ukrainian psyche, by all accounts Ukrainians generally have had the reputation of being an easy-going, warm-hearted people. Many western Ukrainians have, in the past, been flexible regarding their allegiance to the East (Russia) or the West (Europe).

However, sadly there remains a dark stain on the historical social fabric of Ukraine, in the form of its Nazi ideologues, who participated in the genocide of Jews in World War II in the most brutal fashion. Given the depths of Russia's suffering at the hands of Nazis in World War II, it finds this Nazi influence in Ukraine, which today is directed against Russians, intolerable.

UKRAINE IN THE USSR AND AFTER ITS DISSOLUTION

Ukraine had an enormous influence on Russian political and cultural life over many centuries. In addition to Kiev being Russia's first capital and Ukraine being the birthplace of the Russian Orthodox Church, key leaders of the Soviet Union were Ukrainians: Nikita Khrushchev and Leonid Brezhnev led the Soviet Union for almost thirty years. Mikhail Gorbachev, the last president of the Soviet Union (1985 to 1991), was profoundly consequential in that he oversaw the break-up of the Soviet Union. Ukrainians have always been an indispensable part of the social and cultural fabric of Russia.

At the same time, following the dissolution of the Soviet Union in 1991, Ukraine was sometimes regarded as the former Soviet republic most likely to pivot toward stronger ties with Europe, since the majority of the population in the western part of the country were oriented toward Europe because of their Russophobia. Official government pronouncements from Kiev began to state that Ukraine was a "European" rather than a "Eurasian" country.[23]

But by the end of the 1990s, the Ukrainian economy was in tatters, and social and political upheaval had undermined its hoped-for transformation into a European-styled state. In addition, it faced several challenges that strained its relations with Russia. One was Russia's request that it disarm

23. "Independent Ukraine."

the Soviet Union's stockpile of nuclear weapons on Ukrainian soil. Then there was the issue of the status of the Crimean peninsula, which had been arbitrarily placed under the jurisdiction of the Ukrainian Soviet republic by Khrushchev in the 1950s, even though it is overwhelmingly Russian and has been a part of Russia for most of its history.

Post-independence Ukraine was also plagued by severe social crises. Crime, including organized crime, increased dramatically, and Ukraine became heavily involved in the illegal drug trade and the trafficking of Ukrainian women for the international sex trade. Millions of people fell into poverty, and life expectancy plummeted. Politicians and governments were mired in corruption, criminality, and cronyism. A few oligarchs became extremely wealthy, and gained greater and greater control over Ukraine's political and economic life. Ukraine joined the ranks of the world's most corrupt nations.

Ukraine's ethnic Russian population found itself in a very difficult predicament in the post-independence period. Although they constituted only around a quarter of the population, they had held a "psychological majority" in Soviet-era Ukraine.[24] In independent Ukraine, however, their rights were progressively eroded. They were shocked when the Russian language was removed as one of the official languages of Ukraine, even though most Ukrainians speak Russian as well as the very similar Ukrainian language. But much worse was to befall them.

After years of political intrigue, scandals, attempted overthrows, imprisonment of politicians, and growing unrest, early in 2010 Victor Yanokovych was elected as Ukraine's president. He had the support of the Russian-Ukrainian population and Ukrainians more open to peaceful relations with Russia, while his rivals were linked to the right-wing nationalists and Nazis in the western part of the country, who wanted stronger ties with Europe.

Yanokovych's government soon agreed to extend Russia's lease of the port of Sevastopol in Crimea, and in return Ukraine received a reduction in the price of Russian natural gas. The Ukrainian government further improved relations with Russia in June of 2010, when it officially abandoned the goal of joining NATO. These moves infuriated the US and NATO, and precipitated a growing political crisis within Ukraine—along with an American Empire plot for regime change.

---

24. Tuminez, "Nationalism, Ethnic Pressures," 91.

THE 2014 MAIDAN COUP AND ITS AFTERMATH

The forces in Ukraine which sought closer ties with Europe and the suppression of the country's Russian minority were outraged when, in November 2013, a planned "association agreement" with the European Union was rejected by Yanokovych just days before it was scheduled to be signed. This accord would have created closer political and economic ties between the EU and Ukraine, but when Yanokovych read the fine print he saw that it included an IMF loan that would have imposed harsh austerity measures on the country, leading to worsening poverty.[25] Meanwhile, Russia offered an agreement which guaranteed much more favorable economic arrangements, and Yanokovych opted to accept this pact, or at least to try to blend the two proposals.

Street protests erupted in Kiev, in which it initially appeared that students who wanted to pivot to Europe were prominent. Police attempted to disperse the protesters in Kiev's Maidan ("Independence Square"), but the protests continued and the demonstrators occupied Kiev's city hall and demanded that Yanukovych resign. What soon became obvious was that the protesters were not only infiltrated but led by far-right Nazi groups, most notably the Azov Battalion, along with smaller Nazi militias such as the Right Sector and the Aidar Battalion. They were supported and funded not only by Ukrainian oligarchs but by the US, through the CIA, which was directly involved in the escalation of violence. This was a classic American Empire regime change operation.

On February 20, 2014, the violence escalated dramatically, with some police firing on crowds of rioting protesters. However, there is also clear evidence that the Nazi forces had snipers firing from buildings above the square, as out-of-control violence suited their purposes.[26] More than twenty were killed and hundreds injured, and the EU and US placed sanctions on the Yanokovych government, even though much of the violence was perpetrated by the Nazi groups.

A tentative deal was brokered by the EU between Yanokovych and the opposition which called for early elections and an interim unity government, terms which Yanokovych accepted. However, the Nazi elements who were by now the real power brokers rejected the deal, threatened Yanokovych's life, and forced him to flee the country. This was now a successful CIA-backed coup.

25. "Ukraine Suspends Talks on EU Trade Pact."

26. See the research by Katchanovski, "Snipers' Massacre on the Maidan," and "Far Right in Ukraine."

An audio recording surfaced from this time of the Russia-hating Victoria Newland, a key player in Ukraine policy in the Obama administration. She was also a deputy Secretary of State in the Biden administration until her March 2024 resignation, and one of the masterminds behind the present conflict. In this phone call, Newland discussed with the US ambassador to Ukraine who should be Ukraine's new post-coup president and who should be in his cabinet.[27]

Following the coup, Ukraine took a decidedly dark turn. Nazi groups like the Azov Battalion were incorporated into the Ukrainian military, even though they were known for torturing or killing anyone with whom they disagreed. Their tactics have been compared to those of the ISIS terrorist group. The Azov Battalion had previously been designated by the US as one of the top three extremist organizations in the world, but in response to the Ukraine-Russia conflict it has since been removed from that list altogether, even though it is more extremist than ever.

In addition to being brought into the military, Nazi groups also found their way into the national police, intelligence services, parliament, the media, and other organs of government. Subsequently, Russian-language schools were closed. Russian-language radio and television stations and print media were shut down. Russian Orthodox churches were confiscated, even though they had been cherished centers of worship in Ukraine for over a thousand years. Political parties affiliated with the Russian minority were banned.

In March 2014, a referendum was held in Crimea in which 97 percent of the population voted to rejoin Russia.[28] As noted earlier, the Crimean Peninsula had long been a part of Russia but had arbitrarily been placed within the USSR's Ukrainian territory in the 1950s. Experiencing first-hand Ukraine's growing persecution of ethnic Russians, the citizens of Crimea concluded that their only way to ensure a secure future lay with Russia. Their referendum was deemed free and fair by election observers, but Ukraine, the US, and its European allies were furious and vowed revenge.

Following the loss of Crimea, later in 2014 the Azov Battalion and other Nazi militias in the Ukrainian military, along with regular Ukrainian military units, began what would be an eight-year war against the Russian territories in eastern Ukraine, known collectively as the Donbas. After their rights were severely eroded by the virulently anti-Russian post-coup government, these peoples had also held referenda, which confirmed by huge majorities their choice to be independent republics—the People's Republics of Donetsk and Luhansk.

27. "Ukraine Crisis: Leaked Phone Call."
28. "Official Results."

Between 2014 and early 2022, the Ukrainian military assault killed more than 15,000 people in the Donetsk and Luhansk regions, tortured or killed many of those captured as prisoners of war, and the citizens of Donetsk and Luhansk endured almost daily shelling of their homes, schools, day care centers, businesses, open air marketplaces, town squares, factories, hospitals, and clinics. As their suffering worsened during this eight-year war, the two breakaway republics in the Donbas pleaded with Russia to come to their aid.

However, Russia refrained from even formally recognizing the two republics, much less intervening militarily, because it had signed the Minsk Accords and was waiting for them to be implemented. Between September 2014 and February 2015, Russia, Ukraine, France, and Germany had signed the Minsk 1 and Minsk 2 agreements, which mandated that Ukrainian hostilities against the citizens of the Donbas cease, and that Ukraine recognize Donetsk and Luhansk as autonomous regions and withdraw its military forces and weapons. The then German chancellor Angela Merkel admitted in late 2022 that Ukraine and the EU signatories to the Minsk Accords had no intention of implementing them; they signed them only to stall for time so that Ukraine could build up its military forces with the help of NATO.[29]

It is tragic that Ukraine never implemented the Minsk Accords it had signed and that the fighting continued, with tens of thousands of Ukrainian troops bombarding the Donbas day in and day out. Its eight-year offensive ruined the Donbas economy, forced millions of people to flee their homes and become internally displaced, and turned the conflict zone into one of the world's most heavily mined areas. By late 2021, Ukraine had built up its forces at the front to approximately 100,000 soldiers, heavily armed and trained by the US and NATO, and it had become clear that they were preparing for a massive invasion of the Donbas to vanquish the Russian population once and for all.

THE NATO PROBLEM

The North Atlantic Treaty Organization (NATO), established after World War II to defend Europe against a hypothetical Soviet Union attack, is a military force led by and in the service of the American Empire. Its member states are vassals of the United States. Viewing it as an alliance of sovereign nations obscures the fact that it is a tool of US imperial foreign policy in

---

29. Schwarz, "Former German Chancellor Merkel Admits."

its stated quest for world domination, or what the US calls *full spectrum dominance*.[30]

Regrettably, when NATO no longer had the Soviet Union to defend against after the USSR dissolved in 1991, it became offensive in nature, defying its charter. NATO member nations must integrate their militaries under US command in any conflict and offer up their citizens as troops for America's wars. NATO relentlessly bombed Belgrade, Serbia, in 1999 for seventy-eight straight days. It fought alongside the US in its wars in Iraq, Afghanistan, Libya, and Syria. It has even attempted to establish NATO proxies in countries like Colombia in South America. In short, NATO is an arm of the American Empire and its foreign policy, far exceeding its original defensive mandate.

After the collapse of the Soviet Union and the end of the first Cold War, instead of NATO disbanding as it should have, the opposite occurred. There was no "peace dividend," as the world was promised, and no honoring of the West's pledge to Russia that NATO would not expand. US Secretary of State James Baker's famous promise, in a meeting with Russian President Gorbachev on February 9, 1990, that NATO would "not expand one inch eastward"[31] was at the heart of security guarantees given by Western leaders to Gorbachev and other Russian leaders in the early 1990s. Such pledges were given to reassure Russia after it agreed not to stand in the way of Germany's reunification and the dismantling of the Soviet republics. These promises have been verified in documents recently declassified by the US National Security Archive.

But Russia's trust was betrayed. Instead of honoring the promises made to Russia by the US and its NATO allies, NATO stampeded east toward the borders of Russia, adding fourteen new member states. America's decision in 2006 to eventually bring Ukraine into NATO posed an existential threat to Russia, as this would mean a hostile, Nazi-infiltrated, NATO-armed country at its doorstep. By December 2021, as the American professor of international relations at the University of Chicago, John Mearsheimer, has pointed out, a heavily NATO-armed Ukraine had become a de facto member of NATO, crossing a red line for Russia.[32]

---

30. Originally, *full spectrum dominance* was a military term which described military control over all aspects of an enemy territory—land, air, water, psychological, etc. During the George W. Bush presidency, under the influence of so-called "neo-cons" like Dick Cheney, John Bolton, and Paul Wolfowitz, it came to mean global dominance by the US Empire. For a scholarly analysis of the origins and implications of this concept, see Ryan, *Full Spectrum Dominance*.

31. "NATO Expansion: What Gorbachev Heard."

32. Mearsheimer, "Causes and Consequences of the Ukraine War," 24.

On this basis, Professor Mearsheimer concluded, in a speech in June 2022, that "the US bears primary responsibility for what is happening today in Ukraine."[33] Throughout NATO's eastward expansion, a number of American military experts and diplomats had warned that this expansion was unwarranted, dangerous, and unfair to Russia and that the inclusion of Ukraine in NATO would be the final straw that would lead to war. Russia could not be expected to tolerate NATO weapons systems, possibly including nuclear warheads, on its border with a bellicose Ukraine whose corrupt government hated Russia and its own Russian citizens.

Despite these warnings, the US continued to expand its own military bases surrounding Russia and to push for military expansion in NATO countries close to and bordering Russia. (One can imagine how Americans would feel if Mexico were dotted with dozens of Russian military bases adjacent to the US border, armed with heavy weaponry.) The American Empire chose this path because it has the hubris to demand Russia's undoing so that it can no longer be seen as a threat to American imperial hegemony. Ukrainians are nothing but pawns in this extremely dangerous and heartless imperial project.

In the weeks and months leading up to Russia's incursion into Ukraine on February 24, 2022, Russia made serious attempts to avoid war. On December 17, 2021, it circulated to the US and NATO governments an important document which spelled out a proposed revamped security framework for Russia and the NATO countries.[34] It called for NATO not to expand to Ukraine or other former Soviet republics bordering Russia, such as Georgia, and to remove heavy offensive weapons systems in NATO countries bordering Russia.

This document decried the fact that the US and NATO had violated their obligations enshrined in the principle of *indivisibility of security* agreed to by the Organization for Security and Cooperation in Europe (OSCE),[35] to which Russia is a signatory. As Russia's security proposal pointed out, the OSCE's foundational principles, which all NATO states and Russia have pledged to uphold, include the equality of all signatories, which means that *the security of one nation cannot be strengthened at the expense of another*. NATO's eastward expansion and militarization up to Russia's borders have clearly come at the expense of Russia's security and thus violate the OSCE's indivisibility of security principle.

---

33. Professor Mearsheimer made this comment in a speech given at the University of Chicago, "Why is Ukraine the West's Fault?"
34. "Russia's Security Guarantees Proposal."
35. de Brichambaut, "Indivisibility of Euro-Atlantic Security."

Disastrously, the US and NATO refused to engage with Russia on this important December 2021 security proposal, the implementation of which would have prevented the war in Ukraine and brought stability to the region. The US was particularly dismissive, in effect tossing this serious proposal into the rubbish bin without a glance. Russia was facing its worst existential crisis since World War II, being surrounded by hostile NATO countries with their vast build-up of weapons and military forces, and with the Ukrainian army poised for a full-scale invasion of the Donbas with a force of 100,000 soldiers. Russia continued to attempt to find a diplomatic solution, but the US and NATO would not engage in any dialogue, and Ukraine, entirely under the thumb of the American Empire, was coached at every turn to fight Russia militarily rather than make any concessions to safeguard the rights of its Russian population.

THE REAL UKRAINE TODAY

Initially, in the early days of the Ukraine-Russia conflict which started in late February 2022, it appeared that Ukrainian President Zelensky was open to negotiations with Russia, and he sent a negotiating team to meet with Russian counterparts in Istanbul, Turkey, in March. A tentative agreement was reached in early April that would have ended the war almost as soon as it had started, but the US and UK warned Zelensky not to implement it but to follow a military path only, backed by US and NATO money, weapons, and advisors. It is not clear how sincere Zelensky may have been in these negotiations but, in any event, he is a mere puppet of the American Empire and thus not a free agent. Making this statement calls for background and context.

Ukraine is a nation riddled with the corruption of wealthy oligarchs who have operated in collusion with the United States, largely through the CIA. Perhaps none has had more influence on the Zelensky government than Igor Kolomoisky, one of the chief kingpins behind the disastrous state of affairs that is today's Ukraine. Kolomoisky has been one of the richest oligarchs in Ukraine. He has (or had until the war with Russia concealed access to information) majority or outright ownership of major television and other media outlets, the film industry, banks, and other business enterprises, most importantly the largest private natural gas company in Ukraine, Burisma.

Burisma, of course, is the company where President Biden's son Hunter received an astronomical monthly pay-out (variously reported as $40,000, $50,000, or even $80,000) to sit on its board of directors, beginning in 2014 after the coup. Hunter Biden was lured into this position by Kolomoisky in order to secure access to then Vice President Joe Biden, whom President Obama had designated as his point person on Ukraine. The e-mails discovered in Hunter Biden's infamous laptop reveal the extent of his corrupt dealings with Ukrainian oligarchs, especially Kolomoisky.[36]

Kolomoisky has always been rabidly anti-Russian, and he personally funded and was instrumental in organizing the Nazi Azov Battalion, despite the fact that, like Zelensky, he is himself Jewish (Russians replaced Jews as the Ukrainian Nazis' target). He also craved political power for himself. After the Maidan coup in 2014, he was rewarded for his financial and organizational support for the coup by being made governor of one of Ukraine's regions or *oblasts*. He soon became the most influential power broker in Ukraine's government.

In this role, Kolomoisky was nothing if not clever. He wanted someone he could control in the president's office and came up with a brilliant plan to make that happen. In 2015, as a 70 percent owner of Ukraine's largest television corporation, Media Group, he developed a TV comedy series called *Servant of the People* and recruited a comedian named Volodymyr Zelensky to play the leading role of the president in this series. He spent millions of dollars promoting the series, artificially manufacturing its popularity. A few years later, he created a political party with the same name, Servant of the People, and recruited Zelensky as its presidential candidate.

When Zelensky won the presidential election in 2019, it was in part because, during his campaign, he spoke of being the president of peace, bringing unity between east and west and ending Ukraine's war against the people of the Donbas. However, this was mere campaign rhetoric to get himself elected. It was not the playbook he was obligated to follow once he was in office. Kolomoisky and other oligarchs were the puppet masters, pulling the strings on behalf of Nazi organizations and American backers. But although Zelensky was only a puppet, he did very well for himself. He was suddenly a millionaire. He owns multiple properties around the world and was outed in the Pandora Papers as being involved in numerous illegal international financial schemes.[37]

---

36. See Morris and Fonrouge, "Smoking-Gun Emails." This information was found in the laptop which Hunter Biden abandoned at a computer repair shop at the height of his cocaine addiction. The e-mails provide critical information about his influence peddling with corrupt Ukrainian oligarchs, with serious implications for his father. Yet the Biden election campaign, US mainstream media, and social media companies dismissed the laptop revelations as "Russian disinformation," even though the *Post* provided ample evidence of their veracity. The *New York Times* and the *Washington Post* finally grudgingly admitted in March 2022 that the e-mails and other information in the laptop are authentic and in no way connected to Russia.

37. Loginova, "Pandora Papers Reveal Offshore Holdings."

Zelensky has been in way over his head as Ukraine's president during this terrible time. Not only does he have no political experience; he is unable to stand up to the dark forces which hold the actual power in his country. Yet one of the most unbelievable aspects of the propaganda that took hold of the American mainstream media after Russia's entry into the war in 2022 has been the adulation of Zelensky. Until the war began going badly in 2023 and Zelensky's public behavior became increasingly unpalatable, he was idolized like a movie star (which, granted, he used to be). He was portrayed as America's Great New Hero, a present-day Winston Churchill. His speeches to Western parliaments and the US Congress were greeted with fawning standing ovations. There was no interest in the media in uncovering who he really is.

Based on the research I have been able to gather, Zelensky can be summed up as a second-rate comic actor, with past experience in porn films, who is self-absorbed, corrupt, and perhaps mentally unstable. He has continued to rake in millions during the war and to enjoy an opulent lifestyle. He has appeared increasingly unhinged as the war has gone very badly for Ukraine, killing an estimated half a million Ukrainian soldiers, and has continued to cling to his magical thinking that Ukraine can actually defeat the larger, better equipped, better trained Russian military.

This is the manufactured hero of the American Empire whose compliant media convinced the majority of Americans to adore as an exemplar of freedom and courage. As I write this, Ukraine has, for all intents and purposes, lost the war, its economy is shattered, and it is in no sense a democracy. Zelensky has banned all political parties but his own; Ukraine has no press freedom; it allows no dissent; it has a "kill list" targeting journalists and others who speak the truth about or question the war; and there is internal political intrigue, with rumors of coups and internal power struggles.

Once the war began going disastrously for Ukraine, the US commenced efforts to push Zelensky to establish some kind of off-ramp (a Korea-style armistice or "freeze"). However, the Russians would be unlikely to trust any such overture, since the agreement tentatively reached between Ukraine and Russia in Istanbul in the early weeks of the conflict, which would have ended the war and saved hundreds of thousands of lives, was sabotaged by the US. The US and NATO have proven themselves, time and time again, to be utterly untrustworthy in their dealings with Russia.

This is the monstrous situation the American Empire has created in its obsession with weakening Russia. Empire has no heart; it is *for death* by its very nature. And this war, which the American Empire planned and urged into being since 2014, is *for death* in the extreme. America's Machiavellian involvement does not let Russia off the hook for the death and destruction it has caused. But it is also important to expose the role of the American Empire in this catastrophe. As *for-life* Christians, we cannot countenance this nightmare of *for-death* evil.

JUS AD BELLUM AND THE UKRAINE-NATO-US WAR WITH RUSSIA

We recall that the first category of just-war theory is *jus ad bellum*, which calls for a morally justifiable reason to go to war. Here war can be justified if its purpose is to right a "gross injustice" being perpetrated against a nation or group of people. Let me reiterate that, as a pacifist who is *for life*, I cannot morally justify the war between Russia and Ukraine/NATO/US solely on the basis that it is a war, which is inherently *for death*. It has caused the destruction of human life, livelihoods, communities, and the environment. The loved ones of those killed on both sides will never get their loved ones back.

That being said, if one analyzes this war in terms of just-war theory's *jus ad bellum* doctrine, it is possible to make a case that the current iteration of the war in Ukraine (since Russia's entry in February 2022) can at least partially be justified on the part of Russia. Given the historical and geopolitical context and the machinations of the US empire I have laid out, it is clear that Russia and the Russian population in Ukraine have in fact faced an existential threat to their security which has constituted a "gross injustice."

It is thus preposterous for the American Empire to claim that Russia's armed incursion into eastern Ukraine in February 2022 was "unprovoked." From a pacifist perspective, Russia should have found ways to protect its security, and that of the Russian population in Ukraine, other than war. However, it is undeniable that it has been seriously "provoked" since at least 2014, and arguably since the 1990s. When NATO expanded eastward country by country, placing scores of military bases and heavy weaponry at Russia's doorstep, it provocatively threatened Russia's security. When it made Ukraine a de facto NATO nation, armed it to the teeth, and supported its eight-year war against the people of the Donbas, it crossed a red line which many experts had warned would be a provocation that Russia could justifiably resist.

If Ukraine's army and Nazi militias had been allowed to mount their planned full-scale attack on the Donbas as they were poised to do in early 2022, several US military experts have conceded that this would have been the reverse equivalent of the 1962 Cuban Missile Crisis, when the USSR installed missiles capable of carrying nuclear warheads in Cuba, ninety miles from Miami. At that time, the US was widely thought to be justified in threatening the USSR with war and blockading Cuba's waters. The US considered the USSR's missiles in Cuba an existential threat to its security, just as Russia considered Ukraine's US/NATO-backed military build-up on its border an existential threat to its security, not to mention the security of its Russian brothers and sisters in eastern Ukraine.

Given all of these factors, a *jus ad bellum* analysis would conclude that Russia can claim justification for attempting to right the "gross injustice" perpetrated against its Russian compatriots in eastern Ukraine. Its legal justification for its "special military operation" in Ukraine (a designation carefully chosen to avoid the legal consequences of a full-scale declaration of war) was based on Article 51 of the United Nations Charter. Article 51 states that a country has the legal right to engage in military action in an act of defense of its own or its allies' territory, including pre-emptive military action in the face of a threat of imminent attack.[38]

Under this framework, however, once the stated objectives of Russia's "special military operation" have been achieved—liberating Russian areas which have suffered under Ukrainian attacks and repression since 2014 and whose citizens do not wish to be part of Ukraine and voted overwhelmingly in 2022 to rejoin Russia—Russia's military campaign would have no further legal warrant under just-war theory. A full-scale invasion and occupation of the entire country of Ukraine is not justified under Article 51.

The legal justification for Russia's current "special military operation" also takes into account the fact that Ukraine's war against the Russian population in Donbas had *already been taking place for eight years* prior to Russia's intervention in early 2022. Since this war was started by Ukraine in 2014, Ukraine has legally been the aggressor, and Russia is therefore the defender of the Russian population. I heard several interviews with people in the Donbas in early 2022 who described Russia's intervention as "ending our eight-year war." This was a war that was replete with many Ukrainian atrocities, atrocities condemned even by the OSCE, a pro-NATO organization.

I will make only a brief comment on the other aspect of just-war theory, *jus in bello*—right conduct in war. This doctrine asserts that in a just war, the combatants may not target civilians or commit torture against enemies, including prisoners of war. There have been charges of war crimes on both sides of this conflict, but as a pacifist I would argue that war itself is a crime against humanity. All of the soldiers who constitute the opposing armies are wrongly killed or wounded. It is warring nations' *leaders* who order soldiers to go into battle and to kill as many of the enemy as possible.

---

38. United Nations Charter, Article 51.

The "fog of war" makes it almost impossible to definitively determine at this point whether war crimes as defined under the Geneva Conventions have been committed in Ukraine. Independent investigators have debunked a number of such claims against the Russian military and exposed war crimes by the Ukrainian military, but neutral investigations need to be carried out after the war. The Red Cross and other observers have reported that the Russian military treats its prisoners of war well, in accordance with the Geneva Conventions, but that the same cannot be said for the Ukrainian military, which has been filmed torturing and executing Russian prisoners of war. But beyond the treatment of war prisoners, I am still left with the underlying question, How can there be "right conduct" when war consists of destroying life?

A PACIFIST RESPONSE

I return now to a Christian pacifist response to this war, the only *for-life* position I am able to embrace. It is difficult to have a clear notion of what a pacifist response might consist of in this terrible situation in Ukraine now that war has already wreaked havoc on the country and on innocent Ukrainians and Russians alike. By the time war has broken out, pacifists have few options other than acts of civil disobedience to try to persuade warring countries to change course.

Perhaps pacifists should be non-violently disrupting activities through "sit-ins" at the American weapons manufacturers that profit from the weapons that have been sent to Ukraine to enable this war, corporations like Raytheon, Lockheed Martin, RTX, Northrop Grumman, and Boeing, who together made nearly US$200 billion in profit in 2022.[39] Politicians who have supported this imperial proxy war should also be protested, with the same intensity as that seen in the growing numbers of citizens who are presently protesting Israel's war against Palestinians.

Pacifist activism is, again, most effective when it is designed to *prevent* conflict from becoming outright war. It should have been more visible, more vocal, and more fervent in the months leading up to the Russian entrance into the war in Ukraine in 2022 and indeed during the eight years, beginning in 2014, in which the Ukrainian military was attacking the Donbas with US/NATO-supplied weapons. Public acts of non-violent resistance to stop US support for this war are certainly still urgently needed. Lawmakers who have supported the war should be publicly challenged, and this is in

---

39. Echols, "America's Top Five Weapons Contractors."

fact occurring at some of their campaign stops and town halls during the 2024 election season.

In short, Christian pacifists need not only to participate in but to take a leading role in bold non-violent action to stop this nightmare—boycotts, challenging politicians, pressure campaigns, and joining in sustained public acts of civil disobedience. As part of this commitment, Russian and Ukrainian leaders must be urged relentlessly to sit together, face to face, around a table of peace, listening to and speaking to one another as fellow human beings and searching together for a *for-life* way forward.

My fervent prayer is also that Ukrainian citizens will tire of their country being destroyed and of being lackeys of the American Empire. They will tire of being an expendable pawn in the American Empire's imperial designs against Russia. Resistance is already taking place in a growing number of Ukrainian cities, led by mothers of dead, missing, and mistreated[40] soldiers and by those resisting further mobilization for military service.

Justice is most enduring when it arises from below, as the powerful have a very limited vision of justice, even in the best of times. And so my hope is that the Ukrainian people, along with peace-loving allies from around the world, will find a non-violent way to insist on a path to peace between their country and Russia, beginning with changing the Ukrainian government. All peace-loving *for-life* people everywhere should support such resistance in every way possible, and Christian pacifists should take the lead in living out this commitment.

A SAD SUMMARY

To summarize my portrayal of the war in Ukraine as a consequence of the *for-death* American imperial project to weaken its Russian enemy, buttressed by decades of American and European betrayals of Russia's trust, several tragic conclusions can be drawn:

---

40. There is growing anger among Ukrainians, especially mothers of soldiers, that their family members in the army are kept on the front lines indefinitely and not allowed periods of rest and recuperation (this happens because so many soldiers have been killed that there are few left to replace fighters at the front). There is also anger that men in their sixties, the disabled, women—even pregnant women—and very young men are being conscripted and sent to the front with almost no training. I have seen videos of these citizens being grabbed on the street or dragged from cars and buses and shoved into vans by military recruiters. Increasing numbers of soldiers are themselves complaining openly about their neglect and ill treatment, some of whom are refusing to fight, surrendering, fleeing, or defecting to Russia.

- If the American Empire had not been bent on subduing any country it perceives as a threat to its hegemonic power, there would have been no war in Ukraine.
- If the American Empire had moved to dissolve NATO when the USSR collapsed and NATO was no longer needed, there would have been no war in Ukraine.
- If the American Empire had followed the advice of its military experts and diplomats who argued that NATO should not expand eastward, and that Ukraine should never be admitted to NATO as that threatened Russia's legitimate security concerns, there would have been no war in Ukraine.
- If the American Empire had not enabled the Maidan coup in 2014 that installed a rabidly Russia-hating, Nazi-permeated government, there would have been no war in Ukraine.
- If the American Empire had pushed Ukraine to implement the Minsk Accords it had signed, there would have been no war in Ukraine.
- If the American Empire, in the lead-up to the phase of the war that began in February of 2022, had said to Ukraine, "do everything in your power to find a diplomatic solution," rather than "make no concessions whatsoever," there would have been no war in Ukraine.
- If the American Empire had not sabotaged the peace agreement forged between Ukraine and Russia in Istanbul in early April 2022, the war in Ukraine would have been short-lived.
- If the American Empire and its subservient NATO allies had not flooded Ukraine with hundreds of billions of dollars and weapons, there would have been no war in Ukraine.

But because America is an empire, however much it is fraying at the seams, these moral "if" possibilities never arise in the minds of those who wield imperial power. Empire is incapable of being *for life for all* because it is premised on a belief in "unequal relationships" among nations. The lives of those dying on the battlefield, and of their shattered loved ones, simply do not matter to the American warmongers pulling the strings of power in their imperial wars or to the military leaders who send their citizens into battle. This is the hard and heartbreaking lesson of empire. My faith leads me to say "no" to this war and to all wars, because killing can never be *for life*, and empire can never be anything other than evil.

12

Father Abraham Was a Colonizer (and the Road Leads to Gaza)

SOME READERS MAY RECALL the popular Sunday school children's song, "Father Abraham."[1] This song evidently migrated around the world because the children in the churches I pastored in Jamaica sang this song, and my children also sang it growing up on the Pacific Theological College campus in Fiji. In the song, we hear that we are all Father Abraham's sons. Leaving aside the obvious problem that Father Abraham's daughters are missing from this tale, and that little girls in churches all over the world have had to identify themselves as "sons" while singing the song, this song has another theological problem. The reason it can claim that we are all Father Abraham's sons is because, as Christians, we have been adopted into the Abrahamic religious family. We are therefore all heirs of a fundamentally colonialist story led by Father Abraham.

I was very troubled as a teenager attempting to read the Bible from cover to cover, when I came across the gruesome stories in the Old Testament of the Israelites' conquest of the promised land. There I read about the Israelites conquering this or that people by obliterating every man, woman, and child, destroying everyone and all their animals. Since I knew instinctively that God is always *for life*, I wondered, "How could God condone and even command such acts?" I could not answer that question, and this story

---

1. Some sources assert that this song is of unknown origin and therefore in the public domain, while others claim it was written by the Dutch songwriter Pierre Kartner around 1970. To avoid any potential copyright issues, I have chosen not to quote the song's lyrics.

of conquest created a jarring contradiction with my understanding of God as the God of love, justice, and mercy for all.

These biblical atrocities took place in the land of Canaan, situated in what we would today call the southern Levant, which includes present-day Israel, the West Bank and Gaza, Jordan, and southern portions of Syria and Lebanon. It was inhabited not just by the Canaanite tribe, descendants of the son of Ham, Noah's grandson, but by numerous other people-groups. Over time, a variety of Semitic tribes had filled the land of Canaan, including Amorites, Girgashites, Hittites, Hivites, Jebusites, Perrizites, and others.

Among these many people-groups who lived in Canaan were the Amalekites. I heard this name uttered recently by Benjamin Netanyahu, the prime minister of Israel, who referred to the Palestinians as Amalekites and vowed that they would suffer the same fate as the biblical Amalekites. When I looked them up, I found this verse in 1 Sam 15:3, where God speaks through his prophet Samuel: "Now go and attack Amalek and utterly destroy all that they [the Amalekites] have; do not spare them, but kill both man and woman, child and infant, ox and sheep, camel and donkey." There could not be a more glaring depiction of genocide.

ABRAHAM THE COLONIZER

I have been fortunate to learn much from the Pacific Islander theologians who are at the forefront of the focus on decolonization in theology. Two Old Testament scholars in particular have taken the Abrahamic bull by the horns, so to speak, and their conclusions are powerfully relevant for what is happening today in Israel-Palestine. In my reflection, I will draw on recent work by the Samoan Afereti Uili and the Tongan Jione Havea. I begin with a provocative piece by Afereti Uili, "Abraham and the 'Curse' of James Cook."[2] Uili begins by asserting that

> Abraham, like James Cook [the explorer who initiated the colonizing project of the British in the Pacific Islands], is a representative figure of a religion that was part of a colonising culture... While the story of Abraham is a colonising narrative from the perspective of the Canaanites, the Hittites and the Amorites (Gen 12, 13), the narratives of both Abraham and James Cook can also be understood as a curse from the perspective of the colonised peoples of Oceania.[3]

---

2. Uili, "Abraham and the 'Curse' of James Cook."
3. Uili, "Abraham and the 'Curse' of James Cook," 18.

He then goes on to flesh out this claim with the following declaration:

> The Bible's claim that Canaan was Abraham's promised land is a claim based on a belief that Abraham's god had sovereign authority over and rights to the land of Canaan and, by extension, the whole earth. It did not matter that the land was already inhabited. What mattered for the writers of the biblical narrative was that the god of Abraham could promise land already inhabited by others to whomever that god wished.[4]

With Uili's bold assertions in mind, we need to take a fresh look at Father Abraham. After all, Abraham is considered the religious "founding father" for Jews, Muslims, and Christians who were adopted into the Abrahamic tradition. It is therefore imperative that we know who our presumed spiritual father really was.

Abraham was a foreigner in relation to Canaan, hailing originally from a place called Ur in southern Mesopotamia, populated by a branch of the people-group known as Terah. At some point, he and his extended family migrated from Ur north to Haran in Syria. However, after some time Abraham and his wife Sarai, along with his nephew Lot, suddenly left Haran and began travelling south toward Canaan. Genesis 12:1–3 tells us why Abraham left, as Uili explains:

> He was commanded by God to do so. God's command in vs 1 is not a timid or a hesitant call. The double imperative of the Hebrew (*lek leka*) signals a very strong and direct command for Abraham to 'leave' and to 'go forth' from his land, his family and his father's house, to the land God would show him. . . According to God, Abraham will find a new land yet to be revealed to him. In so doing, he will become a great nation.[5]

When Abraham first sets off, he may be thought of as an explorer, leaving for an unknown land. It is when he arrives in Canaan that God tells him, "To your offspring I will give this land" (Gen 12:7). He then becomes a colonizer.

What is strikingly clear is that this unfolding story is *not* the story of the people who were living in Canaan when Abraham arrived. It is the story of an incoming chosen people, who would become the Israelites, not the story of those whom they had to conquer in order to occupy their land—the un-chosen. Uili compares God's gift of Canaan to Abraham and his chosen people to the Doctrine of Discovery that guided the great European

---

4. Uili, "Abraham and the 'Curse' of James Cook," 18.
5. Uili, "Abraham and the 'Curse' of James Cook," 21.

colonizing projects around the world, with its appeal to the *divine bestowal of land*, whereby God gave the colonizers divine licence to conquer and settle in the lands of the un-chosen.

Uili points out the difference in wording when describing Abraham and his family's initial detour to Egypt because of a crippling drought, versus their eventual arrival in Canaan. Their time in Egypt is described as a "sojourn"—a temporary stay—while their arrival in Canaan is to their home.[6] Abraham is now a "settler" in Canaan (Gen 13:12). This is the beginning of what we today call *settler colonialism*. Uili makes several telling points about this state of affairs:

> The promises given to Abraham seem to assume that this was a land with no people, an empty land, although the narrative clearly mentions their presence. Was Abraham supposed to simply ignore them? The first time God mentions the people of the land is in chapter 15, when the promise of the possession of land is reiterated and more pronounced. This time around, not only is the promised land enlarged (15:18), but a whole host of people of the land are now identified by God. But as far as the story goes, this presence of the people of the land in the 'promised land' did not appear to be any concern of God at all. Even now that God has mentioned them, there is no instruction or advice from God on how Abraham should behave in relation to them.[7]

In Gen 15:18–20, God does enumerate a number of indigenous peoplegroups residing in Canaan, but only in passing: "On that day the Lord made a covenant with Abram, saying, 'To your descendants I give this land, from the river of Egypt to the great river, the River Euphrates, the land of the Kenites, the Kenizzites, the Kadmonites, the Hittites, the Perizzites, the Rephaim, the Amorites, the Canaanites, the Girgashites, and the Jebusites.'" This was at least an acknowledgment that the promised land was no "empty land," unlike the claim made by the early Zionists who began their own settler colonialism project in twentieth-century Palestine.

The fact that God is aware of the presence of indigenous peoples dwelling in the land and yet appears totally disinterested in them runs counter to everything we affirm about God being lovingly woven into the very fabric of all peoples and all creation. Uili concludes that "Their mention [the indigenous inhabitants of Canaan] by God is merely to give notice of their

---

6. Uili, "Abraham and the 'Curse' of James Cook," 22.
7. Uili, "Abraham and the 'Curse' of James Cook," 24.

eventual displacement by Abraham and his seed."[8] This is an exclusivist God, who only seems to care about the welfare of one small group of people, Abraham's people, who are to receive the blessing of their own land regardless of the fact that this necessitates their takeover of the land as conquerors and colonizers.

Uili's study of Gen 12–13 leads him to draw the following conclusions:[9]

- Abraham's right to possession of the land of Canaan is "based on a divine imperative." The God of Abraham has the authority to "give land to anyone anywhere."

- Although not only Abraham and his descendants but "all the families of the earth" are ostensibly to be blessed through Abraham's possession of the promised land, he only has minimal interactions with the peoples whom he dispossesses.

- There is some intermarriage and inevitable encounters with those who are not wiped out, yet "With all the wealth Abraham had during times of famine, he never once shared any of it with his neighbours, the people of the land he is taking over as his possession." Uili compares this to "the self-satisfying nature of colonisation and its hunger for wealth."

- In other words, God "never seems to consider in his plans for Abraham the welfare of the people of the land who will be displaced." Relating this to the imperial mindset of dismissal of the colonized peoples of the Pacific Islands, Uili recalls the present-day plight of the West Papuans and the people of New Caledonia (Kanaky) and French Polynesia (Maohi Nui), with implications for other colonized island groups in Pasifika.

It is beyond sobering to confront the awful reality that our founder Abraham was, in the ancient Israelites' faith story which became a part of sacred Scripture, anointed by God to receive as his divine inheritance a promised land through the conquest and dispossession of the indigenous peoples who called that land home.

---

8. Uili, "Abraham and the 'Curse' of James Cook," 25.

9. The quotations in the following bullet points are found in Uili, "Abraham and the 'Curse' of James Cook," 27.

IN THE BIBLICAL COVENANTS, THE CHOSEN ALWAYS WIN

The Tongan Old Testament scholar Jione Havea explores the problem of "chosen-ness" in the biblical covenants (Noahide, Abrahamic, Mosaic, Davidic), in "Covenant: Chosen, Cover, Contest."[10] He argues that "A covenant favours *the chosen one* and consequently disfavours the unchosen others... The favoured and their supporters do not (care to) see (value in) those who are disfavoured as a consequence of the covenant."[11]

At the same time, as we saw in Uili's study, the biblical narratives do at times mention the un-chosen—the conquered and colonized indigenous peoples whom even God names as being "in the land" of Canaan when Abraham arrived. Although they have no voice, Havea suggests that the fact that they are "registered" (named) "invites readers to say and do something about their place as disfavoured subjects in the covenant events. Do they deserve being disfavoured? Is the covenant fair and just? For whom?"[12]

In his discussion of the Abrahamic covenant with God, Havea chooses to dissect the story of a human covenant within the larger covenant between God and Abraham regarding the promised land—namely, the covenant between Abraham and Abimelech described in Gen 21:22–34. This was "a covenant between a king of the indigenous people of the land (Abimelech) and an alien who has been covenanted by God (Abraham)... From the outset, Abraham is favoured."[13] Without going into this rather convoluted story, suffice it to say that Abraham cheated Abimelech twice. As Havea puts it, "Abraham caused the trouble, then he mediated for the lifting of the trouble, for which Abimelech rewarded Abraham, who consequently, to borrow a contemporary image, 'laughed all the way to the bank.'"[14]

The point in Havea's retelling of this story is that readers of the biblical narratives of covenant are always predisposed to favor those whom God has chosen. In the story of Abraham and Abimelech, readers of the biblical account automatically favor Abraham because he was God's representative in his covenant with the chosen people. Havea does not mince words as he makes this point clear:

> This narrative favors Abraham, but the narrative is also clear that he is a cheat and an alien to the storied land, and the covenant

---

10. See Havea, "Covenant."
11. Havea, "Covenant," 34.
12. Havea, "Covenant," 34.
13. Havea, "Covenant," 35.
14. Havea, "Covenant," 35.

> covers up his cheats. The covenant event conditions readers . . . to sympathise with Abraham. In the covenant between Abimelech and Abraham in Gen 21, Abimelech is cheated but readers do not see it as such—the eyes of readers are covered—because Abraham is the favoured subject . . . In this way, the covenant functions as a mechanism for covering up for the elected and for control over the dis-elected.[15]

Because God's covenants always favor the chosen, the faithful inheritors of the covenants (we who read Scripture) are likewise expected to favor those whom God has chosen. The un-chosen are peripheral to or absent from our concern. This has been the pattern of colonial projects throughout history. Those whose lands are confiscated and resettled by colonizers are inconsequential. Theirs is not a story worth telling.

My response to the biblical narratives of conquest and settler colonialism sanctioned by covenants with God is that these are human stories, told by the winners of those conquests. They are human portrayals of a God of a chosen people, narrated and eventually written down by those same chosen people. Despite the conviction of biblical literalists that God somehow magically wrote every word of Scripture, dictating to the scribes who copied these words perfectly onto scrolls, the Bible is the story of and by a people struggling through their faith journey.

This is of course not a monolithic story. There are other strands beyond the one we are examining here. The Old Testament is not simply a story of divine blessing for the chosen people in their promised land. There was always a push-pull between the Israelites' special status as a chosen people and the perils and pitfalls which that status engendered. This ambiguity explains why the prophets emerged: to chastise the Israelites for their injustices perpetrated against the weak. It is why there are many psalms and stories of lament in Hebrew Scripture. It is why the eventual period of the monarchy led to the defeat of the northern and southern kingdoms and the forced exile of the people of Israel, first to Assyria and then to Babylon.

Every group of people tells the story it wants to hear and sometimes also confesses and ponders its failures. Some Old Testament scholars believe that the emergence of what we call the Old Testament in written form, in roughly the "books" we have today, actually occurred fairly late, as the result of the destruction of the monarchy and the soul-crushing experience of exile. The people of Israel wanted to remind themselves that they had been elected as God's chosen people over all other peoples of the earth. They wanted to believe that the promised land was their sacred inheritance, given

---

15. Havea, "Covenant," 35.

to them by God regardless of the destruction this caused for the land's inhabitants. But this story of chosen-ness is theologically dangerous, because the chosen in the biblical story believed that they had to invalidate those whom they named as un-chosen, and so they told themselves that it was God who was behind the un-choosing.

That is our human story, the story we create because of our "human nature." But it is not the story of the God who is *for life*. It is not a narrative that acknowledges the interrelational divine presence that permeates the very being of every creature and place. The story which peoples throughout history have told themselves about being divinely chosen and favored has led to a history of our planet marked by innumerable narratives of conquest and colonization. This leads us to what is occurring today in what was once the ancient land of Canaan. The Palestinians today are indeed the Amalekites of the Old Testament, as Prime Minister Netanyahu has dismissively and cruelly proclaimed.

FATHER ABRAHAM TAKES US TO PALESTINE

It is a sign of the times that I find it necessary to bring the biblical narratives described above into the present situation in Palestine and Israel only by first making a strong disclaimer that I am not in any way anti-Semitic. The arbiters of the American Empire—its politicians, national security state apparatchiks, and media stenographers—along with America's strongest ally, Israel, routinely label anyone who speaks out for the rights of the occupied Palestinian people "anti-Semitic." This even includes Jewish people who stand up for the Palestinian cause (such as the organization Jewish Voice for Peace, which has organized some of the most effective protests in the US against Israel's war on Palestine), as anachronistic as it is to refer to Jews as anti-Semitic.

I have long admired Jewish literature, arts, and intellectual life, and treasured my Jewish friends, and I have, in genuine empathy and horror, soaked up everything I could possibly learn about the Nazi Holocaust against the European Jews. I supported Israel's desire to have a homeland following the Holocaust. I agreed with many others that the extreme trauma of the Holocaust meant that the survivors should have a place to live in which they could feel safe.

At the same time, I knew that something had gone terribly awry in the process of the European Jewish twentieth-century occupation of Palestine and its declaration in 1948 that it was now the nation-state of Israel. I knew that, despite the "empty land" claims by early Zionists, whose goal was to establish Israel as a Jewish state, the land of Palestine which they came to occupy was anything but empty. Like the same ancient land of Canaan when Abraham arrived, there were people living there. I knew, without knowing anything like the full story, that something fundamental needed to change to enable European Jewish settlers and Palestinians to live side by side as the closely related Semitic cousins they are.

As an adult, I began to come to grips with what was really going on in Palestine-Israel, its tragic modern history, and the ways in which a line can be traced from the twisted theology of divine "chosen-ness" that allowed the ancient Israelites to claim the land of Canaan as their exclusive promised land. What we see today in Israel and Palestine is a direct legacy of the sense of entitlement that accompanies the assumption of chosen-ness. As we saw in the story of Abraham's covenant with God, being a chosen people has historically meant the conquest, occupation, and at times obliteration of the un-chosen. The un-chosen cease to exist as equals living together in a kindom in which all are God's family. This became the mindset of the Zionists who created the State of Israel at the expense of the Palestinians whose home it was, and who now call Palestinians "human animals" and "Amalekites" worthy of destruction.

Palestine, the Jewish Diaspora, and Zionism

Drawing on the work of several Jewish[16] and Palestinian[17] intellectuals, I will attempt in this section to provide succinct answers to the questions "Who are the Palestinians?" and "Who are the Zionists?" The ethnic origins of the Palestinian people can be traced to the same Semitic[18] peoples who have lived in this land—a good portion of the original ancient land of Canaan—for millennia and whom we encounter in Scripture. Over time, Palestine came under the influence not only of external empires but other neighboring Semitic groups, especially Arabs.

Religiously, after the growth of Islam following the Arab Muslim conquest of the Levant in 638 CE, Palestine came to be a diverse community

---

16. These include Ilan Pappé, Miko Peled, Gideon Levy, Norman Finkelstein, Max Blumenthal, and others.

17. These include Ali Abunimah, Rashid Khalidi, Mustafa Barghouthi, and others, and Palestinian Christian theologians like Naim Ateek.

18. Ancient *Semitic peoples* included Arabs, Akkadians, Canaanites (and the varied tribes that inhabited ancient Canaan), Hebrews, some Ethiopians (the Amhara and the Tigrayans), and Aramaeans. For this reason, it is incorrect to label those who have a racist hatred of Jews "anti-Semitic," for that would mean they hated all Semitic peoples. See "Semites."

of Muslims, Jews, and Christians. Palestine was of course the birthplace of Christianity. Most people in the West believe that all Palestinians today are Muslims, but there is still a Palestinian Christian minority, descendants of the earliest Christians, who are devoted champions of Palestinian liberation and have produced their own distinctive liberation theology.[19]

Zionism, the ideology of the *rebirth of the Jewish nation*,[20] was initiated by European Jews in the nineteenth century who sought to reestablish Jewish sovereignty in the original promised land. Most of its leaders were secular Jews who used the theology of the promised land and the chosen people to entice diasporic Jews to return but whose own goals were more political than religious.

Zionism cannot be understood without an appreciation of the phenomenon of the Jewish diaspora, since Zionism has also been called a *rejection of diaspora life*.[21] The reasons for the growth of the vast Jewish diaspora over many centuries, perhaps the most widespread outward migration in history, are varied. A complex set of factors predisposed Jews to begin migrating from their historic promised land, which had come to be known as Palestine. They were already widely dispersed as early as the first century CE, from Greece to Egypt, to various outposts of the Roman Empire. The reasons seem to range from a search for greater economic security to a desire to escape domination by the various empires which made their presence felt in Palestine. I will highlight a few key turning points in this history.

Following the Arab Muslim conquest of Palestine and the wider Levant in the seventh century, there was an increase in Arab migration into Palestine, leading to intermarriage between indigenous Palestinians and Arabs (fellow Semites) and the growth of the Muslim population. By the eleventh century, the percentage of Jews in Palestine had declined substantially due to a combination of the rising Muslim population and Jewish migration. The Jewish population further decreased following the killing of both Jews and Muslims during the brutal Christian Crusades in the medieval period. The Muslim influence in Palestine increased further after the Turkik Ottoman Empire spread through the Levant in the sixteenth century. Although Jews

---

19. Essential reading today for anyone interested in Palestine should be the work of the Palestinian liberation theologian Naim Ateek, especially his *A Palestinian Theology of Liberation*, and *A Palestinian Christian Cry for Reconciliation*. Ateek is the founder of the Sabeel Ecumenical Liberation Theology Center in Jerusalem, which connects Christian theology with grassroots activism. For more recent developments in Palestinian theology, see Munayer and Munayer, *Decolonising Palestinian Liberation Theology*.

20. Stemhell, *Founding Myths of Israel*, especially 3–36.

21. Schweid, "Rejection of the Diaspora in Zionist Thought," 133ff.

could freely worship and engage in commerce under the Ottoman Empire, they were heavily taxed, leading to yet another surge in outward migration.

But already by the Middle Ages, the combination of external domination and the quest for a more prosperous life had led to a significant dispersion of Jews from Palestine to Europe (and also to Russia). Many of them flourished in Europe, often as merchants and traders, and made significant contributions to European life. Although they tended to settle in their own Jewish enclaves, there was some intermarriage with European populations, and today Jews with European backgrounds have an average of 30 percent European ancestry.[22]

This has meant that most of the Jews who migrated back to Palestine in the modern era have been distinctly European, both ethnically (seen in the fact that they are lighter-skinned and have more European features than the remnant of indigenous Jews in Palestine) and culturally. Former Prime Minister Ehud Barak famously declared that European Jews returning to Palestine had created "a villa in the jungle."[23] The Zionist settler colonialism in Palestine has thus been colonialism with a European flavor, creating an added layer of resentment among Palestinians and in the broader Middle East.[24] The Jewish settlers' cultural identity is seen as European, not Middle Eastern.

Zionism had been a growing force among European Jews since the late nineteenth century, and by the early twentieth century it had gained significant momentum. The year 1917 was a turning point. The British Empire had engaged in military operations in Palestine during World War I in its campaign to overthrow the Ottoman Empire, under whose umbrella Palestine still existed.[25] In order to gain Jewish support for this war effort, the British *Balfour Declaration* promised the Zionists that they could have a Jewish national home in Palestine. The Balfour Declaration was not a sign of the British Empire's ideological support for Zionism but a calculated move in the chess game which was the imperial design for the entire Middle East.[26]

22. Wade, "New Light on the Origins of Ashkenazi."

23. This phrase originated with former prime minister Ehud Barak, in a 1996 speech in which he said, "We [Israelis] live in a modern and prosperous villa in the middle of the jungle." Berman, "After Walling Itself In." The phrase became popularized by other Israeli leaders as a way of distinguishing the European Jews of Israel from the Semitic/Arab cultures of the Middle East.

24. Just one of many examples of this resentment is the fact that Israelis participate in Eurovision, the annual European-wide singing competition, even though Israel is part of the Middle East, not Europe.

25. For a history of this period, see, for example, Bruce, *The Last Crusade* and Grainger, *The Battle for Palestine*.

26. Among the many studies of the Balfour Declaration and the role of the British

From the Balfour Declaration to the State of Israel

There were many layers of intrigue and imperial manipulation in the years that followed the Balfour Declaration, leading up to the self-proclamation of the State of Israel in 1948. As always, the meddling of empire (in this case, the British Empire) did not make things better for the indigenous inhabitants of Palestine. Although the Balfour Declaration called for religious and cultural protections for Palestinians, stating that "nothing shall be done which may prejudice the civil and religious rights of existing non-Jewish communities,"[27] this did not include political and sovereignty protections. This ambiguity aided and abetted Zionism's project, which never included safeguarding the Palestinians' rights to live as free and equal citizens in their own land. Like the ancient Israelites' conquest and occupation of Canaan, the Zionists who led the Jewish occupation of Palestine saw the Palestinians as an "un-chosen" thorn in the side to be extracted and tossed aside.

When the British captured Jerusalem in December 1917, 90 percent of the population of Palestine were Muslims, four percent were Christians, and six percent were indigenous Jews.[28] Palestine became a British Mandate, in effect a colony of empire. By 1922, the first British census of Palestine showed that the Jewish population had grown to 12 percent, thanks to growing numbers of Jews arriving from the European diaspora.[29] The Zionist project still consisted of a small group of incoming occupiers, just as Abraham's occupiers started out small in Canaan, but this was in the process of changing.

Zionist resistance to the British Mandate in the years between the two world wars coalesced around an alliance consisting of a number of Zionist paramilitary organizations, most significantly Haganah, Irgun, and Lehi, whose actions have been labelled by numerous historians as terrorism. The most famous of their terrorist attacks was the bombing of the King David Hotel in Tel Aviv on July 22, 1946, which killed ninety-one and wounded forty-six people of various nationalities, including British officers, Arabs, and others.[30] Zionist disregard for the lives of the "un-chosen" was becoming increasingly apparent.

Empire in the Zionist project to create the State of Israel, see, for example, Adelson, *London and the Invention of the Middle East*; Brysac and Meyer, *Kingmakers*.

27. "Balfour Declaration."
28. Wenger, "Jerusalem."
29. Wenger, "Jerusalem."
30. For an analysis of the King David Hotel bombing and other terrorist operations of Zionist paramilitary groups, see Bell, *Terror Out of Zion*.

The Holocaust in Europe in the 1940s, in which six million Jews were massacred by the Nazis, stimulated the mass migration of European Jews to Palestine. Not all of them were Zionists. Many displaced survivors of the Holocaust were severely traumatized, and some found themselves on ships headed for Palestine almost by accident, often after failed attempts to migrate to the United States and other Western-aligned countries. The British had grown tired of trying to manage the Mandate amidst Zionist terrorism and Palestinian rebellion and finally turned this messy situation over to the United Nations.

On November 29, 1947, the UN General Assembly passed a resolution calling for Palestine to be partitioned between Jewish and Palestinian communities. Palestinians did not accept this partition, as it would mean the permanent loss of large portions of their land, farms, and historic villages and landmarks, and their resistance paved the way for the Zionists to unilaterally declare the establishment of the State of Israel.[31] On May 14, 1948, "on the day in which the British Mandate over Palestine expired, the Jewish People's Council gathered at the Tel Aviv Museum, and approved the . . . proclamation declaring the establishment of the State of Israel."[32] This proclamation, crafted with no consultation with or consideration of the needs of the Palestinians, amounted to a declaration of divine chosen-ness: "This is our promised land, and we are the only ones entitled to it."

The Ethnic Cleansing of Palestinians by the State of Israel

As millions of Jews migrated to Israel after World War II, settler colonialism steadily evolved into outright ethnic cleansing of the Palestinian population, which eventually led to the State of Israel being deemed an *apartheid state*.[33] Hundreds of illegal Jewish settlements were erected on land legally set aside for Palestinians, settlements in which growing numbers of Zionists enacted

---

31. United Nations, "Question of Palestine."

32. Jewish People's Council, "Declaration of Establishment of State of Israel."

33. *Apartheid* was the Afrikaans term for the separation of whites from blacks and mixed-race natives of South Africa. It denied non-whites many basic rights, brutalized them in numerous ways, and led to black resistance that finally ended apartheid in 1994 with the election that saw Nelson Mandela, leader of the anti-apartheid struggle, become the first black president. Apartheid defines an inherently unequal society, in which one or more groups of people are considered inferior to a ruling group, which denies them equal rights and forces them to live in separate enclaves (as in the black townships and set-apart "homelands" in apartheid South Africa, and Gaza and the West Bank in Israel).

the most extreme forms of ethnic cleansing. Heavily armed, these settlers formed militias which displaced, terrorized, and killed many Palestinians.

Although the underlying Zionist agenda of erasing the Palestinian population had existed since the first Zionist leaders began arriving from Europe and plotting the establishment of the State of Israel, this project became full-blown in 1948 with what Palestinians call the *naqba*—"the catastrophe." The *naqba* and successive waves of persecution have been brilliantly documented and analyzed by Ilan Pappé in his acclaimed book, *The Ethnic Cleansing of Palestine*.[34] This is particularly compelling because he is himself an Israeli Jewish historian, who has for years bravely fought for Palestinian rights.

During the *naqba* in 1948, approximately 750,000 Palestinians who were indigenous inhabitants of the land were forcibly removed from their homes, becoming refugees in places like Jordan, Lebanon, Syria, and Egypt, or internally displaced in refugee camps, the largest of which is Jabalia in the Gaza Strip. Pappé describes this as one of the largest forced migrations in modern history and as the founding ideology of the State of Israel.

In addition to this massive displacement, several thousand Palestinians were massacred, and hundreds of villages and farms were destroyed. Villages were bombed, many homes demolished with bulldozers, and mines were laid amidst the rubble so that if Palestinians returned to try to salvage some of their belongings they would be blown to bits. The demolitions also included hundreds of groves of olive trees, which had been tended by Palestinians for thousands of years. All of these atrocities were part of the systematic plan of the Zionists to remove the Palestinians from their midst. There was no real place for them in the Jewish state of Israel; they were the un-chosen.

A detailed synopsis of the escalation of the Zionist project to rid their promised land, Israel, of the Palestinian "people of the land" is beyond the scope of this discussion, but I include here a very brief overview.[35] Following the *naqba* of 1948, a second war by Israel against the Palestinians in 1967 resulted in what the Palestinians call *al-naksa* ("the setback"), and in this operation another 300,000 Palestinians lost their homes. Israel formally occupied the West Bank, East Jerusalem (which it illegally annexed along with nearby villages), the Gaza Strip, and the Golan Heights (part of Syria). This period also marked a more formalized upsurge in illegal Jewish settlements on confiscated Palestinian land.

---

34. Pappé, *Ethnic Cleansing of Palestine*.

35. Details of this history of escalation are helpfully summarized in "Hostilities in Gaza and Israel," and I have drawn on their research in this overview.

In 1993, the Oslo Accords were signed in Washington, DC by President Bill Clinton, the Palestinian leader, Yassar Arafat, and the Israeli prime minister, Yitzhak Rabin (who was subsequently assassinated by a Zionist), following secret negotiations in Norway. This led to the establishment of the Palestinian Authority (PA) in 1994, which was intended to oversee internal Palestinian governance in the West Bank and Gaza. The PA came into force under the signatures of the Israeli government and the Palestine Liberation Organization (PLO), an umbrella association of several Palestinian political movements. It was intended to be a temporary interim arrangement that would pave the way for the establishment of a Palestinian state after five years, based on the borders that existed between Israel and the Palestinian territories prior to the 1967 war, with East Jerusalem as its capital.

There have been two major problems with this intended roadmap to a Palestinian state. First, the Palestinian Authority has no real power, as it is under the control of the Israeli military, and many Palestinians feel that Fatah, its ruling party, has been subservient to Israel and has not fought as it should for Palestinian rights. This explains why Hamas became the more popular political party and why most Palestinians today have little faith in the Palestinian Authority.

Second, Israel has shown that it never intended to fulfil its commitments in the Oslo Accords. Instead of freezing its illegal settlements on Palestinian lands in 1994, as mandated by the accords, it vastly expanded them, erected huge walls arbitrarily boxing in Palestinians in the West Bank, and bypassed roads in the West Bank and East Jerusalem to create a de facto annexation of territories meant to be in the future state of Palestine.[36] The walls have cut some Palestinian villages in half, separating farmers from their farms and olive groves, and at times even from family members.

In 2005, Israel withdrew its ground forces from Gaza, a twenty-five-mile-long strip of Palestinian habitation along the Mediterranean coast, one of the most densely populated areas on earth, 70 percent of whose 2.3 million inhabitants are internally displaced refugees. It has been called the world's largest concentration camp, as its residents are literally fenced in, with almost no freedom of movement in or out of Gaza. After the Israeli military left Gaza in 2005, it continued to control its airspace, water, and land crossings. In 2006, Hamas, the second largest Palestinian political organization, was elected to govern Gaza, after which Israel imposed a land, air, and sea blockade. (Interestingly, both Israel and the US initially supported and partially funded Hamas, believing that splitting the Palestinians between Hamas and Fatah would weaken the Palestinian Authority.)

---

36. "What is the Palestinian Authority."

Accelerating Deterioration

Since 2006, the humanitarian and economic situation in Gaza has been described by the United Nations, Red Cross, and other humanitarian bodies as "hell on earth." There have been periodic incursions and bombing campaigns by the Israeli military, both indiscriminate and targeted sniping against civilians, and clashes with the military wing of Hamas and other resistance groups, most notably in 2008–2009, 2012, 2014, 2021, and 2022. Zionists and the Israeli military refer to these upscaled attacks as "mowing the lawn,"[37] which is a genocidal way of speaking. The Palestinian resistance has also staged several *intifadas* (grassroots uprisings) in response to the escalating oppression.

The United Nations Special Rapporteur for Human Rights, Michael Lynk, issued a dire warning in October 2018 that "with an economy in free fall, 70 percent youth unemployment, widely contaminated drinking water and a collapsed health care system, Gaza has become 'unlivable.'"[38] The situation for Palestinians also steadily deteriorated in the West Bank, East Jerusalem, and the Golan Heights, which Israel forcibly took from Syria during the 1967 war. In these Palestinian enclaves, Israeli soldiers routinely demolish Palestinians' homes, shoot at Palestinians, including children, and invade the homes of Palestinians to arbitrarily arrest people. Around 10,000 Palestinians are held in Israeli prisons in "administrative detention," without being charged or tried in a court of law. Some have been held in this way for over 30 years. Others have been released after several years, sometimes only to be cruelly re-arrested the following day. Children are among these detainees.

The UN has reported that 2023 was the deadliest year for Palestinians in the West Bank since the beginning of incident reporting in 2005. In the first half of 2023 alone, the UN verified "the highest daily average of settler-related incidents ever recorded, leaving 1,105 Palestinians displaced."[39] These incidents, including Israeli settlers raiding Palestinian villages, demolishing houses, and beating or shooting Palestinians, have been described as *pogroms* (defined in the *Oxford English Dictionary* as "an organized massacre

---

37. "This metaphor was used in Israel to describe its Operation Cast Lead assault on Gaza in 2008–2009 that killed over 1,400 Palestinians, which one hardline Zionist brushed off at the time by saying: 'It's unfortunate, but every once in a while you have to mow the lawn.'" Niva, "Operation 'Mow the Lawn.'" The inference is that periodically the Israeli military needs to bomb and attack Gaza so as to "cut everything back to nothing." I am reminded of the question I raised in chapter 9, "Lawn Transformations," regarding our human propensity for excessive control.

38. Lynk, "Question of Palestine."

39. UN OCHA, "Displacement of Palestinian Herders."

of a particular ethnic group"). The most far-right government in Israel's history has pushed ahead with further annexation plans, including settling another 500,000 Israelis in the West Bank on confiscated Palestinian properties.

PALESTINE RISES UP AND ISRAEL RESPONDS

On October 7, 2023, the world was shocked when fighters from the military wing of the Hamas government in Gaza, Izz ad-Din al-Qassam (commonly known as al-Qassam),[40] breached the border fences and raided Israeli territory. Although its soldiers are well-trained, al-Qassam has no heavy weapons, no navy or air force, no tanks, only small arms and rockets. It entered Israel by foot, bicycle, motorcycle, and hang glider, followed by other smaller militias. Several Israeli army bases, police stations, and two *kibbutzim* (Israeli communal farms, heavily militarized) were attacked. The Israeli army was only able to regain control on October 9.

Although originally the media reported that 1,400, then 1,200 Israelis (and a small number of foreign nationals) had been killed and over 5,400 injured, the official number of Israeli deaths has since been lowered again, estimated at around 1,000 as of this writing. More than 200 Israelis were taken to Gaza as hostages, as leverage to bring about a prisoner exchange with Palestinians detained in Israel, an exchange which has been only partially successful to date.

Follow-up reporting, even by Israeli news sources, has shown that a good number of the Israelis killed during the al-Qassam attack were actually killed in "friendly fire" incidents by the Israeli military. This is evident in that they were killed and burned by missiles fired from helicopters or tanks, neither of which al-Qassam possesses. The full picture of these three days of fighting will only become clear in time, but what is already clear is that the anguish of the loved ones of all who were killed or wounded will live forever. The attack has been portrayed by Israel and the US as a terrorist attack by Hamas, all of whose fighters are labelled terrorists. However, although there have been some attacks in the past by Hamas-affiliated militants which can be characterized as terrorism, today's al-Qassam is a trained military resistance force.

40. It is inaccurate to refer to the Palestinian resistance force as "Hamas," as Hamas is the political party which was duly elected to govern in the Gaza Strip. When the US and Israel speak of these fighters as "Hamas," this is a way of branding the government in Gaza as nothing but terrorists, which is an unfair characterization. For this reason, I will be referring to the Palestinian resistance force by its correct name, al-Qassam.

Israel and its supporters say that their extreme response to the al-Qassam incursion is justified because Israel "has the right to defend itself." Israel certainly has the legal right to defend its citizens and to repel armed attacks. However, the Geneva Conventions also stipulate that occupied people have a legal right to armed resistance against their occupiers, under just-war principles. This means that occupiers cannot claim self-defense to justify their response to acts of resistance to their illegal occupation. Israel's justification for its disproportionate response to the al-Qassam attack is akin to a long-time abuser's justification for strangling his partner, when she resists his abuse by kicking, scratching, and biting him, by arguing that he was only defending himself.

As a pacifist who embraces a *for-life* ethic, I reiterate that I reject all acts of violence. Clearly the decades of accelerating violence perpetrated by Israel against Palestinians have had a dehumanizing impact on some of those who have been on the receiving end of this violence, driving them at times to violent acts which are outside the norms of just-war principles, such as the taking of hostages. Each new generation of Palestinian children who have witnessed the killing and persecution of their families and friends is more militant than the previous generation.

At the same time, members of the Israeli Defense Force (IDF) have also been dehumanized by the decades of violence and ethnic cleansing directed against Palestinians. I have read and listened to interviews with former IDF soldiers who now agonize over the ways in which their aggression against Palestinians has dehumanized them. This kind of aggression dehumanizes everyone involved.

In this horrific state of affairs, the al-Qassam attack which Israel and its American ally call a "terrorist attack" is framed by Palestinians as a "concentration camp breakout." It is therefore important to attempt to put the events following October 7, 2023, into perspective. My summary below of what happened in the aftermath of the October 7 attack is corroborated by information collated by Diakonia, the International Humanitarian Law Centre,[41] and other independent sources. By the time this work is published, much more will have occurred, but this is a very brief summary of the essence of what happened in the initial aftermath of the attack by al-Qassam.

As of late May 2024, it was confirmed that over 36,000 Palestinians had been killed in Gaza during Israeli attacks; this death toll includes more than 15,000 children, 11,000 women, and hundreds of health workers and journalists; an additional 81,000 had been injured.[42] Tragically, these numbers

---

41. "Hostilities and Escalating Violence."
42. "Israel-Gaza War."

will be much higher by the time this book is published. Many thousands more remain missing, their bodies trapped beneath the rubble. Journalists and medical personnel have been especially singled out by the Israeli military, and the figure of more than 100 journalists killed, often by snipers, is far more than in any war in modern history.[43] The most shocking killings are those of children. UN Secretary-General António Guterres stated in the early weeks of the war that "Gaza is becoming a graveyard for children."[44]

The humanitarian situation in Gaza since the October 2023 outbreak of hostilities, already precarious in the extreme, has been catastrophic. By October 11, Israel had imposed an electricity blackout on Gaza. Fuel-run generators were used to try to keep hospitals and other critical infrastructure running, but this was short-lived as fuel ran out and could not be resupplied due to the closure of all border crossings.[45] A few fuel imports had been permitted by Israel by mid-November. Karim Khan, the prosecutor of the International Criminal Court, stated clearly that "willfully impeding relief supplies to civilians may constitute a war crime."[46] By early December, the World Food Program had documented

> . . . inadequate food consumption in 97% of households in northern Gaza and 83% of households in southern Gaza. Furthermore, 48% of residents in the north and 38% in the south suffer from severe hunger, and only around 1.8 and 1.5 litres of clean water per day. 90% of Gazans in the north and two thirds in the south reportedly had to go one full day and night without food; 18% and 13% respectively indicated that they endured this for over 10 days in the last month. . . Half of Gaza's population is starving.[47]

Since then, widespread starvation and disease have become a shocking reality in Gaza. UNRWA Commissioner-General Philippe Lazzarini reported that "Every little girl and boy I met in an UNRWA shelter asked me for bread and water."[48] The UN High Commissioner for Human Rights, Volker Türk, issued a statement on December 1, 2023 decrying the "apocalyptic" humanitarian situation in Gaza.[49] By mid-December, 1.9 million Palestinians in Gaza, 85% of the population, had been displaced from their homes.

43. "Journalist Casualties in the Israel-Gaza War."
44. "Gaza is Becoming a Graveyard for Children."
45. Cited in "2023 Hostilities and Escalating Violence."
46. "Statement of ICC Prosecutor Karim A. A. Khan."
47. "Statement by the World Food Programme."
48. Lazzarini, "Statement at the Joint Emergency Summit."
49. UN OCHCR, "Comment by UN High Commissioner for Human Rights."

Lazzarini called this "the largest displacement of Palestinians since 1948."[50] As I write this, the number of displaced has risen to over 90 percent, and hundreds of thousands of Gazans are starving.

This is only a brief and incomplete synopsis of the devastation and clear-cut war crimes wreaked by Israel on Palestinians in Gaza in the first few months following the al-Qassam incursion into Israel on October 7, 2023. It does not take into account the escalation of attacks on Palestinians in the West Bank, both by Israeli police and military and by armed Israeli settlers. This has included murders, beatings, detentions, and the destruction of Palestinians' homes.

I have found the apocalyptic scenes in Gaza to be almost unbearable to watch. Seeing video clips of Palestinian children wailing for their dead parents, describing the blown-off heads of their siblings and friends and the loss of their bombed homes brings me each time to unstoppable weeping. I keep hearing in my head the cry of one little Palestinian boy, "This is not a life!" The agony of Israelis who have lost family members is equally unbearable.

But the overall situation of the Palestinians—the end result of the Zionist belief that Jews are the chosen people who deserve to have the promised land all to themselves—seems to me to be the absolute worst inversion of the interrelational *for-life* ethic that is meant to guide our shared life on this planet. It has been called genocide, and I end this chapter with a reflection on what genocide is and what it means in this situation.

THE GENOCIDE STARTED IN CANAAN AND IS NOW IN PALESTINE

In this final section, I am guided in part by the work of the Center for Constitutional Rights, which has compiled extensive research on genocide.[51] Supporters of Israel have been angered that Israel's assault on the Palestinians has been depicted by so many as genocide, and in return they have charged that it is Hamas which seeks the genocide of the Israeli people. Most Palestinians, however, simply long to live in peace in their own homeland. It is true that, for many Palestinians, what they have endured at the hands of the Israelis for the past seventy-five years has led them to the view that the current state of Israel—as an apartheid state that wants them to disappear—should no longer exist in its present form. However, Palestinians have

---

50. Lazzarini, "UNRWA Situation and Response."
51. See "Genocide of the Palestinian People."

never had a problem with Israelis as Jews; the problem is not Judaism but Zionism.

But what about Israel's goals for the Palestinians? The association of Israel with the genocide of the Palestinian people merits analysis, as it is the worst charge imaginable. The term *genocide* was first coined in 1944 by the Jewish Polish legal scholar Raphael Lemkin. As Lemkin wrote,

> ... the term does not necessarily only signify mass killings. More often it refers to a coordinated plan aimed at destruction of the essential foundations of the life of national groups, so that these groups wither and die like plants that have suffered a blight. The end may be accomplished by the forced disintegration of political and social institutions, of the culture of the people, of their language, their national feelings, and their religion. It may be accomplished by wiping out all basis of personal security, liberty, health, and dignity. When these means fail, the machine gun can always be utilized. . . Genocide is directed against a national group as an entity, and the attack on individuals is only secondary to the annihilation of the national group to which they belong.[52]

The UN Convention on the Prevention and Punishment of the Crime of Genocide specifies that genocide includes acts "committed with intent to destroy, in whole or in part, a national, ethnic, racial, or religious group, including: (a) killing members of the group; (b) causing serious bodily or mental harm to members of the group; (c) deliberately inflicting on the group conditions of life calculated to bring about its physical destruction in whole or in part; or (d) imposing measures intended to prevent births within the group."[53]

Most contemporary scholars of genocide concur that Israel's policies and actions toward the Palestinian people do in fact constitute genocide, based on the above commonly accepted criteria. These policies "range from the 1948 mass killing and displacement of Palestinians to a half-century of military occupation and, correspondingly, the discriminatory legal regime governing Palestinians, repeated military assaults on Gaza, and official Israeli statements expressly favoring the elimination of Palestinians."[54]

Human rights experts, including the Israeli Jewish historian Ilan Pappé, have described the "incremental genocide" of Palestinians, in the service of the Zionists' long-range goal of the "ultimate destruction of Palestinians

---

52. Lemkin, "Genocide—A Modern Crime."
53. "Convention on Prevention and Punishment."
54. Shaw, "Palestine in an International Historical Perspective," 7.

as a national group."⁵⁵ This has included not only the steady escalation of indiscriminate killings, destruction of homes and property, and extrajudicial imprisonment of Palestinians, but the "normalization of the Israeli annexation of Palestinian territory and the exile or absorption of the national group of people who identify as Palestinian. International law is clear that an occupying power may not annex the people or territory it occupies."⁵⁶

In early 2024, a legal case charging Israel with genocide against the Palestinians was brought by South Africa at the International Court of Justice, headquartered in The Hague. On January 26, 2024, the court issued a provisional cease-and-desist order against Israel, until a formal trial can be held at a later date, covering all actions, military and otherwise, judged as genocidal. All member nations of the UN are expected to support this order. Israel has indicated that it will not be following the Court's ruling, and this could have dire consequences not only for Israel but for the main backer of its genocidal project, the United States.

Why have so many Israelis, Americans, and some of their allies in the West refused to condemn this genocide for what it is? One might also ask, why were so many Germans in the 1930s and early 1940s unable to recognize the Nazi "final solution" for the Jews for what it was? Going back to the beginning of this chapter, why did Abraham and his early band of Israelites not recognize that their conquest of the peoples of the land of Canaan included genocide? Why did they put the commandment for this crime against humanity into the voice of God?

These are the kinds of ultimate questions which I find extremely difficult to answer. Having many millennia of history from which to learn, why do we as human communities find it so hard to learn and so easy to forget? I think often of the commonplace remarks I have heard from the Jewish Holocaust survivors I have watched in the remarkable video archives of the Shoah Foundation, which conducted extensive interviews with these survivors in the 1990s to record their experiences before they died.

One insight in particular has stayed with me as the result of my many hours of listening to these survivors, who were children or teens during the Holocaust, most of whom lost their parents, siblings, and extended families while managing miraculously to survive the concentration camps. When asked what was the most important lesson they had taken away from the Holocaust, all of the interviewees said, in one form or another, "something like this (genocide) must never happen again."

55. Pappé, "Brief History of Israel's Incremental Genocide." See also Lendman, "Israel's Slow-Motion Genocide in Occupied Palestine."

56. "Genocide of the Palestinian People." See also Article 2(4), United Nations Charter.

Zionists in Israel today also use the phrase "never again," but they mean "never again for Jews," not "never again for anyone." The supreme irony of the present situation is that the Zionists have forgotten that genocide must never happen to anyone. They are unable to see the awful parallels between the Jewish experience leading up to the Nazis' "final solution" in Europe and the experience of the Palestinians today.

Having read numerous books about the Jews forced into the Warsaw Ghetto by the Nazis during World War II, for example, I cannot escape the parallels between that experience and the present experience of the Palestinians living in the Gaza Ghetto—detainment behind walls or fences, denial of the necessities of life, denial of freedom of movement, starvation, disease, indiscriminate killing. Both the Jews in the Warsaw Ghetto and the Palestinians in Gaza finally, in despair, resorted to armed resistance. Of all people, the Jewish people know what genocide is, and yet the Zionists who control Israel, along with the majority of Israeli citizens, do not seem to be able to translate their own collective history of genocide into an awareness of what Palestinians are experiencing at the hands of the State of Israel.

How can the present slaughter of Palestinian innocents and the many decades of the incremental ethnic cleansing of Palestinians by Israel come to an end? Already as I write this, the war has wider regional involvement, with attacks on northern Israel by the Palestinian Hezbollah army in Lebanon (and retaliatory attacks in southern Lebanon by Israel), attacks on US military bases in Iraq and Syria (and retaliatory bombings by the US military), attacks by Israel on Iranian targets in Iraq and Syria (and Iran's retaliation), and Yemen's refusal to allow ships traveling to or from Israel to travel through the Red Sea (which has provoked American and UK bombing of Yemen). Israel seems to have no plan other than the obliteration of the Palestinians.

There remains, on paper, the Oslo Accords vision of a so-called "two-state solution," but the agreed upon pre-1967 war borders have been so breached by Israel, and so many illegal Israeli settlements built in the territories set aside for the Palestinian state, that it is difficult to imagine how two states, Israel and Palestine, might be carved out of this disaster. In an ideal world, the present-day iteration of most of what was the ancient land of Canaan would agree to be the democratic nation of Palestine, with every citizen, Israeli and Palestinian, Jewish, Muslim, and Christian, having equal rights, equal participation in civic life, equal respect, and equal peace and security in their shared land. That would be a *for-life* way forward.

As I reflect again on the biblical history of the chosen people who erased or colonized the indigenous peoples of Canaan, it seems to me that the greatest sin of the assumption of chosen-ness is that it robs the chosen of any empathy with the un-chosen. When a prominent Israeli politician refers to Palestinians as "human animals," and when the prime minister of Israel calls the Palestinians "Amalekites," all empathy has been lost. And when we lose empathy, we lose our humanity. We have been utterly captured by our "human nature" (our preoccupation with self-promotion and power), such that we can no longer live as interrelated beings whose moral compass is a *for-life* ethic that applies to all creatures and all creation.

Israel, of course, is not the only nation which has succumbed to this de-humanization. And there are also individuals who live like this—narcissists and bullies who have no regard for anyone other than themselves. Far too many nations and extremist organizations have been trapped in this same brutalizing way of life—the Nazi Azov Battalion in Ukraine, the Turks who committed genocide against the Armenians, the Tutsis who committed genocide against the Hutus in Rwanda, Buddhist nationalist extremists in Myanmar who practice ethnic cleansing against the indigenous Rohingya, Pol Pot's genocide in Cambodia—the list is far too long.

It must also be said that the role of the American Empire in the present genocide against the Palestinians cannot be ignored or downplayed. The US is Israel's closest ally, and it has supplied Israel with many billions of dollars' worth of weapons. It is American bombs and missiles that rain down daily on the Palestinians. Israel has always served the American Empire's aims in the Middle East, functioning as a surrogate military base in the region. The American Empire now has Palestinian blood on its hands and has lost whatever waning credibility it had in the eyes of most of the world. Its support for Israel may ultimately turn out to be the death knell of its crumbling imperial project.

A particularly tragic by-product of the Zionist genocide of the Palestinian people is the damage it is doing to the Jewish religion. Because the Zionists created the State of Israel as an explicitly Jewish state, this means that the genocidal actions of Israel may be seen by the world as a reflection of the religion of Judaism. Despite the scriptural narrative of the brutal conquest and settler colonialism initiated by Father Abraham in Canaan, that is not the only story of the Jewish people's faith journey. The Jewish religion is a theologically rich story of a particular people's quest to be a faithful people, a story that is also part of our story as Christians who follow Jesus, a faithful Jew from Palestine. The present disaster of Israel's genocidal project against the Palestinians shows the dangers of aligning any nation-state with a particular religion, for the sins of the state will sully and demean the designated religion.

The biblical story of Abraham and the "chosen" path of the ancient people of Israel is a very old story, and sadly it is a story that seems to never end. Israel's genocide in Palestine should prompt all of us to do everything we can to make the Israel-Palestine story the last chapter in this kind of narrative. All of God's creatures are called to an interrelational life of mutual love and respect; no one group is more divinely chosen than any other. We should never choose only ourselves, our ethnic group, our nation, our religious group, for that leaves many others un-chosen, and the self-chosen give themselves no choice but to dismiss, belittle, and ultimately hate and destroy the un-chosen. We should know better. As a species, we need to recover what it means to be humans who are intricately and intimately interwoven into the *for-life* divine design for our life together on this planet.

13

What If?

At the heart of this work has been my conviction that theology is to be *lived*. It is not abstract thinking but an engagement of our minds and hearts with praxis—with the lived experience of our relatedness to ourselves, others, creation, our communities, our societies. The necessary follow-up to the "so what?" question that has guided our theologizing is "what if?" What is our actual vision of an interrelated life grounded in a *for-life* ethic? It is one thing to critique what has gone wrong, our personal and collective sins of estrangement from our *for-life* calling, but another to envision an actual life of "right relationships." The latter is where I want to end this work.

My envisioning here is, of course, context-specific, and it is also specific to who I am as a person. My vision of "the good life" will not be identical to yours. But I encourage you to engage in your own *for-life* envisioning exercises and to let that be a part of your daily life and future commitments. It is easy to be overwhelmed at times by the sinful state of the world, the wars and threats of wars, the poverty and other social injustices, the ecological crisis, the "unequal relationships," the relational difficulties we all encounter. We need to counteract that disquiet, bordering at times on despair, by *imagining*.

This is not mere day-dreaming. This is honestly asking "what if" we were to live an abundant kindom life in every aspect of our existence. To those who say, "don't be naïve, the dreams you have will never happen," I say, "not unless we try." This is an invitation to "suspend disbelief" for a moment, to dare to imagine the kind of world we would ideally love to inhabit, rather than succumbing to a cynical or resigned acceptance of our present dystopian existence. I see my "what if" imagining in the pages that follow not as fantasy but as clear-headed envisioning that flows from my conviction that God has given us a livable, do-able *for-life* ethic to follow.

I am envisioning this *for-life* praxis mainly in the context of the culture of my birth, my native America, even though I have left America for good and live in Aotearoa New Zealand, particularly in its connectedness to my beloved Pasifika. I situate my envisioning in America because it is the context I know best and because America remains so impactful in the world as the only remaining empire, which still causes a lot of damage even though its days as an empire are numbered. At the same time, many of the "what-if" scenarios I envisage here should spark associations with lived experience in other contexts, and that is my ultimate goal.

Just as this book has been an outward-spiraling reflection on the many facets of interrelated life, which all overlap and impact each other, so I allow my *what-if* imagining to flow from the personal, the interpersonal, and the communal to society, creation, and the world at large. This imagining obviously cannot cover all aspects of our interrelated life. This is only a small sampling of "what-ifs."

I begin with the personal, but of course the personal is in no way confined to our individual selves, as though "who we are" as persons could be separated from our relatedness to others. As individuals living in postmodernity, we experience at times a crushing sense of isolation from others—not so much in our remaining indigenous communities but certainly in our individualist Eurocentric societies. I believe the best antidote to this experience of alienation and loneliness, a state in which we struggle to manage the complexities of life on our own, including our feelings and fears, lies in the belonging, mutual encouragement, and empowerment experienced in kindom faith communities.

I would therefore like to see our existing churches re-envisioned as mutual support, empowerment, public witness, fellowship, and spiritual enrichment hubs. Church members would, in the first instance, support one another through regular times of gathering for the sharing of prayer and *life*—the "what is going on" in one another's daily lives. Those brought low by times of personal crisis could count on their fellow kindom dwellers to listen, to provide shoulders to cry on, and to access appropriate life-saving resources as needed. Every congregation would be reconfigured into clusters of small, intimate groups to facilitate this mutual support.

But kindom congregations would not only cater for each other's personal and interpersonal needs. They would be acutely attuned to their neighborhoods and communities. Their doors would be open every day, their facilities would be fully utilized by life-affirming community groups or organizations, and church members would be available to meet with anyone who comes through the doors seeking help or solace. They would also be intentional about going out to the places where people find themselves most in need. They would be advocates, a voice for the voiceless in their communities. They would offer compassionate care and solidarity, both in and beyond their church facilities, for the poor, the homeless, drug addicts, at-risk youth, immigrants, refugees, disabled persons, and more. Everyone would be welcome and no one would be alone.

I am aware of rare cases where this actually happens. I know of a church in an American city which turned its Sunday school classrooms in its education wing into living quarters, installed showers, and invited the homeless who were encamped in their parking lot to stay in these facilities. There they received food, shelter, pastoral care, access to medical care, and assistance finding jobs and a permanent place to live. Some of these people began to come into the sanctuary on Sunday mornings to join in worship, and this formerly middle-class white congregation found itself spiritually renewed and rejuvenated as its formerly "me" vs. "them" mindset became "us." I wish every church could be like that.

Kindom communities would not be housed only within church buildings. Like the Basic Ecclesial Communities and Intentional Christian Communities, some would meet in more intimate and informal spaces. They might emulate the pattern of the earliest Christian communities in the book of Acts, who gathered in people's homes to worship, pray, learn, and share food and life—not just with each other but with the wider community. I have been a part of several such intentional Christian communities, and the intimacy and shared vulnerabilities of these expressions of church cannot be matched in terms of creating a sense of belonging and empowerment, taking individuals' spiritual, emotional, and material needs seriously, and equipping one another to move out into the world to bring kindom *life* to others.

In my vision of a rebirth of kindom faith communities in the American context, both the BEC/ICC model and the more traditional churches which still have buildings would be intentional about widening their circles of relationships, encountering and loving "others," no matter who they may be. Denominations (larger manifestations of church) would embrace both expressions of church and offer full support for the non-institutional communal forms of kindom life.

How should we live and participate in the broader relational networks in our societies? Rather than simply hoping that we can elect politicians who will legislate in a *for-life* way, we should not, in the first instance, place too much of our focus on electoral politics. In order to live out a societal *for-life* ethic, we need to focus most of our energy on building grassroots populist movements that advocate for the common good. As they gain sufficient momentum and support, they will be able to model and further the justice we need in every aspect of our social relationships. These grassroots social movements will be held together by their unbreakable commitment to the common good.

These movements will be characterized by a combination of *acts of caring* and *acts of resistance* against the "powers and principalities." I am seeing hopeful signs in the United States regarding movements grounded in *acts of caring*. Networks of *mutual aid* are growing across the country as people of goodwill come together to help the most vulnerable by sharing food, housing, transportation, and the means to pay for necessities like electricity and medicine. Many of these mutual aid initiatives go beyond emergency assistance. They include equipping individuals and communities to grow their own food in community gardens, find or create employment, and organize to fight for a viable social "safety net" and an overturning of the social injustices which plague society. This is grassroots empowerment and activism. Our churches must join with community organizers and other religious and humanitarian groups to greatly expand these efforts.

The *acts of resistance* component of building a *for-life* social order can take many forms. For example, there should be widespread boycotts of the products of corporations that harm the wellbeing of people and planet. These could include corporations like Monsanto, whose fertilizers and other chemical products are toxic and cancer-causing, and the giant agricultural corporations that not only sell unhealthy foods but mistreat their workers. Corporations and businesses that do not allow their workers to unionize, or that refuse to reduce their carbon footprint, or that support US *for-death* domestic and foreign policies should all be boycotted.

We must also be willing to engage in sustained non-violent acts of civil disobedience to challenge the corrupt business-as-usual in the halls of power. We are long past the time when it is enough to engage in occasional "woke" protest marches that last for a few hours but produce no lasting change. Although protest marches are valuable tools for calling attention to pressing injustices, they may run the risk at times of making the marchers feel righteous but involving no risk or sustained commitment to persevere in the face of police brutality or arrest. There is certainly merit in public protest as a sign of solidarity with those who suffer injustice, but we must also be willing to pay the cost of personal sacrifice for disrupting the routines of the powerful.

Beyond the basics of *acts of caring* and *acts of resistance*, what follows is a sampling of concrete changes that would emerge in a *for-life* oriented America. First, the new economic system that emerges from our grassroots activism would be socialist rather than capitalist. This would not mean no private enterprise, but it would mean no massive, monopolistic corporations. They would be broken up and whittled down so that smaller enterprises, mostly worker-owned, can flourish. Basic services (health, infrastructure, utilities, education, public safety) would be provided by the government through a fair taxation system. The wealthy would be taxed proportionate to their actual wealth, and all tax loopholes that enable them to stash their cash in tax havens around the world would be closed. There would be limits to how wealthy individuals can be.

In this new social order, everyone would live a life free of poverty. Citizens would be entitled to a GBI (Guaranteed Basic Income). Those who are employed would be guaranteed a generous living wage, and everyone would be provided with government-funded services such as health care and education. Those who work part-time would have supplemental income from the government to ensure that their livelihood is viable. Those who work in their homes as homemakers or caregivers, self-employed people like artists or writers, and disabled persons would receive a full living wage. Homelessness would be outlawed. The millions of empty abandoned houses across the United States would be refurbished and millions of new housing units constructed, so that everyone has decent housing in which to live.

Workers would be entitled to a working life that is safe, healthy, and in which they have agency. As one example, Big Ag (the gigantic agricultural corporations mentioned earlier that create pesticide-laden foods, pollution, cruelty to animals, and mistreatment of workers) would be replaced with government-subsidized, locally owned and managed eco-sustainable agricultural collectives. Across the board, in every business or industry, workers would have the option of collective ownership of what they produce through worker cooperatives. Where such cooperatives are not feasible, unions would be encouraged, facilitated, and legally protected. This revolution in the societal mindset regarding what it means to be a worker would ensure that workers not only have a voice but a stake in their working life.

Along these lines, the nation would move toward a four-day work week. This is in part an acknowledgement that machines are increasingly replacing manual labor previously carried out by humans. But a shorter work week would have the benefit of giving workers the opportunity to spend more quality time with their loved ones and to pursue creative interests outside the workplace, thus contributing greatly to their overall wellbeing and the flourishing of their communities. Everyone would be guaranteed at least a month of annual paid vacation, flexible working arrangements (work-from-home, flexible working hours, workplace childcare, etc.), generous sick leave and compassionate leave, and paid maternity and paternity leave for up to a year.

Prioritizing the common good also includes providing simpler and more humane ways of helping people to manage their finances and their health. Non-profit, customer-owned "people's banks" would be set up in every community across the country. Many of these could be housed in rejuvenated and expanded post offices, which would be a fully government-owned and operated public service, easily accessible to every citizen. Every county, no matter how small or rural, would have its own non-profit community hospital, providing free health care services to everyone.

Instilling a sense of human dignity would further extend to the way law enforcement works and the way prisoners are treated. Local, state, and federal police would undergo a radical transformation, from their present racist and violent way of policing to a humane approach to safeguarding personal and community safety. Although the passage of the Fourteenth Amendment to the constitution in 1868 technically guaranteed equal protection under law for all Americans, we know that policing continued to be extremely brutal for African Americans and other people of color. We see the bitter harvest of this history of policing today in the persistent police brutality and disregard for the basic human rights of many who are apprehended, especially black and brown people.

In order to address this travesty, everyone involved in law enforcement would, in a *for-life* society, undergo serious and sustained retraining. Those with violent or racist tendencies would be re-educated or weeded out. Police would be intensively trained in the de-escalation of potentially violent situations. Many functions presently handled by police would be shifted to others, such as mental health professionals, social workers, and mediators trained in conflict resolution. Police forces would be de-militarized and de-weaponized. Police would use non-lethal forms of restraint, such as the safe use of tasers, rather than guns.

As a *for-life* society, we would undertake a radical reframing of how we understand and treat lawbreakers. One aspect of our desperately needed prison reform might be to revitalize and reframe the concept of the *penitentiary*. The penitentiary (from the Latin *paenitentia*, meaning "repentance") would be a place where one is removed from society for a time in order to reflect on and repent for the crimes one has committed. The goal of such repentance would be restoration, which entails making amends for one's wrongdoing.

This is *restorative justice* rather than *retributive justice*. We recall from chapter 5 that retributive justice simply punishes, while restorative justice rebuilds "right relationships" between offenders and those they have wronged. Many crimes in a *for-life* society could be handled solely through restorative justice programs. Drug offenders, who occupy a large proportion of our prison population today, would be given rehabilitation and mental health treatment rather than prison sentences. Private for-profit prisons would be abolished, as they exist only to cage as many people as possible while providing as few services as possible. The death penalty would be abolished, as a *for-life* ethic cannot tolerate taking the life of another human being.

A vital step in the construction of this new society would be the dismantling of the military-national security state complex. The United States would emulate something like the Costa Rica model, which says "we do not want or need an army, as we will never attack anyone." Although, as a Christian pacifist, I would not want to see any armed military force, I recognize that a more realistic possibility for the near future might have to be a vastly reduced *defense force only*, committed simply to defending America from external attack and assisting with national emergencies via a National Guard.

This reorientation away from war and toward peace would reduce our defense budget and military forces by at least 75 percent—savings which would be diverted to *for-life* policies and programs that support the common good. Offensive weapons systems and all nuclear weapons would be destroyed—a "swords to ploughshares"[1] policy. "Swords to ploughshares" facilities would be set up across the country, which would dismantle now un-needed weapons and re-purpose them for peaceful uses. Buy-back programs for privately owned guns would entice gun owners with generous financial incentives that would benefit their families, moving the society toward the day when guns would no longer exist. Meanwhile, all high-capacity and assault weapons would be banned and strict licensing systems put in place to deny gun ownership to mentally unstable persons and those with criminal records.

The dismantling of military weapons can happen without risk to the nation if America ceases to be an imperial bully. The image that comes to mind is that of a bully on the school playground. The worse the bully behaves, the more his victims band together to collectively challenge him. If he stops being a bully, they have no need to attack him. If the US says "we will

---

1. This is a reference to the prophetic vision of a just society in Isa 2:4: "They shall beat their swords into ploughshares, and their spears into pruning hooks; nation shall not lift up sword against nation; neither shall they learn war anymore." Micah 4:4 also describes a vision of a world free of war, in which people "shall all sit under their own vines and under their own fig trees, and no one shall make them afraid."

not meddle in your country or steal your resources, and we will not attack anyone," we will no longer have enemies who wish to harm us.

What would this mean in practical terms? The US would close its 900+ military bases around the world and most of its bases on US soil. It might continue to have a very small peacekeeping presence, in the short term, in countries where it has security treaties, like South Korea. However, because now all of our efforts abroad would be focused on diplomacy and peacemaking, we would work to strengthen the presence and effectiveness of United Nations peacekeeping forces wherever there are lingering conflicts.

American foreign policy would be very clear: we would have diplomatic relations with every country—dialogue is always more productive than isolation. Our diplomacy would be centered around seeking to understand other cultures and nations—their histories, their core values, their hopes and dreams, and their insecurities. Economic sanctions against other countries would cease. They have never achieved their desired goal of making people so miserable that they rise up and oust their governments; they have only harmed innocent people and increased hatred of America.

In our *for-life* way of relating to other nations, we would support other countries with generous aid, in every form other than military aid (no more weapons sales or gifts to anyone), based on two criteria: (1) *Are you working in a concerted way to combat the climate crisis?* And (2) *Are you working in a concerted way to build a "for-the-common-good" culture in your country?* Of course, these two criteria must first begin to be applied at home. America needs to honestly address these questions itself as its new guiding principles.

In recognition of the new "fair world order" that is already emerging across the world, we would embrace its core principle of multipolarity, in which we would have a constructive role to play as an equal partner alongside every other nation. Given this new way of relating to the world, most of the Pentagon complex would be transformed into national institutes for diplomacy, conflict resolution, and peace-building. Young Americans could be trained for a period of national public service in such institutes and equipped for peace-building initiatives at home and abroad. The CIA would be dismantled. Surveillance of American citizens and citizens of other countries would cease. Censorship would cease. Freedom of speech and freedom of the press would be restored and protected, with new guidance put in place to define what constitutes news versus opinion.

Our most urgent task domestically would be to *declare a climate emergency*, and a new vitally important government department would be created to address this crisis. The government would invite proposals for climate change mitigation and restoration from scientists and underwrite their diverse efforts to tackle the crisis from all sides. Initiatives would urgently be put in place to wean the country off of fossil fuels and replace them with renewable energy sources. Every community that loses jobs due to the closure of fossil fuels industries would be guaranteed job replacements in renewable energy enterprises, such as manufacturing wind turbines, solar panels, lithium batteries, and so on.

The government would financially underwrite and oversee a major new national initiative in which millions of Americans would be employed to implement the proposals of the climate scientists, and it would pay these workers well. This could be roughly patterned after Franklin D. Roosevelt's Citizens Conservation Corps set up during the Great Depression, only on a much larger scale. These projects could be managed at the local or state level; universities, colleges, non-profit organizations, and religious communities could help to facilitate or sponsor some of these efforts.

Here are just a few examples of how these initiatives might work: some cadres would be working to plant algae, which soaks up CO_2, along coastlines. Others would be planting millions of locally indigenous trees all across the country. Others would be engaged in ocean, river, and stream clean-up and restoration. Others would be rewilding habitats to return them to eco-sustainability. Others would be planting and managing "urban farms" in towns and cities across the country, which would not only absorb CO_2 but help to combat our urban "food deserts." Others would be refitting homes, schools, and businesses with renewable energy sources.

Because we would be devoting so much less of our national treasury to militarism and war, there would be more than sufficient funds to pay for climate recovery, universal health care, housing for all, government-funded education at all levels, humane immigration reform, reform of the prison and criminal justice systems, and other *for-life* initiatives. There would be ample funds left over to provide humanitarian aid, and aid in support of climate change mitigation, to other countries, based on the two foreign policy principles articulated above.

Massive changes in our institutions of government would be essential to root out the corruption that has gravely undermined our governance. New laws would be required to prevent lawmakers from being beholden to lobbyists and corporate donors rather than to their constituents—lobbyists and corporate donors would be outlawed. Elections would be publicly financed. New laws would be required to ban racist gerrymandering of electoral districts. New election integrity practices would be put in place to ensure that no citizen is disenfranchised and that every vote is counted. It might even be advantageous to require all adult citizens to vote as their civic duty. This would ensure that everyone has an ownership stake in their country, rather than being powerless non-participants.

The electoral system would need to be radically reconstructed to make it more democratic and participatory. Proportional representation would elevate the voices of smaller parties. In this system, if a party earns 5 percent of the vote, for example, it would have 5 percent of the seats in the legislature. This kind of truly representative government is much more democratic than the present corrupt, corporation-bought, dysfunctional electoral system. True democracy will be focused on the common good, not the special interests of powerful elites.

There is much more to be said about this vision of a *for-life* America, but this is a small beginning designed to stimulate further envisioning in the minds of readers. At its heart, it is a vision built on humility and compassion for all rather than hubris, greed, and *me-ism*. From a theological perspective, it is a vision rooted in an ethic that is unequivocally and unconditionally *for life for all*—all creatures and all creation. It is a vision that prioritizes the common good over the obsession of the powerful with maintaining their power and privilege at all costs.

What would it mean for America to be guided by humility and dedication to the common good? It would mean letting go of the unbearable pressure of having to pretend that the United States is the most important, most powerful, greatest nation in the world. It would mean making this declaration: "We don't need to be an empire. We don't want to be an empire. We are going to stop saying that America is the best nation in the world—what arrogance! We are going to work toward a new American exceptionalism built not on imperial power and might but on love and care for our neighbors, nearby and far away. Instead of being *for the power and dominance of the few*, we choose to be *for life—for everyone and everything*. We choose to respect and safeguard the human community and all of creation. We are ready to repent, atone, and embrace a new loving way of being in the world."

This entire book has been pushed along by a "what-if" vision. It has been a search for a lived theology that is interwoven into the whole of life. Otherwise, what is the point of theology? What is the point of faith? Faith empowers us to see beyond our limited "human natures" that tell us to put ourselves first. Faith overcomes the fears that prevent us from having the courage to be *for life* in every fiber of our being and in every aspect of our lived experience. Faith reminds us that we are all a part of that divine spark which first created light out of the darkness of the primordial "deep." Our gratitude for that miraculous gift of life means that we must be and act *for life* in all of its vast and diverse expressions. That gratitude should make us ask "what if" questions in every situation, and find our home in kindom communities which can help us answer those questions. May it be so.

Bibliography

Adelson, Roger. *London and the Invention of the Middle East: Money, Power, and War, 1902–1922.* New Haven: Yale University Press, 1995.

Ah Siu-Maliko, Mercy. *Embodying Aga Tausili: A Public Theology from Oceania.* Lanham, MD: Lexington, 2021.

Aizenman, Nurith. "How the US Gun Violence Death Rate Compares with the Rest of the World." NPR, Oct 31, 2023. https://www.npr.org/sections/goatsandsoda/2023/10/31/1209683893/how-the-u-s-gun-violence-death-rate-compares-with-the-rest-of-the-world.

Alava, Andreína Chávez. "An Army of Women Is Building Venezuela's Housing Revolution." *Venezuelaanalysis*, Mar 8, 2023. https://venezuelanalysis.com/analysis/15722/.

Aris, Ben, and Ivan Tkachev. "20 Years of Russia's Economy under Putin, by the Numbers." *BNE IntelliNews*, Aug 19, 2019. https://www.themoscowtimes.com/2019/08/19/long-read-russias-economy-under-putin-in-numbers-a66924.

Ateek, Naim. *A Palestinian Christian Cry for Reconciliation.* Maryknoll, NY: Orbis, 2008.

———. *A Palestinian Theology of Liberation: The Bible, Justice, and the Palestine-Israel Conflict.* Maryknoll, NY: Orbis, 2017.

Atwood, Eunice. "How Does Theology Call Us to Challenge Poverty?" Joint Public Issues Team, Oct 2022. https://jpit.uk/challengepoverty-theology#:~:text=God's%20character%20reveals%20a%20God,for%20people%20experiencing%20economic%20injustice.

Augsburger, David. *Pastoral Counseling across Cultures.* Philadelphia: Westminster, 1986.

Baiden, Peter, and S. K. Tadeo. "Investigating the Association between Cyberbullying Victimization and Suicidal Ideation among Adolescents." *Child Abuse and Neglect* 102 (April 2020) 104–41.

Barker, David. "In American Politics Today, Even Fact-Checkers Are Viewed through Partisan Lenses." Scholars Strategy Network, 2021. www.https://scholars.org/scholar/david-barker.

Barry-Igivisa, Wardley D. "The Language of Trees and Clams." In *From the Deep: Pasifiki Voices for a New Story*, edited by James Bhagwan, Elise Huffer, Frances C. Koya-Vaka'uta, and Aisake Casimira, 49. Suva, FJ: Pacific Theological College, 2020.

Beckham, Barry. *Garvey Lives! The First Produced Play about Black Moses.* Silver Spring, MD: Beckham, 2017.

Bell, J. Bowyer. *Terror Out of Zion: The Fight for Israeli Independence.* Piscataway, NJ: Transaction, 1996.

Berman, Lazar. "After Walling Itself In, Israel Learns the Hazards of the Jungle Beyond." *Times of Israel*, Mar 8, 2021. https://www.timesofisrael.com/after-walling-itself-in-israel-learns-to-hazard-the-jungle-beyond/.

"Biography of Allan Boesak." Blackpast, 2015. https://www.blackpast.org/global-african-history/people-global-african-history/allan-boesak-1946/.

"Black Lives Matter." https://www.blacklivesmatter.com/.

Boesak, Allan. "Theological Reflections on Empire." *HTS Teologiese Studies/Theological Studies* 1 (2009) 291–99.

Bradstock, Andrew. "Recovering the Common Good: The Key to a Truly Prosperous Society." Public lecture, Centre for Theology and Public Issues, University of Otago, Dunedin, New Zealand, Jan 21, 2013.

"A Brief History of the Israeli Occupation of Palestine." *TRT World*, 2020. https://www.trtworld.com/magazine/a-brief-history-of-the-israeli-occupation-of-palestine.

Brock, Brian. *Wondrously Wounded: Theology, Disability, and the Body of Christ.* Studies in Religion, Theology and Disability. Waco, TX: Baylor University Press, 2020.

Brotton, Melissa J., ed. *Ecotheology in the Humanities: An Interdisciplinary Approach to Understanding the Divine and Nature.* Lanham, MD: Lexington, 2016.

Bruce, Anthony. *The Last Crusade: The Palestine Campaign in the First World War.* London: John Murray, 2002.

Brueggemann, Walter. *Journey to the Common Good.* Louisville, KY: Westminster John Knox, 2010.

Brysac, Shareen B., and Karl E. Meyer. *Kingmakers: The Invention of the Modern Middle East.* New York: W. W. Norton, 2009.

Brzezinski, Zbigniew. "The Cold War and Its Aftermath." *Foreign Affairs* 4 (1992) 31–49.

———. *The Grand Chessboard: American Primacy and Its Geopolitical Imperatives.* 2nd ed. New York: Basic, 2017.

Butler-Bass, Diane. *Freeing Jesus: Rediscovering Jesus as Friend, Teacher, Savior, Lord, Way, and Presence.* San Francisco: HarperOne, 2021.

———. "The Kin-dom of God." Red Letter Christians, Dec 15, 2021. https://www.redletterchristians.org/the-kin-dom-of-god/.

Carter, Warren. *Matthew and Empire: Initial Explorations.* Harrisburg, PA: Trinity, 2001.

Chibuye, Lackson, and Johan Buitendag. "The Indigenisation of Eco-theology: The Case of the Lamba People of the Copperbelt in Zambia." *HTS Teologiese Studies/Theological Studies* 1 (2020) 60–67.

Chomsky, Noam, and Edward S. Hermon. *Manufacturing Consent: The Political Economy of the Mass Media.* Reprint ed. New York: Pantheon, 2002.

Clark, Jawanza. *Reclaiming Stolen Earth.* Maryknoll, NY: Orbis, 2022.

Cochard, Roland. *Consequences of Deforestation and Climate Change on Biodiversity.* Lausanne: University of Lausanne, 2011.

Cohen, Dan, and Max Blumenthal. "The Making of Juan Guaidó: US Regime Change Laboratory at Work." *Telesur English*, Jan 29, 2019. https://www.telesurenglish.net/news/The-Making-of-Juan-Guaido-US-Regime-Change-Laboratory-At-Work-20190129-0021.html.

Cohen, Stephen. *American Perceptions and Soviet Realities.* Revised ed. New York: W. W. Norton, 1986.

———. *Failed Crusade: America and the Tragedy of Post-Communist Russia.* New York: W. W. Norton, 2001.

———. *Rethinking the Soviet Experience: Politics and History.* Oxford: Oxford University Press, 1986.

———. *Soviet Fates and Lost Alternatives: From Stalinism to the New Cold War.* New York: Columbia University Press, 2009.

Conradie, Ernst M., and Hilda P. Hoster, eds. *T&T Clark Handbook of Christian Theology and Climate Change.* London: Bloomsbury, 2020.

"Convention on the Prevention and Punishment of the Crime of Genocide—Article II." United Nations Treaty Series, Jan 12, 1951. https://treaties.un.org/doc/Publication/UNTS/volume%2078/volume-78-I-1021-English.pdf.

"Country Profile: Venezuela." UN Data. https://data.un.org/CountryProfile.aspx/_Docs/Country Profile.aspx?Cr Name=Venezuela%20(Bolivarian%20 Republic%20of.

Cox, Harvey. *The Future of Faith.* New York: HarperOne, 2010.

———. *The Secular City: Secularization and Urbanization in Theological Perspective.* 4th ed. Princeton: Princeton University Press, 2013.

———. *When Jesus Came to Harvard: Making Moral Choices Today.* New York: HarperOne, 2006.

Crawford, Neta C. *The Pentagon, Climate Change, and War: Charting the Rise and Fall of US Military Emissions.* Cambridge, MA: MIT Press, 2022.

Creamer, Deborah. "Theological Accessibility: The Contribution of Disability." *Disability Studies Quarterly* 4 (Fall 2006). https://dsq-sds.org/index.php/dsq/article/view/812/987.

"Cyberbullying: What Is It and How to Stop It." UNICEF, 2022. https://www.unicef.org/end-violence/how-to-stop-cyberbullying.

"The Dangers of Sexting." Canopy, Mar 7, 2023. https://canopy.us/2023/03/07/sexting-the-impacts-consequences-on-young-people/.

Davidson, Peter. "Empire." In *World History Encyclopedia.* Boston: Houghton Mifflin Harcourt, 2011. https://www.worldhistory.org/empire/.

de Brichambaut, Marc Perrin. "The Indivisibility of Euro-Atlantic Security." Organization for Security and Cooperation in Europe (OSCE). Partnership for Peace Research Seminar, Vienna Diplomatic Academy, Feb 4, 2010. https://www.osce.org/files/f/documents/ 5/f/41452.pdf.

Early, Christian, and Ted Grimsrud, eds. *A Pacifist Way of Knowing: John Howard Yoder's Nonviolent Epistemology.* Eugene, OR: Cascade, 2010.

Echols, Connor. "America's Top Five Weapons Contractors Made US$196 Billion in 2022." Responsible Statecraft, Aug 8, 2023. https://responsiblestatecraft.org/2023/08/07/americas-top-5-weapons-contractors-made-196bin2022/#:~:text=The%20top%205%20for%202022,Aviation%20Industry%20Corporation%2C%20and%20Boeing.

Eilers, Kent. "Theology and the Experience of Disability." *Theology Forum*, November 13, 2017. https://theologyforum.wordpress.com/2017/11/13/theology-and-the-experience-of-disability-a-review/.

Eisland, Nancy. *The Disabled God: Towards a Liberatory Theology of Disability.* Nashville, TN: Abingdon, 1994.

"Energy Usage Per Capita by Country." US Energy Information Administration, 2021. https://www.eia.gov/international/data/world/total-energy/total-energy-consumption?pd=47&p=0 2&u=2&f=A&v=mapbubble&a=-&i=none&vo=value &t=C&g=01&l=249-ruv20evs&s=3 15532800000&e=1609459200000&ev.

Fitch, David. *The Church of Us versus Them*. Ada, MI: Brazos, 2019.

"Flashback: President Bush on Putin's 'Soul.'" *NBC News*, Mar 27, 2014. https://www.nbcnews.com/video/flashback-president-bush-on-putins-soul-208352323648.

Florer-Bixler, Melissa. "The Kin-dom of Christ." *Sojourners*, Nov 2018, 1–4.

Freel, Chrystia. "Ukrainian Role Admitted in 1941 Babi Yar Massacre." *Washington Post*, Oct 6, 1991. https://www.washingtonpost.com/archive/politics/1991/10/06/ukrainian-role-admitted-in-41-babi-yar-massacre/2befa2af-0706-4f4e-bc9f-f992074f9698/.

Freire, Paulo. *Cultural Action for Freedom*. Cambridge, MA: Harvard University Press, 1972.

———. *Education for Critical Consciousness*. London: Bloomsbury Academic, 2021.

———. *Pedagogy of the Heart*. London: Bloomsbury Academic, 2021.

———. *Pedagogy of the Oppressed*. 5th ed. London: Penguin, 2017.

Gaventa, William C. *Disability and Spirituality: Recovering Wholeness*. Studies in Religion, Theology and Disability. Waco, TX: Baylor University Press, 2018.

"Gaza is Becoming a Graveyard for Children." United Nations press release, Nov 7, 2023. https://turkiye.un.org/en/251952-guterres-%E2%80%9Cgaza-becoming-graveyard-childre n%E2%80%9D.

"The Genocide of the Palestinian People: An International Law and Human Rights Perspective." Center for Constitutional Rights, 2016. https://ccrjustice.org/sites/default/files/attach/2016/ 10/Background%20on%20the%20term%20genocide%20in%20Israel%20Palestine%20Context.pdf.

Giddens, Anthony. *The Consequences of Modernity*. Cambridge, MA: Polity, 1990.

"Global Abortion Policies Database: Country Profile—Fiji." World Health Organization. https:// abortion-policies.srhr.org/country/fiji/.

"Globalization." *Merriam-Webster Dictionary Online*, 2018. https://www.merriam-webster.com.

Gordon, Michael. "Russia and IMF Agree on a Loan for $10.2 Billion." *New York Times*, Feb 23, 1996. https://www.nytimes.com/1996/02/23/world/russia-and-imf-agree-on-a-loan-for-10.2-billion.html.

Grainger, John D. *The Battle for Palestine, 1917*. Woodbridge, UK: Boydell, 2006.

Greer, Peter. "Stop Helping Us: A Call to Compassionately Move beyond Charity." In *For the Least of These: A Biblical Answer to Poverty*, edited by Anne Bradley and Art Lindsley, 221–40. Grand Rapids, MI: Zondervan Academic, 2015.

Groody, Daniel G., ed. *The Option for the Poor in Christian Theology*. Notre Dame, IN: University of Notre Dame Press, 2007.

Grov, Christian, et al. "Perceived Consequences of Casual Online Sexual Activities on Heterosexual Relationships." *Journal of the National Library of Medicine* 2 (Apr 2011) 429–39.

Guthrie, Woody. "This Land is Your Land." Words and music by Woody Guthrie. Sound recording. New York: Ludlow Music Inc., 1940.

Gutierrez, Gustavo. *A Theology of Liberation: History, Politics and Salvation*. 50th anniversary ed., with a new introduction by Michael Lee. Maryknoll, NY: Orbis, 2023.

———. *The God of Life*. Maryknoll, NY: Orbis, 1991.

———. *We Drink from Our Own Wells: The Spiritual Journey of a People*. Translated by Matthew J. O'Connell. Maryknoll, NY: Orbis, 2003.

Haraway, Donna J. *When Species Meet*. Minneapolis, MN: University of Minnesota Press, 2007.

Hauerwas, Stanley. *Dispatches from the Front: Theological Engagements with the Secular*. Durham, NC: Duke University Press, 1994.

———. *The Peaceable Kingdom: A Primer in Christian Ethics*. Notre Dame, IN: University of Notre Dame Press, 1991.

Havea, Jione. "Covenant: Chosen, Cover, Contest." In *reStorying the Pasifika Household*, edited by Upolu Lumā Vaai and Aisake Casimira, 32–39. Suva, FJ: PTC Press, 2023.

Hedges, Chris. *America: The Farewell Tour*. New York: Simon and Schuster, 2018.

———. "American Commissars." *Scheerpost*, Apr 4, 2022. https://scheerpost.com/2022/04/18/hedges-american-commissars/.

———. *Empire of Illusion: The End of Literacy and the Triumph of Spectacle*. New York: Hachette Book Group, 2010.

———. *The Greatest Evil Is War*. New York: Seven Stories, 2022.

———. *The World As It Is: Dispatches on the Myth of Human Progress*. New York: Nation, 2011.

———. *Wages of Rebellion: The Moral Imperative of Revolt*. New York: Nation, 2015.

Herbert, Walter. "Faith-based War: From 9/11 to Catastrophic Success in Iraq." Paper presented, Liberation Theology in the 21st Century Conference, Baylor University, Waco, TX, Oct 11–13, 2006.

Herrera, Remy, and Joelle Cicchini. "U.S. Military Bases and Personnel Abroad." *Journal of Innovation Economics and Management* 2 (2013) 127–49.

Hoekema, David. "A Practical Christian Pacifism." *Christian Century*, Oct 22, 1986, 917–29.

"Hostilities and Escalating Violence in the Occupied Territories." Diakonia: International Humanitarian Law Centre, Dec 13, 2023. https://www.diakonia.se/ihl/news/2023-hostilities-in-gaza-and-israel-factual-account-of-events/.

"Hostilities in Gaza and Israel: A Factual Account of Events." Diakonia: The International Humanitarian Law Centre, Dec 9, 2023. https://www.diakonia.se/ihl/news/2023-hostilities-in-gaza-and-israel-factual-account-of-events/.

Hubach, Stephanie O. "Disability Ministry: What It Is, and Why It Matters." Engaging Disability with the Gospel, 2016. https://engagingdisability.org/disability-ministry-what-it-is-and-why-it-matters/.

Hussain, Waheed. "The Common Good." In *The Stanford Encyclopedia of Philosophy*, edited by Edward N. Zalta. Stanford, CA: Stanford University Press, 2018. https://plato.stanford.edu/archives/spr2018/entries/common-good/.

"Independent Ukraine." *Britannica Online*. https://www.britannica.com/place/Ukraine/independent-Ukraine.

Intergovernmental Panel on Climate Change. "Annual Reports." www.https://www.ipcc.ch/reports/.

Isasi-Diaz, Ada Maria. *En La Lucha/In the Struggle: Elaborating a Mujerista Theology*. Maryknoll, NY: Orbis, 1993.

———. *La Lucha Continues: Mujerista Theology*. Maryknoll, NY: Orbis, 2004.

———. *Mujerista Theology*. Maryknoll, NY: Orbis, 1996.

"Israel-Gaza War in Maps and Charts," May 28, 2024. aljazeera.com/news/ longform/ 2024/5/28/live-tracker.

Jewish People's Council. "Declaration of Establishment of State of Israel, May 14, 1948." Israel Ministry of Foreign Affairs. http://www.mfa.gov.il/mfa/foreignpolicy/ peace/guide/pages/ declaration%20of%20establishment% 20of%20 state%20of% 20israel.aspx.

Johnson, Elizabeth. "Naming God She: The Theological Implications." Boardman Lectureship in Christian Ethics, University of Pennsylvania, 2002. http:// repository.upenn.edu/boardman/ 5.

———. "The Incomprehensibility of God and the Image of God Male and Female." *Theological Studies* 3 (1984) 441–65.

Johnson, Lydia. "Clusters on the Vine: A Case Study of Intentional Christian Community in Contemporary America." DMin thesis, Lexington Theological Seminary, 1989.

———. *Drinking from the Same Well: Cross-Cultural Concerns in Pastoral Care*. Eugene, OR: Pickwick, 2011.

Jones, Bernie D. "Critical Race Theory." In *The Oxford International Encyclopedia of Legal History*, edited by Stanley N. Katz. Oxford: Oxford University Press, 2009. https: //www.oxfordreference.com/display/10.1093/acref/9780195134056.001.0001/ acref-9780195134 056-e-215.

"Journalist Casualties in the Israel-Gaza War." Committee to Protect Journalists, Dec 17, 2023. https://cpj.org/2023/12/journalist-casualties-in-the-israel-gaza-conflict /.

Katchanovski, Ivan. "The Far Right in Ukraine During the 'Euromaidan' and the War in Donbas." *SSRN Electronic Journal* (Sep 2016). https://www.researchgate.net/publi cation/306548367_The_Far_Right_in_Ukraine_During_the_Euromaidan_and_ the_War_in_Donbas.

———. "The Snipers' Massacre on the Maidan in Ukraine." *Academia* (2015). https:// www.academia.edu/8776021/The_Snipers_Massacre_on_the_Maidan_in_ Ukraine.

Keller, Catherine. *Facing Apocalypse: Climate, Democracy, and Other Last Chances*. Maryknoll, NY: Orbis, 2021.

———. *Political Theology of the Earth: Our Planetary Emergency and the Struggle for a New Public*. Insurrections: Critical Studies in Religion, Politics, and Culture. New York: Columbia University Press, 2018.

———. *The Face of the Deep: A Theology of Becoming*. Milton Park, UK: Routledge, 2003.

Kerber, Guillermo. "Climate Change and Southern Theologies: A Latin American Insight." *Belo Horizonte* 17 (2010) 45–55.

"Kingdom of God." In *Britannica Online*, Aug 14, 2023. https://www. britannica.com/ topic/ Kingdom-of-God.

Knaggs, Paul. "Ukraine Parliament Quotes Nazi Collaborator Stefan Bandera." Labour Heartlands, Jan 4, 2023. https://labourheartlands.com/ukraine-parliament- quotes-nazi-collaborator-stefan-bandera/.

Lagi, Rosiana. "Vanua Sauvi: Social Roles, Sustainability and Resilience." In *Relational Hermeneutics: Decolonising the Mindset and the Pacific Itulagi*, edited by Upolu L. Vaai and Aisake Casimira, 187–97. Suva, FJ: University of the South Pacific, 2017.

Latifi, Chessa. "Five Things to Know about Central American Migration." Project Hope, May 11, 2023. https://www.projecthope.org/five-things-to-know-about-central-american-migration/#:~:text=The%20root%20causes%20of%20migration,weather%2C%20 agriculture%2C%20and%20livelihoods.

Lazzarini, Philippe. "Statement at the Joint Emergency Summit of the League of Arab States and the Organization of MIC Cooperation." Press statement, Relief and Works Agency for Palestine Refugees in the Near East (UNRWA), Nov 11, 2023. www.https://palestine.un.org/en/node/7204.

———. "UNRWA Situation and Response to the Escalation in Gaza." Press statement, Relief and Works Agency for Palestine Refugees in the Near East (UNRWA), Dec 11, 2023. https://www.unrwa.org/resources/reports/unrwa-situation-report-32-situation-gaza-strip.

Lebron, Christopher J. *The Making of Black Lives Matter: A Brief History of an Idea*. 2nd ed. Oxford: Oxford University Press, 2023.

Lemkin, Raphael. "Genocide—A Modern Crime." *Free World* 39 (1945). http://www.preventgenocide.org/lemkin/freeworld1945.htm.

Lendman, Steve. "Israel's Slow-Motion Genocide in Occupied Palestine." In *The Plight of the Palestinians*, edited by William A. Cook, 29–38. London: Palgrave, 2010.

Light, Michael T., Jingying He, and Jason P. Robey. "Comparing Crime Rates between Undocumented Immigrants, Legal Immigrants, and Native-born US Citizens." In *Proceedings of the National Academy of Sciences*, Dec 7, 2020. https://www.pnas.org/doi/full/10.1073/pnas.2014704117.

Loginova, Elena. "Pandora Papers Reveal Offshore Holdings of Ukrainian President and his Inner Circle." Organized Crime and Corruption Reporting Project (OCCRP), Oct 3, 2021. https://www.occrp.org/en/the-pandora-papers/pandora-papers-reveal-offshore-holdings-of-ukrainian-president-and-his-inner-circle.

Lusama, Tafue Molu. "*Vaa Fesokotaki*: A Theology of God for a New Oceanian Climate Change Story." PhD thesis, Pacific Theological College, 2021.

Lynk, Michael. "The Question of Palestine." Press release, United Nations Special Rapporteur for Human Rights Office, Oct 14, 2018. https://www.un.org/unispal/document/gaza-unliveable-un-special-rapporteur-for-the-situation-of-human-rights-in-the-opt-tells-third-committee-press-release-excerpts/.

Maliko, Selota. "Restorative Justice: A Pastoral Care Response to the Issue of *Fa'atea Ma Le Nu'u* (Banishment) in Samoan Society." PhD thesis, Otago University, 2016.

Markley, John. "What Is Classical Theology?" Language Humanities, 2023. https://www.languagehumanities.org/what-is-classical-theology.htm.

Marshall, Christopher. *Compassionate Justice: An Interdisciplinary Dialogue with Two Gospel Parables on Law, Crime, and Restorative Justice*. Eugene, OR: Cascade, 2012.

"Mass Shootings by Country." Wisevoter, 2022. https://wisevoter.com/country-rankings/mass-shootings-by-country/.

Maté, Gabor. *The Myth of Normal: Trauma, Illness and Healing in a Toxic Culture*. New York: Penguin Random House, 2022.

———. *When the Body Says No: Exploring the Stress-Disease Connection*. Hoboken, NJ: Wiley, 2011.

McFague, Sallie. *The Body of God: An Ecological Theology*. Minneapolis: Augsburg, 1993.

Mearsheimer, John J. "The Causes and Consequences of the Ukraine War." *Horizons* 21 (Summer 2022) 12–27.

———. "Why Is Ukraine the West's Fault?" Public lecture, University of Chicago, June 23, 2022. http://bit.ly/UCHICAGOytAbout#UChicago.

Monbiot, George. "How Many of Those Calling for Putin's Arrest Were Complicit in the Illegal Invasion of Iraq?" *Guardian*, Mar 20, 2023. https://www.theguardian.com/commentisfree/2023/mar/20/putin-arrest-illegal-invasion-iraq-gordon-brown-condoleezza-rice-alast air-campbell-russia.

Morris, Emma-Jo, and Gabrielle Fonrouge. "Smoking-Gun Emails Reveal How Hunter Biden Introduced Ukrainian Businessman to VP Dad." *New York Post*, Oct 14, 2020.

Morris, Lindsey. "Blood for Bananas: United Fruit's Central American Empire." *Roots of Contemporary Issues*. Pullman, WA: Washington State University, 2015. https://history.wsu.edu/rci/sample-research-project/.

Moyer, Melinda. "Undocumented Immigrants Are Half as Likely to Be Arrested for Violent Crimes as U.S.-Born Citizens." *Scientific American*, Dec 7, 2020. https://www.scientificamerican.com/article/undocumented-immigrants-are-half-as-likely-to-be-arrested-for-violent-crimes-as-u-s-born-citizens/.

Munayer, John S., and Samuel S. Munayer. *Decolonising Palestinian Liberation Theology: Methods, Sources and Voices*. Edinburgh: Edinburgh University Press, 2022.

Muscan, Mary. "Media Violence: Advice for Parents." *Pediatric Nursing* 6 (Nov–Dec 2002) 585–91.

Naeem, Zaheed. "Health Risks Associated with Mobile Phone Use." *International Journal of Health Sciences* 4 (Oct 2014) 5–8.

Nasilisili, Sereima. "Custodianship: Re-righting Ecological Ethics towards Sautu." In *reStorying the Pasifika Household*, edited by Upolu Lumā Vaai and Aisake Casimira, 74–80. Suva, FJ: PTC Press, 2023.

"NATO Expansion: What Gorbachev Heard." National Security Archive, 2017. https://nsarchive.gwu.edu/briefing-book/russia-programs/2017-12-12/nato-expansion-what-gorbachev-heard-western-leaders-early.

Ng, Kate. "The History of the Word 'Woke' and Its Modern Uses." *Independent*, Jan 22, 2021. https://www.independent.co.uk/news/uk/home-news/woke-meaning-word-history-b1 790787.html.

Niva, Steve. "Operation 'Mow the Lawn.'" Middle East Research and Information Project, December 12, 2012. https://merip.org/2012/12/israels-operation-mow-the-lawn/.

Notzon, F. C., Y. M. Komarox, S. P. Ermakov, C. T. Sempos, J. S. Marks, and E. V. Sempos. "Causes of Declining Life Expectancy in Russia." *Journal of the American Medical Association* 10 (Mar 11, 1998) 793–800.

Nowrasteh, Alex. "Criminal Illegal Immigration Rates Fall Along the Border." Cato Institute, Oct 31, 2021. https://www.cato.org/blog/criminal-illegal-immigration-rates-fall-along-border#:~:text=In%20FY2021%2C%20only%20about%201.9,were%20criminals%20Figu re%201.

"Official Results: 97% of Crimea Voters Back Joining Russia." *CBS News*, Mar 17, 2014. https://www.cbsnews.com/news/official-results-97-of-crimea-voters-back-joining-russia/.

Palu, Valamotu. "Tapa Making in Tonga: A Metaphor for God's Care." In *Weavings: Women Doing Theology in Oceania*, edited by Lydia Johnson and Joan A. Filemoni-Tofaeono, 62–71. Suva, FJ: South Pacific Association of Theological Schools, 2003.

Pappé, Ilan. "A Brief History of Israel's Incremental Genocide." In *On Palestine*, edited by Noam Chomsky and Ilan Pappé, 147–54. Chicago: Haymarket, 2015.

———. *The Ethnic Cleansing of Palestine*. London: Oneworld, 2010.

Pohue, Marc. "Navigating with the Womb of Life: An Opu-Eco-Theology from Maohi Nui." PhD thesis, Pacific Theological College, 2022.
"Post-Humanism." The Ethics Center, 2023. https://ethics.org.au/ethics-explainer-post-humanism/.
Primrack, Brian A., et al. "Social Media Use and Perceived Social Isolation among Young Adults in the U.S." *American Journal of Preventative Medicine* 1 (Mar 2017) 1–8. https://www.ajpmonline.org/article/S0749-3797(17)30016-8/fulltext.
"The Question of Palestine and the UN General Assembly." United Nations Data Collection. https://www.un.org/unispal/data-collection/general-assembly/#:~:text=The%20question%20of%20Pales tine%20was,under%20a%20special%20international%20regime.
Ransby, Barbara. *Making All Black Lives Matter: Reimagining Freedom in the Twenty-first Century*. Oakland, CA: University of California Press, 2018.
Rawls, John. *A Theory of Justice*. Revised ed. Cambridge, MA: Harvard University Press, 1999.
Reilly, Katie. "The Times Donald Trump Insulted Mexico." *Time*, Aug 31, 2016. https://time.com/4473972/donald-trump-mexico-meeting-insult/.
"Right to Vote: Suffrage for Women, African Americans and Native Americans." State Historical Society of Iowa. https://history.iowa.gov/history/education/educator-resources/primary-source-sets/right-to-vote-suffrage-women-african#:~:text=19th%20Amendment %20to%20 the%20U.S.%20Constitution%2C%20August%2026%2C%201920/.
Ropeti-Apisaloma, Marie. *Nafanua Theology: A Samoan-Christian Argument for Women in Ordained Ministry*. Suva, FJ: PTC Press, 2022.
Ruether, Rosemary R. *America, Amerikkka: Elect Nation and Imperial Violence*. London: Equinox, 2007.
Russell, Letty. *Church in the Round: Feminist Interpretation of the Church*. Louisville: Westminster John Knox, 1993.
———. *The Future of Partnership*. Philadelphia: Westminster, 1979.
"Russia's Security Guarantees Proposal to US and NATO." Russian Foreign Ministry, Dec 17, 2021. https://tass.com/politics/1421141.
Ryan, Maria. *Full Spectrum Dominance: Irregular Warfare and the War on Terror*. Stanford, CA: Stanford University Press, 2019.
"The Sabbath Year and the Year of Jubilee (Leviticus 25)." Theology of Work. https://www.theologyofwork.org/old-testament/leviticus-and-work/the-sabbath-year-and-the-year-of-jubilee-leviticus-25/.
Samuelu, Piula A. "Decolonising Grace: A *Faapalepale* Restorative Theology from a Samoan Perspective." PhD thesis, Pacific Theological College, 2022.
Schaefer, Jane. "Environmental Degradation, Social Sin, and the Common Good." In *God, Creation, and Climate Change: A Catholic Response to the Environmental Crisis*, edited by Richard Miller, 69–94. Maryknoll, NY: Orbis, 2010.
Schaeffer, Katherine. "Key Facts About Americans and Guns." Pew Research Center, Sep 13, 2023. https://www.pewresearch.org/short-reads/2023/09/13/key-facts-about-americans-and-guns/.
Schneider, Laurel. *Beyond Monotheism: A Theology of Multiplicity*. London: Routledge, 2004.

Schwarz, Peter. "Former German Chancellor Merkel Admits the Minsk Agreement Was Merely to Buy Time for Ukraine's Arms Build-up." World Socialist Website, Dec 21, 2022. https://www.wsws.org/en/articles/2022/12/22/ffci-d22.html.

Schweid, Eleazer. "Rejection of the Diaspora in Zionist Thought." In *Essential Papers on Zionism*, edited by Jehuda Reinharz and Anita Shapira, 133–60. New York: NYU Press, 1996.

Second Amendment. *Constitution of the United States*. https://constitution.congress.gov/constitution/amendment-2/#:~:text=Constitution%20of%20the%20United%20States,Second%20Amendment&text=A%20well%20regulated%20Militia%2C%20being,Arms%2C%20shall%20not%20be%20infringed.

"Semites." In *Britannica Online*. https://www.britannica.com/topic/Semite.

Shaw, Martin. "Palestine in an International Historical Perspective on Genocide." *Holy Land Studies* 13 (2010) 1–7.

Singh, Stacy. "A Biblical Response to Poverty." Institute for Faith, Work and Economics, 2018. https://tifwe.org/christian-poverty-long-term/.

Sprinkle, Preston. "Disability and the Church." Theology in the Raw, Jan 12, 2023. https://theologyintheraw.com/disability-and-the-church/.

"Statement by the World Food Program on the Growing Humanitarian Catastrophe in Gaza." World Food Program, Dec 5, 2023. https://www.wfp.org/news/statement-world-food-programme-growing-humanitarian-catastrophe-gaza.

"Statement of ICC Prosecutor Karim A. Khan on the Situation in the State of Palestine and Israel." International Criminal Court, Dec 7, 2023. https://www.icc-cpi.int/news/statement-icc-prosecutor-karim-khan-kc-cairo-situation-state-palestine-and-israel.

Stemhell, Zeev. *The Founding Myths of Israel: Nationalism, Socialism, and the Making of the Jewish State*. Princeton: Princeton University Press, 1998.

Sundberg, John. "Eurocentrism." In *International Encyclopedia of Human Geography*, edited by Rob Kitchin and Nigel Thrift, 3:638–43. Amsterdam: Elsevier Science, 2009.

Swinton, John. *Who Is the God We Worship? Theologies of Disability: Challenges and New Possibilities*. Berlin: Walter de Gruyter, 2011.

"Three Ways the 1994 Crime Bill Continues to Hurt Communities of Color." *American Progress*, May 10, 2019. https://www.americanprogress.org/article/3-ways-1994-crime-bill-continues-hurt-communities-color/#:~:text=While%20the%20bill%20contained%20a,disparities%20in%20criminal%20justice%20involvement.

Tombs, David. *Latin American Liberation Theology*. Boston: Brill Academic, 2002.

"Top Causes of Poverty Around the World." Concern Worldwide, Mar 2022. https://www.concern.net/news/causes-of-poverty.

Tuminez, Astrid S. "Nationalism, Ethnic Pressures, and the Breakup of the Soviet Union." *Journal of Cold War Studies* 4 (Fall 2003) 81–136.

Tuwere, Ilaitia Sevati. *Vanua: A Fijian Theology of Place*. Suva, FJ: Institute of Pacific Studies, University of the South Pacific, 2002.

Uili, Afereti. "Abraham and the 'Curse' of James Cook." In *reStorying the Pasifika Household*, edited by Upolu Lumā Vaai and Aisake Casimira, 18–31. Suva, FJ: PTC Press, 2023.

"Ukraine Crisis: Leaked Phone Call Embarrasses U.S." *BBC News*, Feb 7, 2014. https://www.bbc.com/news/world-europe-26072281.

"Ukraine Suspends Talks on EU Trade Pact as Putin Wins Tug of War." *Guardian*, Nov 21, 2013. https://www.theguardian.com/world/2013/nov/21/ukraine-suspends-preparations-eu-trade-pact.

"Union Membership of US Workforce." News release, US Bureau of Labor Statistics, Jan 23, 2023. https://www.bls.gov/news.release/pdf/union2.pdf.

United Nations Charter, Article 51. https://www.un.org/en/about-us/un-charter/full-text#:~:text=Article%2051,maintain%20international%20peace%20and%20security.

United Nations Office for the Coordination of Humanitarian Affairs (OCHA). "Displacement of Palestinian Herders amidst Increasing Settler Violence," Sep 23, 2023. https:/www.ochaopt.org/content/displacement-palestinian-herders-amid-increasing-settler-violence.

United Nations Office of the High Commissioner for Human Rights (OCHCR). "Comment by UN High Commissioner for Human Rights, Volker Türk, on Resumption of Hostilities in Gaza." Press release, Dec 1, 2023. https://www.ohchr.org/en/press-releases/2023/12/comment-un-high-commissioner-human-rights-volker-turk-resumption-hostilities.

United Nations Trust Fund for Human Security. *Climate Change*, 2023. https://www.un.org/humansecurity/climate-change/.

Urofsky, Melvin J. "Jim Crow Law." In *Britannica Online*, Feb 29, 2024. https://www.britannica.com/event/Jim-Crow-law.

US Conference of Catholic Bishops. "Respect for Unborn Human Life: The Church's Constant Teaching." https://www.usccb.org/issues-and-action/human-life-and-dignity/abortion/respect-for-unborn-human-life.

Vaai, Upolu Lumā. "E Itiiti a Lega Mea—Less Yet More: A Relational Development Paradigm of Life." In *Relational Hermeneutics: Decolonizing the Mindset and the Pacific Itulagi*, edited by Upolu Lumā Vaai and Aisake Casimira, 215–31. Suva, FJ: University of the South Pacific, 2017.

———. "Faith and Culture." In *Christianity in Oceania*, edited by Kenneth R. Ross, Katalina Tahaafe Williams, and Todd M. Johnson, 225–33. Edinburgh: Edinburgh University Press, 2021.

———. "Relational Hermeneutics: A Return to the Relationality of the Pacific Itulagi as a Lens for Understanding and Interpreting Life." In *Relational Hermeneutics: Decolonizing the Mindset and the Pacific Itulagi*, edited by Upolu Lumā Vaai and Aisake Casimira, 17–40. Suva, FJ: University of the South Pacific, 2017.

———. "Theo-ethical Reflections from Oceania: Changing the Story of the Pacific Household of God." Paper presented, 11th Assembly of the World Council of Churches, Karlsruhe, Germany, Aug 31–Sep 8, 2022.

———. "Tino Theology." In *The Relational Self: Decolonizing Personhood in the Pacific*, edited by Upolu Lumā Vaai and Unaisi Nabobo-Baba, 223–41. Suva, FJ: University of the South Pacific, 2017.

———. "We Are Earth: reDIRTifying Creation Theology." In *reStorying the Pasifika Household*, edited by Upolu Lumā Vaai and Aisake Casimira, 40–54. Suva, FJ: PTC Press, 2023.

———. "'We Are, Therefore We Live'—Pacific Eco-Relational Spirituality and Changing the Climate Change Story." Policy Brief # 56, Toda Peace Institute, Oct 2019. https://toda.org/assets/files/resources/policy-briefs/t-pb-56_upolu-luma-vaai_we-are-therefore-we-live.pdf?v=0.

Velasquez, Manuel, Claire Andre, Thomas Shanks, and Michael J. Meyer. "The Common Good." Mark Kula Center for Applied Ethics, Santa Clara University, 2021. https://www.scu.edu/mcae/publications/iie/v5n1/com mon.html.

"Venezuela: 3m New Homes for Those on Low Incomes and Another 2m by 2025." Antidote to Gloom, Mar 11, 2020. https://antidotecounteragent.wordpress.com/2020/03/11/venezuela-3m-new-homes-for-those-on-low-incomes-and-another-2m-by-2025/.

Wade, Nicholas. "New Light on the Origins of Ashkenazi in Europe." *New York Times*, Jan 14, 2006.

Waqainabete, Jeremaia. *Christian Environmentalism: An Ecological Approach to Earth Keeping*. Suva, FJ: World Wide Fund for Nature-Pacific, 2018.

Weil, Sydney. "How Does Water Use in the United States Compare with that in Africa?" African Wildlife Foundation, Aug 3, 2023. https://www.awf.org/blog/how-does-water-use-united-states-compare-africa#:~:text=Every%20day%2C%20the%20average%20Ameri can,count%20on%20it%20being%20sanitary.

Weisbrot, Mark, and Jeffrey Sachs. "Economic Sanctions as Collective Punishment: The Case of Venezuela." Center for Economic and Policy Research, Apr 25, 2019. https://cepr.net/report/economic-sanctions-as-collective-punishment-the-case-of-venezuela/.

Wenger, Martha. "Jerusalem: A Primer." Middle East Research and Information Project, May–Jun, 1993. https://merip.org/1993/05/jerusalem-a-primer/#:~:text=About%2090%20percent%20of%20the,dramatically%20in%20the%20nineteenth%20century.

"What Is Celtic Spirituality?" The Celtic Center. www.thecelticcenter.org/what-is-celtic-spirituality.

"What Is the Palestinian Authority and What Is Its Relationship with Israel?" *Al Jazeera*, Nov 10, 2023. https://www.aljazeera.com/news/2023/10/11/what-is-the-palestinian-authority-and-how-is-it-viewed-by-palestinians.

Whitney, Rod. "US Provides Military Assistance to 73% of World's Dictatorships." *Truthout*, Sep 23, 2017. https://truthout.org/articles/us-provides-military-assistance-to-73-percent-of-world-s-dictatorships/.

Wolff, Richard. Interview. *Activism*, 2022. https://www.filmsforaction.org/watch/richard-d-wolff-bankruptcy-protection-debt-jubilee-students-debt-and-the-credit-system/.

———. *Occupy the Economy: Challenging Capitalism*. San Francisco: City Lights, 2012.

World Council of Churches. "Indigenous Theologians' Reflections on the WCC 10th Assembly Theme," Sep 29, 2012. https://www.oikoumene.org/en/resources/documents/wcc-programmes/unity-mission-evangelism-and-spirituality/just-and-inclusive-communities/indigenous-people/wcc-10th-assembly-theme.

Wright, Christopher J. H. *Old Testament Ethics for the People of God*. Downers Grove, IL: InterVarsity, 2004.

———. *The Mission of God: Unlocking the Bible's Grand Narrative*. Downers Grove, IL: IVP Academic, 2018.

Wylie-Kellermann, Bill. *Principalities in Particular: A Practical Theology of the Powers That Be*. Philadelphia: Fortress, 2017.

Yoder, John Howard. *Original Revolution: Essays on Christian Pacifism*. Elkhart, IN: Herald, 2003.

———. *The Politics of Jesus*. 2nd ed. Grand Rapids: Eerdmans, 2002.

Yoon, Mi Yung. "Explaining U.S. Intervention in Third World Internal Wars, 1945–1989." *Journal of Conflict Resolution* 4 (Aug 1997) 580–602.

Yunkaporta, Tyson. *Sand Talk: How Indigenous Thinking Can Save the World*. San Francisco: HarperOne, 2020.

Yusa, Michiko. "Henotheism." In *The Encyclopedia of Religion*, edited by Mircea Eliade, 6:267. New York: Macmillan, 1987.

www.ingramcontent.com/pod-product-compliance
Lightning Source LLC
Chambersburg PA
CBHW051053230426
43667CB00013B/2277